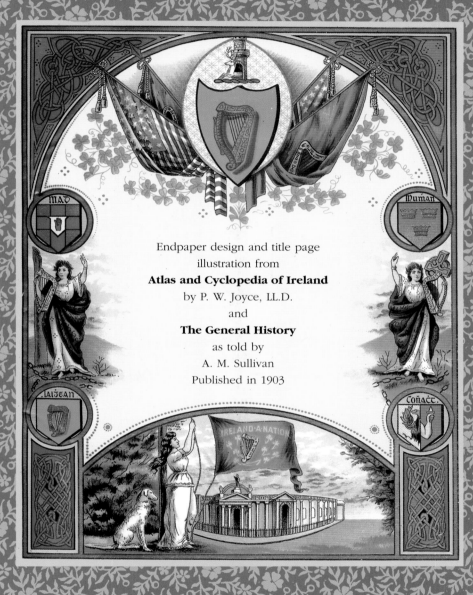

Endpaper design and title page
illustration from
Atlas and Cyclopedia of Ireland
by P. W. Joyce, LL.D.
and
The General History
as told by
A. M. Sullivan
Published in 1903

THE TIMECHART
HISTORY
OF
IRELAND

THE TIMECHART

HISTORY

OF

IRELAND

WORTH PRESS LIMITED
LONDON

First published 2001 by
Worth Press Limited
109 Hawkins House
Dolphin Square
London
SW1V 3NS

ISBN 1-903025-06-0

© Worth Press Limited 2001

CIP catalogue records for this book are available from the British Library and the Library of Congress.

Edited and designed by
Playne Books Limited
Chapel House
Trefin, Haverfordwest
Pembrokeshire SA62 5AU
United Kingdom

Edited by
Gill Davies
Vivienne Kay

Picture research
Vivienne Kay

Editorial assistant
Faye Hayes

Design
David Playne

Typeset by
Playne Books Limited
in Garamond

Printed in Hong Kong

Publisher's note

The publishers hope that this timechart and history of Ireland and its people will help for a greater understanding of the nation's development. While history does have its emotive issues, the timechart has been made up of facts and events, not opinions or comment. The publishers would wish to be informed if any element is incorrect or in any way contentious.

Picture credits

Title page photograph: Bill Doyle

Adam Woolfitt/CORBIS
AKG / Michael Teller
Bettmann/CORBIS
Bill Doyle
Bord Fáilte – Irish Tourist Board
Christies Images Ltd
Collections/Fay Godwin
Collections/Image Ireland/Alain Le Garsmeur
Collections/Image Ireland/Anderson McMeekin
Collections/Image Ireland/Bill Kirk
Collections/Image Ireland/Errol Forbes
Collections/Image Ireland/Geray Sweeney
Collections/Image Ireland/Thomas Ennis
Collections/Michael Diggin
Collections/Michael StMaur Sheil
CORBIS
Hulton Getty
Hulton-Deutsch Collection/CORBIS
Jonathan Potter Ltd – Antique maps
Mary Evans Picture Library
Michael StMaur Sheil/CORBIS
National Museum of Ireland
Peter Newark's Pictures
Playne Photographic
Richard Cummins/CORBIS
Sean Sexton Collection/CORBIS
Werner Forman/CORBIS

The publishers wish to thank Dr Patrick Power and Dr Seán Duffy for their great help and enthusiasm throughout the creation of this book.

Special thanks are also due to:

Bill Doyle
Bord Fáilte – Irish Tourist Board
Janice Douglas
National Museum of Ireland
Northern Ireland Office

Author

Dr Patrick Power

Patrick C. Power was born in Dungarvan, County Waterford, but has lived most of his life in County Tipperary. He was trained as a National Teacher and spent much of his teaching career in Ballyneale National School. In 1964 he graduated as a BA, by 1965 he had earned his MA and in 1971 was conferred with a PhD. by University College Galway of the National University of Ireland. Dr. Power gives lectures and guided tours in Counties Tipperary and Waterford. A great enthusiast for Ireland, its history, archaeology and literature, Patrick C. Power has had over twelve books published, including:
A Literary History of Ireland, The Book of Irish Curses, History of South Tipperary, The Courts Martial of 1798-9, and *Anglo-Irish Poetry 1800-1922.*

Consultant

Dr Seán Duffy

Dr Seán Duffy is a Fellow of Trinity College, Dublin, where he lectures in medieval Irish and British history. He has published widely in both areas, and has a particular interest in Irish relations with Wales, Scotland, and the Isles. His books include *Ireland in the Middle Ages* (1997) and *The Concise History of Ireland* (2000), and he is the editor of the best-selling *Atlas of Irish History* (1997, 2000). Dr Duffy is Chariman of the Friends of Medieval Dublin and organiser of a series of annual symposia on the city's historical and archaeological heritage; the proceedings of the first two of these have been published under his editorship as *Medieval Dublin*, volumes I (1999) and II (2000).

Contents

6

Introduction by Dr Seán Duffy

8

Introduction to the landscape

10

The changing face of power and domination

12

Peoples of Ireland

15

How to use this book

16

The Chart

7000BC-AD550

AD550-1120

1120-1300

1300-1490

1490-1615

1615-1760

1760-1850

1850-1920

1920-1980

1980-2001

35

Peace negotiations

36

Factfinder

53

Glossary

54

The Effects of Geography

56

Towns and cities

60

Religion and culture

64

The Languages of Ireland

65

The Old Irish Laws

66

Music in Ireland

68

Art

72

Irish Folklore and the 'Little People'

74

The influence of the Celts

76

Maps over the centuries

86

Gaelic games and sport

88

Irish Farming

90

Wit and wisdom

92

Literature

98

Libraries and Museums

100

Bibliography

Introduction

A timechart is a particularly appropriate way to approach the history of Ireland. Almost since the dawn of Irish history, with the introduction of Christianity in the fifth century, the Irish kept their own version of the timechart. It began when tables were needed for the purpose of calculating the precise date on which Easter Sunday would fall each year. These tables were kept in vellum manuscripts preserved in monasteries. But the monks who maintained them began to jot down in the margins the occasional event that happened that year.

After a time, they had on their hands quite an extensive record of incidents and happenings of which somebody had thought it worth preserving a memory, and these grew into full-scale compilations of annals. As their name suggests, the annals provide an annual record, set out in chronological order, of the major events of each year. They are the most important body of evidence to survive from medieval Ireland, from the sixth to the sixteenth century, and they allow us to piece together a very detailed picture of the lives of Irish kings – when were they made king, what battles did they fight, who did they marry, when did they die? – and of the history of its famous, and not so famous, monasteries in which the annals were compiled. . . .They are, in fact, medieval timecharts.

And the annals show that the most important dynasty in Ireland in the early

A country of contrasts: calm sunset on the River Boyne and storm clouds gathering over the Burren

medieval period were the Uí Néill, who traced their origin to a perhaps legendary king called Niall of the Nine Hostages. They claimed that the high-kingship was rightfully theirs, and had their symbolic capital at Tara. But their supremacy was threatened in the ninth century when Ireland began to suffer repeated Viking raiding which looked likely to overwhelm the country. Instead, however, the Vikings were gradually integrated into Irish society, and became the engines of trade, establishing a number of towns, including the eventual capital, Dublin.

In the late twelfth century, Ireland was again invaded, this time by people of Anglo-Norman origin. The annals of later medieval Ireland show a country dominated by two peoples who see themselves as distinct nations, their relationship dogged by racial antagonism. Even though many of these Anglo-Normans were assimilated into Irish life over the centuries, they never came to see themselves as Irish, but called themselves 'the English of the land of Ireland'. In fact, they only began to merge with the native population when, from the mid-sixteenth century onwards, both faced the prospect of dispossession by a new wave of English Protestant plantation.

The wars and tensions that have plagued Ireland in the last four centuries are largely a product of this new religious dimension. In the aftermath of the Reformation, the divisions between Rome

and the Protestant churches were played out violently and bitterly on the soil of Ireland. The last great struggle by the native Irish to try to overturn this new English Protestant domination was the Nine Years' War (1593-1603) but the annals record in dejected terms the overthrow of the armies of O'Neill and O'Donnell at the battle of Kinsale in 1601. When they left Ireland for good, in September 1607, in what has become known as the 'Flight of the Earls', the Gaelic order which they represented ceased to exist.

In the annals of Irish history the century that followed was perhaps the bloodiest, and it sowed the seeds of future conflicts which have lasted into our own time. Ulster was extensively 'planted' in the seventeenth century with settlers from England and Scotland, the latter predominantly Presbyterian, but the native population, largely Catholic and disinherited, survived in sufficient numbers to mean that the new Ulster was never going to remain trouble-free for long. Throughout Ireland, the rights of the majority Catholic population were trampled upon and their property-holdings removed, culminating in the harsh legislative restraints introduced in the early eighteenth century known as the Penal Laws.

When the spirit of the American and French Revolutions reached Ireland's shores it led to a large-scale rebellion in 1798 but the response of the British gov-

ernment to Irish unrest was to abolish Ireland's Parliament under the Act of Union of 1800. Although it had always been a symbol of the power of the colonists, in time the loss of the parliament appeared, even to Catholics, as a denial of Ireland's independence.

When they secured full rights of citizenship by the passing of Catholic Emancipation in 1827 – won through the charismatic leadership of Daniel O'Connell – the repeal of the Act of Union became the goal of nationalist Ireland.

Here, however, O'Connell failed and, amid the catastrophe of the Great Famine (1845-9), others began to believe that peaceful protest was not enough. The rebellion by the Young Ireland movement in 1848 was followed by that of the Fenians in 1867, but both were doomed to failure.

Ironically, it was a British Prime Minister, W.E. Gladstone, who first brought hope of change, and the cause of Irish Home Rule was fought instead on the floor of the British House of Commons, led by a new nationalist leader, Charles Stewart Parnell. He joined forces with Michael Davitt's Land League to secure the rights of Irish tenant farmers to ownership of their own land, but the attainment of an Irish Home Rule parliament eluded him.

By the time Home Rule was finally conceded on the eve of the First World War it was too late. A new generation of idealists believed that the establishment of a

Republic was the only answer to Ireland's problems, and an armed rebellion the only way to advance it. Their Rising in Easter 1916 failed in the short term but when the public mood changed in favour of the rebels, a bloody war (1919-21) followed, between British forces and what was now called the Irish Republican Army (IRA), which eventually led to the establishment of the Irish Free State. The Anglo-Irish Treaty signed on 6 December 1921 appeared to give the Irish all that they had sought since they were subjected to English rule in the twelfth century, but the settlement fell far short of an independent Republic and a tragic, if short-lived, Civil War (1922-3) ensued.

In the long run, what was more damaging than the Civil War was the decision to exclude from the Free State six of Ireland's thirty-two counties – those in the north-east which had substantial Protestant populations and where opposition to independence was strongest. The problem with this attempted solution was that the great majority of people in the other twenty-six counties were unwilling to accept partition, while even within the six-county statelet that became known as Northern Ireland, a very considerable minority, mostly Catholics, felt likewise.

The regime that ruled from Stormont, until it was brought to an end by the British government in 1972, was anything but tolerant. It was removed because of its inabil-

ity to reform itself and its unwillingness to grant full Civil Rights and a share of power to the Catholic nationalist minority. Because it turned a deaf ear to peaceful protests by the northern Civil Rights Association, others resorted to more extreme methods. And so, for most of the last third of the twentieth century a resurgent nationalist armed movement, the Provisional IRA, fought a campaign to secure a British commitment to disengage from the six partitioned Ulster counties and to allow a united Ireland to be established. Armed Loyalist groups, a greatly strengthened Royal Ulster Constabulary, and large contingents of British troops attempted to meet fire with fire, but it was a war which neither side could win.

In the end, compromise was inevitable. The Good Friday Agreement of 1998 allowed for the establishment of a cross-community government in Belfast, with a reformed police force, a guarantee of 'parity of esteem' for all sections of society, and with strong North-South institutions to reflect the aspirations of nationalists and republicans. As the twenty-first century dawned the future looked brighter, but only time will tell. How the Ireland of the third millennium AD came to be is what this timechart attempts to show, in as dramatic, attractive, and informative a manner as possible. It is a pleasure to have been associated with its production and to commend it to its readers.

Traditional harvesting and an Army border control

Seán Duffy Dublin, 2001

Introduction to the landscape

An island on the north-west coast of the European mainland, Ireland is the most westerly point in Europe that merchants, visitors, settlers and invaders would ever reach throughout history. It stands on a large shelf of rock, which is shallow in comparison with the main part of the North Atlantic Ocean. This ocean stretches south, west and north of the island and its continental shelf. The shelf abounded in fish, which found an abundance of plankton there to make it a profitable feeding ground. Nowadays, unfortunately, the fish stocks are in danger from over fishing and the use of fine-meshed nets.

The nearest part of Ireland to Great Britain is the Antrim coast which lies relatively close to Scotland, about twenty kilometres away. In this area the two land-masses were joined by what is described as the land bridge. Across this came animals, flora and fauna – and human beings. This land bridge had been eroded by the time the first adders had made their way north from the south of England. Consequently there are no snakes in Ireland – and never have been!

The climate of Ireland is temperate due mainly to the influence of the Gulf Stream. This brings warm seawater to the coast accompanied by the prevailing south-west winds. There is rain in every season. The wettest parts of Ireland are on the west coast in Counties Donegal, West Galway and Kerry. The driest region is in a strip of land off the coast from Dundalk to County Wexford. As a result of the frequent rain the growth of grass is consistent in every season and causes some foreigners to speak of the green or the emerald isle.

Although the summer temperatures can reach 20° C and higher sometimes, the average summer temperatures vary from about 14° C to 16° C. The highest temperatures occur in the south-east and south-west. The coolest temperatures occur in the extreme north of the island. Snow is mainly on high ground and is more likely to fall on the eastern part of the island and the north. Overall, the south-west has a very equitable climate.

The coasts of Ireland vary greatly. The western coast faces the strength and fury of Atlantic storms and is much indented. It is predominantly a rocky coastline with large and impressive cliffs such as the Cliffs of Moher in County Clare. It contains thousands of inlets of the sea, some large as Clew Bay in County Mayo is and very many others which are narrow and shallow. The eastern coast faces the more tranquil Irish Sea and is not as indented as the craggy contours on the west.

Unlike most islands, which have a backbone of mountains and hills, most of the mountains of Ireland are situated near the coast. The only inland mountains are those of Slieve Bloom in County Offaly and the hills of North Tipperary. The mountains form a letter C with a large gap from Dublin to Dundalk. Thus the centre of the island of Ireland consists of low-lying land and is known as the Central Plain.

The River Shannon and its many tributaries drain the Central Plain. It spreads itself over the centre of Ireland in three great lakes, Lough Allen, Lough Ree and Lough Derg. The river flows southwards and enters the sea at Limerick where an estuary carries its waters into the Atlantic Ocean. The Central Plain also contains other large lakes, such as Lough Conn and Lough Mask in County Mayo and Lough Corrib in County Galway. The land west of the River Shannon is of poor quality in many places compared to the land eastwards from it.

The River Boyne and its tributaries drain the Central Plain east of the Shannon basin. The Boyne flows through the rich grazing lands of County Meath and enters the Irish Sea at Drogheda through an estuary about sixteen kilometres long. There are two river-basins in the south. Counties Carlow and Kilkenny are drained respectively by the Rivers Barrow and Nore, which form a confluence near New Ross. This meets the River Suir from County Tipperary and flows into Waterford harbour. The Rivers Blackwater, Lee and Bandon form the second river basin in the south: all of which flow through County Cork while the Blackwater also flows through County Waterford. They enter the sea at different points.

The northern part of Ireland is delineated partially by a system of lakes, which are Upper and Lower Lough Erne, from west to east. Counties Antrim and Down are in the extreme east of the area, which is cut off from the rest by Lough Neagh and the Lower and Upper Bann.

The predominant rock in the Central Plain and in some of the south of Ireland is the sedimentary carboniferous limestone. The collapse of the roofs of great underground caverns in this rock was the origin of the great lakes of the Central Plain. Sandstone forms the commonest rock in much of the south of Ireland. The most common igneous rocks in Ireland are granite in the Wicklow Mountains, south Connemara and the Mountains of Mourne and basalt in County Antrim. In the northeast corner of Antrim, lava which shrunk by contact with water forms the 'Giant's causeway'. Pillars of eight or nine sides are to be seen here.

Dublin, the capital city, is situated on the east coast where the mountainous chain around the island is broken. Its situation on the shores of a good harbour facing England helped to secure its importance as a port and city. From Dublin the main communication system of roads and railway lines stretch out to all parts of Ireland. Belfast, the chief city of Northern Ireland, is also situated by a good harbour, which faces towards Scotland and Northern England. The coalfields of these regions supplied the factories of Northern Ireland with fuel in the past.

The mineral resources of Ireland are limited. Some copper was mined in places such as Bunmahon in County Waterford in the past but the available quantity was too small for large scale exploitation. Successful lead mining is conducted near Navan in County Meath and also in north County Kilkenny. The only coal available in the country was culm (slack) near Lough Allen and in Counties Tipperary and Kilkenny but these mines have been closed now for many years.

The peat bogs of Ireland have always been a notable feature of the island. The greatest of these was the Bog of Allen in Counties Meath, Kildare and Offaly, an area of raised bog that began to grow and expand with the damp climate, which succeeded a drier climate after about 700 BC. Raised bog is found in areas where there was poor drainage. Much of the Bog of Allen has been cleared to provide fuel since the 1930s. Blanket bogs are found mainly in the west of Ireland where the rainfall is heaviest.

In the north-east of County Clare is the Burren, which covers 1300 hectares. It consists of bare limestone terraces or pavements where alpine and Mediterranean flowers grow in the cracks. There are occasional patches of fertile ground here and there in sheltered areas.

This is a beautiful land – a green island, a landscape of mountains, mist, lakes, fields and marsh – surrounded by multiple seascapes; some wild and rocky, some gently shelving with dunes and

windswept beaches. It is a land of contrasts that has inspired myriad legends, a rich burgeoning of music and art and literature, and been the backdrop to a turbulent history. Above all, this is a landscape that has given rise to a people known for their wit and character, their individuality, their strength and loyalty, their Irish style and humour. The story of a nation is the story of its people. The timeline of Ireland traces this history from the very earliest times into the new millennium.

Rocky coastline in County Kerry (left), limestone pavements of the Burren (above) and the lakes, Killarney (below)

The changing face of power and domination

During the time that written records of some kind or other have been kept, that is from about 500 AD until 2000 AD, the island of Ireland has, for about nine centuries, been subject to foreign domination and control. This represents some sixty per cent of that long stretch of time.

AD 500-800

In this period the country was divided into about one hundred small kingdoms, each of which was called a tuath. Male relatives, to the third degree of kinship, elected the king of each tuath. No one could be elected king if he was not physically fit.

There was no central kingship or High King. However, kingdoms tended to coalesce for the common good and generally tuath kings in the provinces of Munster, Connacht, Ulster, Meath and Leinster would recognise one of their colleagues as an over-king.

The king was bound by the native Brehon Law, which was first written down in or about 450 to 550 AD. These laws were not passed or ratified by any king but arose out of the customs of the people over the centuries. All those who were not slaves in this strictly classified society were under their protection. They were administered by the brehons or lawyers and the king could neither repeal nor enforce them. However, the brehons glossed and explained them over the years. Thus the lawyers were independent of the king.

Verdicts were given after discussion of a complaint by a brehon from either side. Each person had an honour price. The chief penalty was based upon this honour price if a person was proven guilty. There were no judges, no prisons, no police and no capital punishment in this native Irish system. The society where it operated was wholly rural and consensus was much easier to achieve in such an environment.

With the introduction of Christianity, monasteries were founded throughout the land. However, they were seen as part of the tuath system and bishops of the first dioceses were of the family that elected the king. The church's efforts to enforce Canon Law, a form of Roman Law, failed. For example, divorce was recognised by the Brehon Law in spite of the official church.

800-1170

In this period Viking raiders settled on the coastline and founded seaports in Dublin, Wexford, Waterford and Limerick. They introduced a governing system, which was the antithesis of the native Irish customs. Their walled towns were the first urban settlements in Ireland and ruled themselves and their hinterlands. The king of each town was the eldest living son of his father. Money was minted, courts were held and

capital punishment and imprisonment introduced. Severe punishments for the non-payment of taxes was also part of the system. Trade links with the seaports in Europe were forged.

This was the first serious challenge to the native Irish establishment. The latter was seen as weak and ineffective in coping with the Viking method of rule and authority. The latter was urban and international, the former was rural and insular. However, the Vikings confined their attentions to the north, east and south coasts and bothered little with Connacht or the interior of the island where the native Irish ruled.

In the 11th and 12th centuries an effort was made to establish a central authority in Ireland. Brian Boru, king of a tuath in the south, made himself master of Munster in both Irish and Viking areas. He went on to subdue the rest of Ireland and was declared High King in 1002.

After his death in battle at Clontarf in 1014 there was almost a century and a half of internecine warfare between various kings to secure the High Kingship. In 1166, after years of bloodshed, Turlough O'Connor of Connacht was acknowledged High King, the second and the last person to hold that title.

1170-1534

In 1170 the first Norman settlements were made in Ireland. The Normans seized the old Viking ports and built towns on the rivers in the interior. The native Irish and the former Viking system were unable to resist the seizure and settlement of the land in all areas except a few remote districts in the south, in Wicklow and inside the Erne lakes and Lough Neagh in Ulster.

The Normans brought the feudal system of land tenure. The king was the ultimate owner of land and granted manors or certain portions of land in exchange for military service to the Crown. Each manor lord had absolute power over his workers or *betaghs*, as they were called in Ireland, and held a manor court.

The king governed Ireland through his viceroys. They held courts where the royal writ ran and judges went about throughout the year hearing cases. For about a century and a quarter this was the state of affairs in 'the land of peace', which did not include Ulster and a few other areas where the Brehon Law was still used.

From about 1316 onwards the authority of the king waned. First of all the invasion of Ireland by Edmund Bruce of Scotland disrupted the country. Then the Black Death plague of 1348 ravaged the land and made the lot of the remaining *betaghs* more tolerable. They could demand better pay and conditions. As the 14th century went on, the authority of the king waned as the Hundred Years War caused further neglect of Ireland. Local lords took over the governance of areas to

keep law and order. The greatest of these were the Earl of Ormond in Kilkenny and part of Munster, the Earl of Kildare in the midlands and the Earl of Desmond in most of Munster.

By the beginning of the 15th century, as the royal authority further weakened, that of the great lords and others strengthened. The Wars of the Roses in England prevented any assertion of the royal authority in Ireland except in and around Dublin. A huge earthwork, called the 'Pale', was built around this area to keep out what were called the 'mere Irish'. The descendants of the Norman settlers were said to be more Irish than the Irish themselves. The cities of Waterford, Cork, Limerick and Galway remained loyal to the crown and were governed like city states.

In the late 15th century and early 16th, Garret, Earl of Kildare, was the only effective ruler of Ireland. The Tudor monarch, Henry VIII who reigned from 1509, adopted a policy to reconquer Ireland.

1534-1603

In this period Ireland was gradually brought into obedience to the monarch. It was essentially an expansion of the authority of the king from the Pale. Furthermore, the link between the Pope and the church in Ireland was officially broken in 1535 by the Irish Parliament when the king was declared head of the church.

After 1534 the Earl of Kildare's lands just outside the Pale were gradually invaded and captured and the royal authority restored there after the final defeat in 1537.

The policy of re-conquering was next extended to Laois and Offaly, when the lands of the Irish there was confiscated and planted with settlers from England after 1553. This was the beginning of the policy of 'plantations', the settlement of people from England and the expulsion of the native people.

In the 1560s the royal authority had been restored in Counties Tipperary and Kilkenny when the Earl of Ormond, who had been reared at the royal court, took over his patrimony and ruled these areas in the royal interests.

The Tudor reconquest was seen as a struggle between Catholicism and Protestantism, and between the king and the pope.

The re-conquering policy was applied next to the heart of Munster when a rebellion of the people of the Earl of Desmond in Munster was stamped out. Huge tracts of land were then confiscated and granted to settlers from England.

The final phases of reconquest began in 1585 when Connacht was 'pacified'. The people in the land behind the Erne lakes and Lough Neagh had never been conquered and this territory was now invaded. From 1595 to 1603 war was waged against Hugh O'Neill of Tyrone and his allies there

Brian Boru

Hugh O'Neill, Earl of Tyrone

Part of the walled city of Limerick 1651

until a treaty allowing them to keep their household lands was signed in 1603. This was the end of the last area of native rule. During this war Irish nationalism was born, which was seen as a Catholic force.

1603-1800

The authority of the king was supreme over the whole island. Ulster was planted with settlers from Scotland and England. Throughout Ireland a great reorganisation of local government took place when new charters were granted to towns. Many new boroughs were created to elect members to the Irish Parliament. The State religion of Protestantism was promoted and laws against the Catholic religion enforced.

There was some respite for Catholics after 1625. Outside Ulster, the vast majority of landowners and gentry were Catholics who were loyal to the king but feared that their lands might be confiscated.

In 1641 a rebellion by the former landowners in Ulster was generally successful. In 1642 the Catholic landowners in the remainder of Ireland took over the rule of the country but in the name of the king. They established the Confederation of Kilkenny, a type of Catholic parliament, whose motto was 'United to God and King'. They saw themselves as supporters of the king against the English Parliamentarians.

In 1649-50 Oliver Cromwell invaded Ireland and defeated the Confederation. Military rule was established and the Irish Parliament abolished. The land of all Catholic landowners was confiscated and granted to soldiers and as a repayment to investors in the long war.

This plantation changed the ownership of land in Ireland radically. The new landlords were alien in race, religion and language to the native Irish people.

In 1660 the Irish Parliament was restored and governed the country until 1800. It was not fully independent but could make laws only with the assent of the king and the English parliament. It was also required to adopt laws enacted in that parliament.

From the late 17th until the early 18th century certain laws deprived Catholics of the right to sit in parliament, hold municipal offices, or commissions in the army. This happened although they were the majority in the country.

In 1800 the parliament had already repealed many of the anti-Catholic laws, which also applied to Dissenters. In that year its own members dissolved the Irish parliament and henceforth the island was governed from Westminster.

1801-1922

In the next century and a quarter there were three violent attempts to dissolve the Union of Great Britain and Ireland – in 1848, 1867 and in 1916-21. All of them failed but the last one led to negotiations that gave a type of Commonwealth status to twenty-six counties out of the thirty-two. The members of these revolutionary movements were almost all Catholics.

There were also a series of measures, which gave the formerly oppressed Catholics experience in self-government and exercising power.

1 In 1929 Catholics were permitted to sit in parliament.

2 The Boards of Guardians, which governed the Poor Law system after 1840, were composed of ex-officio members but also of members elected by those who paid Poor Law rates.

3 The Irish Municipal Reform Act 1840 extended the franchise so that those Catholic property holders had votes and could be elected to corporations and as mayors of cities.

4 The Local Government Act 1899 replaced the Grand Juries of counties by the County Councils and the Town Commissioners – in many cases by Urban District Councils. This also gave women the franchise in certain instances.

These measures gave more classes of people a voice in public administration during the 19th century and the first years of the 20th.

After 1829 the Roman Catholic Church found a new sense of power in Ireland. From this time onwards the hierarchy tended to be former students of St. Patrick's College and did not show the same deference to government as their predecessors who had been educated in mainland Europe.

The hierarchy insisted on weekly church attendance at Mass and large new churches replaced the smaller ones in existence from about 1830 onwards. They made themselves the leaders of the Catholic majority whom they had led in the 18th century. In 1852 Rev. Paul Cullen became Archbishop of Dublin and set out to strengthen the bond between the Irish Church and Rome. The number of priests in Ireland nearly tripled between 1840 and 1870 and the power of the clergy became very great. Their support of the Land League after 1879 caused the bloodless revolution of depriving legally but gradually the all-powerful landlords of their estates. The vast majority of the Irish Catholic clergy were of farming stock.

1922-2000

The Anglo-Irish Treaty of 1921 divided Ireland in two.

Six counties with Belfast as capital had self-rule but remained part of the United Kingdom and sent Members of Parliament to Westminster. It was dominated and ruled by its Protestant majority. This area held the most significant and successful section of Irish industry. The most influential politicians were businessmen.

The other twenty-six counties were ruled by the Dáil in Dublin and were dominated by its Catholic majority. The influential politicians were generally from working-class families. It had links with the Commonwealth and members of the Dáil to take an oath of allegiance to the King of England until 1933. In 1937 a new constitution was adopted stressing the independence of the State but recognising the unique position of the Catholic Church.

These two maps show the effects of plantation – initially in the Tudor period and then under Cromwell when Catholic Irish were forced to move west of the River Shannon

The Archbishop of Dublin was consulted about the constitution before it was presented to the people.

The Irish Catholic foreign missionary movement thrived until the 1960s. Priests and nuns were sent to Africa and India principally, but also to Australia, Canada, the USA and Great Britain, the English-speaking world and the Commonwealth.

The Northern State as part of Great Britain joined in the war effort from 1939 to 1945. Troops were stationed and trained there and warships, cargo ships and military aircraft were produced.

The Southern Irish State maintained strict neutrality but perhaps as many as 20,000 men joined the British armed forces. Thousands also emigrated to work in the war industries.

After the war the Belfast ruled area thrived in the post-war reconstruction for some time. In the south there was large-scale unemployment and much emigration of the youth.

In 1949 the Southern State was declared the Republic of Ireland. Henceforth the President of Ireland issued passports and ambassadors were appointed abroad instead of High Commissioners.

In 1968 a popular Catholic and nationalist movement in the North took peaceful means of protest to end the abuse of power by the permanent Protestant majority. It demanded the end of discrimination by a local and central government system that discriminated against them. In 1972 the Belfast government was suspended and the area was ruled directly by Westminster. When certain Protestant groups acted violently against them and the police did not protect them, the Irish Republican Army waged guerrilla warfare against police and army. It lasted thirty years and ended in a cease-fire in 1964 without victory for either side.

Much of the support for the IRA came at first from the South but in the late 1970s the northern officers took over total direction of the campaign.

The republic slowly reached forward to economic success. Membership of the EEC, EC and EU secured this objective in the 1990s. In 1989 and 1996 the formal post of President of Ireland, filled since 1945 by retired politicians, was taken by two distinguished female lawyers, their Excellencies Mary Robinson and Ms Mary McAleese. They brought a prestige to the office that it not previously held.

Negotiations between the British Government and the Irish Government concerning the governance of the North were held. In 1998 the 'Good Friday Agreement' was made to constitute an assembly in Belfast with all parties represented in government. Although there is delay in putting this into effect, a point has been slowly reached where both republicans (Sinn Féin) and Loyalists regard each other as equal partners. Parity of esteem and power sharing has been formally accepted in a novel experiment.

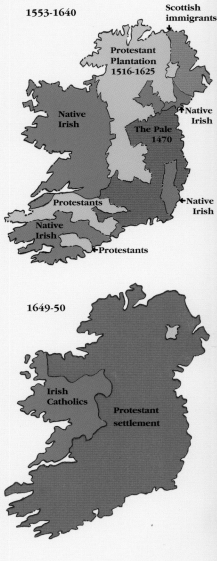

1553-1640

Scottish immigrants

Protestant Plantation 1516-1625

Native Irish

Native Irish

The Pale 1470

Protestants

Native Irish

Native Irish

Protestants

1649-50

Irish Catholics

Protestant settlement

Mary Robinson

Peoples of Ireland

The people of Ireland constitute an amalgam of various racial stocks, who came to settle there over the centuries. It is not known who were the original settlers because there is a lack of native written evidence. The earliest reliable information comes from the geographer Ptolemy and his map, where the information may have been as old as the final years of the pre-Christian era.

The Celts

Since about 400 BC, Celtic immigrants had been settling in Ireland but of the ten names of people that are mentioned, just one, Brigantes, is known from Celtic mainland Europe.

The Celtic peoples who came to Ireland brought with them the La Téne art form and the Q-Celtic form of the Gaelic language. It should be said that none of the ten names above had the letter p, so it can be assumed that they were speakers of Q-Celtic Gaelic. It can be assumed also that they were the ruling class and that an earlier people or peoples lived in the country, speaking a different language which continued for some time.

The earlier people were absorbed fully into the culture of the invaders, at first as a subject race. Modern surnames that stem from the Celtic families include O'Brien, grandson of Brien, McGrath, son of Crath. The first surname among these native people may have been O'Cleary, Ó Cléririgh, the son of the cleric.

The Irish Celts were a rural people whose economy was mainly based on the cow. Their favourite foods seem to have been bread, pork and milk as well as beef.

The latter was generally supplied from bull calves that were slaughtered from November onwards. They also brewed some kind of beer called coirm.

Those gold objects ornamented with the La Téne design which have been discovered are mainly from the earlier Celtic period. By the third and fourth centuries of the Christian Era the influence of the La Téne design had waned. The development of Celtic design proper would emerge and lead to its highest achievement as an art form.

Vikings

The Vikings who settled in Ireland came from Scandinavia – from Norway and Denmark. They were known as 'Fair-haired Foreigners' and 'Black-haired Foreigners' respectively. The two names are preserved in place names, Fingal and Baldoyle, the homestead of the black-haired foreigners. Two of the surviving Viking surnames are the hybrid Cotter, Mac Ottir son of Ottir, and hybrid surnames which contain Mac Giolla, son of the servant of (a saint), as in McKilmurry, son of the servant of Mary. They lived in maritime urban communities and developed a commercial trade, which had not existed previously in Ireland.

They spoke Old Norse, a Teutonic language rather similar to modern Icelandic, and the linguistic ancestor of the other Scandinavian languages – Norwegian, Danish and Swedish.

Anglo-Normans

The Anglo-Normans supplied some of the most common surnames in Ireland. Many of them begin with Fitz meaning son, as in Fitzgerald. Others such as Butler, Prendergast, Power, Wall and B(o)urke were names of the first colonisers from England. Through the manorial system the Normans developed commercial agriculture – hitherto unknown in Ireland, except in the large Cistercian abbeys founded shortly before the Normans came. The Anglo-Normans introduced horse saddles and stirrups to Ireland as well as archers. The native Irish could not oppose their heavy cavalry and longbow men.

The original Anglo-Norman settlers spoke Norman French but those of their grandchildren (and often their children) who had Irish mothers, spoke Gaelic.

An English-speaking colony was settled in parts of South County Wexford in the early days of the Anglo-Norman invasion. They spoke a form of Middle English, which was still alive there in the 19th century. It was called Yola.

English and Scottish settlers

From 1556 to 1654 there were four plantations of English and Scottish settlers made by the British government in Ireland. They spoke English, Lowland Scots English and Scots Gaelic.

The English who settled in Counties Laois and Offaly failed to establish a vigorous colony and the plantation was a failure at first. Meanwhile, the McDonnells from the isles were settled in North County Antrim. They were Gaelic speakers and did nothing to develop agriculture. They were settled as irritants to the independent people of Ulster.

A noble chieftain's feast from a woodcut in John Derrick's 'Image of Irelande' and illustrations of Irish people from a 1616 map

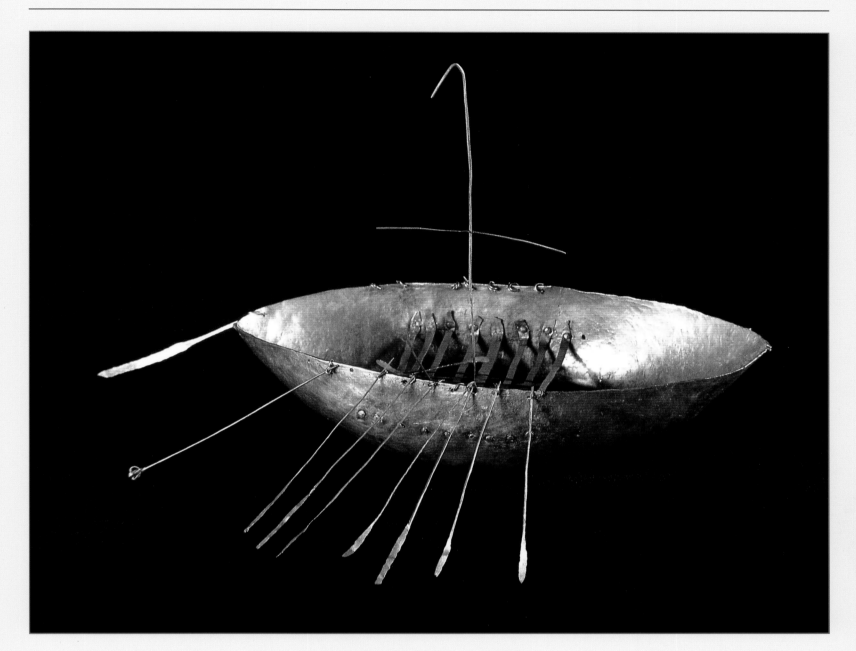

In the sixteenth century, men such as Sir Walter Raleigh and Edmund Spencer, the poet, received estates. In 1586, in the plantation of the Desmond lands in Munster, the planters were expected to introduce eighty-six families each into their estates. It failed because they did not bring in sufficient English people, so they rented land to native Irish tenants,

By contrast, the plantation of Ulster after 1610 was very successful and its effects lasted until the present day. English settlers, many from London, including tradesmen and businessmen, settled in County Derry under the aegis of London companies. Scots from the Lowlands, who spoke their own dialect of English, came to the other counties of Donegal, Tyrone, Cavan, Fermanagh and Armagh.

These people made roads, developed the countryside and generally began to make the area prosperous. This plantation proved eminently successful because people of all classes in society settled and stayed in the area.

In 1654 the Cromwellian plantation was carried out. An English-speaking class of landlords was introduced, some of whom were members of the Cromwellian Army. Others were from towns and cities that had invested in the war. The introduction of workers and tradesmen from England did not prove successful and the few who did come were absorbed into the native Irish population.

Because the landlords were English speakers, this language was followed by the new class of Catholic business-men who were of native Irish families. Gradually but inexorably the English language replaced Gaelic.

Immigration

From the 17th century onwards, people from Great Britain, who served the crown in various capacities, settled in Ireland permanently. These have been mainly civil servants and army personnel.

At the end of the 20th century, people from Asia and Africa and some mainland European States arrived as refugees and settled in the country – mostly in the Republic. For the first time since the foundation of the State, large numbers of asylum seekers of other races have settled in the republic.

Emigration

Over the centuries, largely for reasons of religion or poverty, to seek food, work and a better life, there have been successive waves of emigration.

In the 17th century, between 50,000 and 100,000 Irish left for the American colonies. From 1700 to 1776, 250,000-400,000 went there but during the potato famine years and its aftermath, there was a massive exodus – mainly to the USA but some to Canada. 651,931 arrived in North America during the Famine years (1845-47) – more than half of them landing in New York.

After 1922 many of the Protestant people in the southern Irish State emigrated to England, the Commonwealth or the colonies. They saw no future for themselves under the new regime.

Irish communities have sprung up all around the world, from Argentina to Australia. And wherever and whenever they have left home for new climes, the Irish peoples have taken with them a strong sense of nation and their cultural heritage to other parts of the world.

A miniature gold boat found amongst a hoard of Celtic ornaments in County Derry shows the fine craftmanship of the Celts in the first century AD

Worldwide, the total number of people of Irish descent is over 60 million.

In the United States 43 million claim Irish descent.

In Britain today, there are up to one million people of Irish birth.

30% of the Australian population (around five million) is of Irish descent.

In Argentina, there is an ethnic Irish population of around 300,000.

21 US Presidents have been of Irish descent (including, in recent times, Kennedy, Nixon and Reagan).

Three British Prime Ministers were born in Dublin including the Duke of Wellington.

Irish people preparing to board ship and seek a new life in America

A queue for food on an emigrant ship

How to use this book

This book provides a unique combination of time chart and conventional book pages to create a highly informative document – one that presents all the events, great and small. It covers the history and culture of Ireland in a way that is both clear and accessible.

The Timechart

Gatefolds (pages 16-35)
Each gatefold opens out so that the events through history can be seen as a continuous flow from one page to another.

Under the flaps
Under the flaps of the gatefolds, additional information is available on a selection of subjects related to the appropriate period of time.

Streams
The information in the timechart is separated out into various 'streams':

> **Culture and heritage**
> **Lifestyle**
> **Battle and conflict**
> **Politics, law and religion**

> **Rule**
> **Agriculture and industry**
> **People and personalities**

World events
The narrow stream at the bottom of the chart shows what was happening in the rest of the world at the same time.

Factfinder

In order to help trace information, the Factfinder links events and personalities to dates and places. Thus it acts as a useful summary of events as well as an index to lead the reader to the appropriate date on the chart.

Special subjects

The Timechart has space for only very brief information on any one subject or event. In order to compensate for this, in addition to the historical material under the flaps, certain particular areas of interest have been looked at in more detail in separate pages from the chart. These are:

> **Introduction to the landscape**
> **The changing face of power and domination**
> **Peoples of Ireland**
> **The Effects of Geography**
> **Towns and Cities**
> **Religion and Culture**
> **The Languages of Ireland**
> **The Old Irish Laws**
> **Music in Ireland**
> **Art**
> **Irish Folklore and the 'Little People'**
> **The influence of the Celts**
> **Gaelic games and sport**
> **Irish Farming**
> **Wit and wisdom**
> **Literature**

There is also a section devoted to **Maps over the Centuries**.

Further information

While it is not within the scope of this book to cover all the subject areas of Ireland's history in depth, the comprehensive *Further Reading* and list of *Libraries and Museums* should enable readers to discover more detailed information about particular areas of interest.

Facts and figures

Through the course of history, translation from one language into another or misinterpretation have sometimes led to error and confusion. While the publishers have made every effort to verify facts and figures they cannot be held responsible for any inaccuracies, misunderstandings or controversy! However, they would welcome further information or advice on any such fallible areas in order to update future editions.

Publisher's note

The publishers hope that this timechart and history of Ireland and its people will help for a greater understanding of the nation's development. While history does have its emotive issues, the timechart has been made up of facts and events, not opinions or comment. The publishers would wish to be informed if any element is incorrect or in any way contentious.

To find a specific item in the timechart, refer to the four-way Factfinder on pages 36-53.

The gatefold opens or folds back to provide continuity from the previous page.

The names of the streams are repeated on each page to help readers follow the flow.

A stream of World Events runs through the entire timechart so that the reader can see, for example, that an uprising in Ireland in 1848 was happening at the same time as widespread revolutions in continental Europe.

The streams vary in size as the events or changes require. This in itself is a reflection of the pattern of history and culture – and shows for example, the surge in literature and Gaelic interest at the end of the 19th century.

A *Glossary* on page 53 will help clarify certain terms used.

Information under the flap gives more detail on events or personalities in that period.

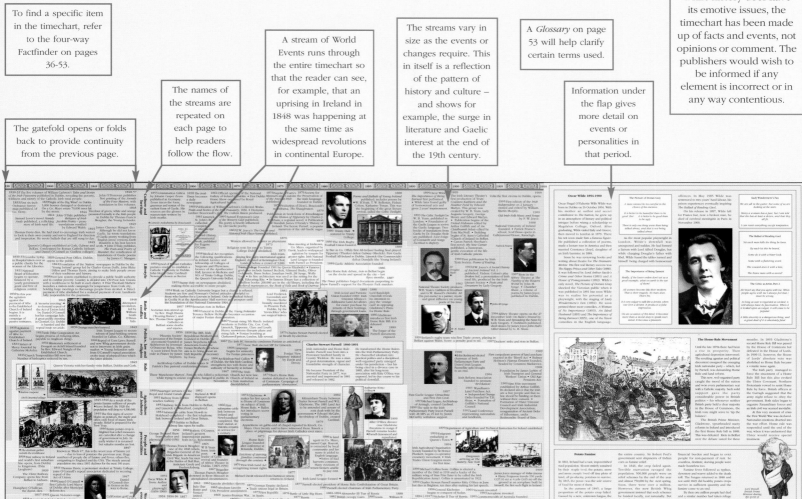

Culture and heritage

7000 BC The first human beings live in Ireland in the Mesolithic Age, surviving on what they hunt, fish or collect in surrounding countryside.

5500 BC End of the early Mesolithic Age in Ireland. Hunters-gatherers use small flint blades called microliths but large polished axes appear in the later Mesolithic Age.

← *Axe*

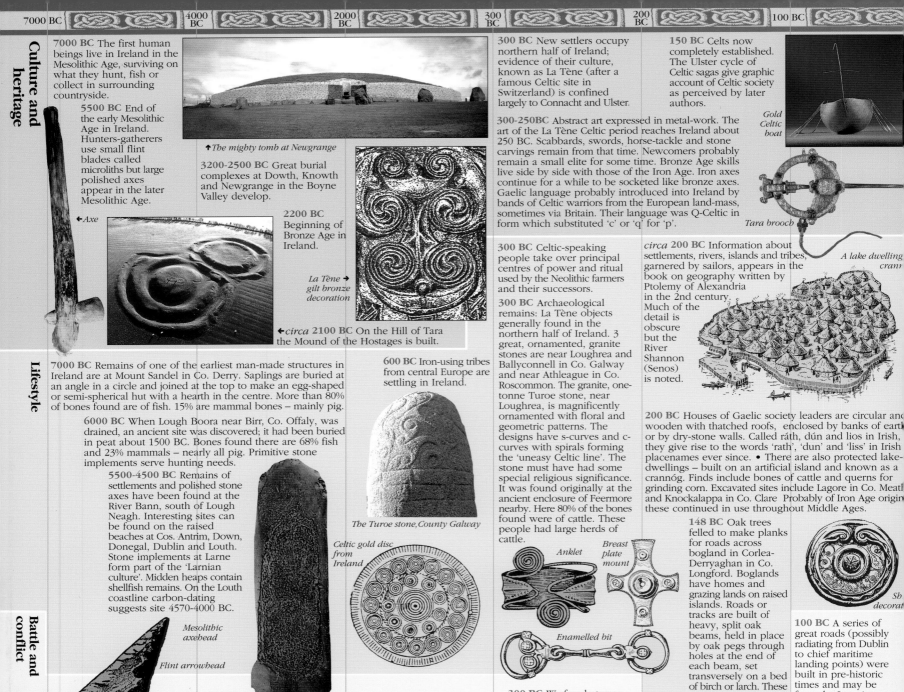

↑ *The mighty tomb at Newgrange*

3200-2500 BC Great burial complexes at Dowth, Knowth and Newgrange in the Boyne Valley develop.

2200 BC Beginning of Bronze Age in Ireland.

La Tène → *gilt bronze decoration*

← *circa 2100 BC* On the Hill of Tara the Mound of the Hostages is built.

300 BC New settlers occupy northern half of Ireland; evidence of their culture, known as La Tène (after a famous Celtic site in Switzerland) is confined largely to Connacht and Ulster.

300-250BC Abstract art expressed in metal-work. The art of the La Tène Celtic period reaches Ireland about 250 BC. Scabbards, swords, horse-tackle and stone carvings remain from that time. Newcomers probably remain a small elite for some time. Bronze Age skills live side by side with those of the Iron Age. Iron axes continue for a while to be socketed like bronze axes. Gaelic language probably introduced into Ireland by bands of Celtic warriors from the European land-mass, sometimes via Britain. Their language was Q-Celtic in form which substituted 'c' or 'q' for 'p'.

Tara brooch

150 BC Celts now completely established. The Ulster cycle of Celtic sagas give graphic account of Celtic society as perceived by later authors.

Gold Celtic boat

Lifestyle

7000 BC Remains of one of the earliest man-made structures in Ireland are at Mount Sandel in Co. Derry. Saplings are buried at an angle in a circle and joined at the top to make an egg-shaped or semi-spherical hut with a hearth in the centre. More than 80% of bones found are of fish. 15% are mammal bones – mainly pig.

6000 BC When Lough Boora near Birr, Co. Offaly, was drained, an ancient site was discovered; it had been buried in peat about 1500 BC. Bones found there are 68% fish and 23% mammals – nearly all pig. Primitive stone implements serve hunting needs.

5500-4500 BC Remains of settlements and polished stone axes have been found at the River Bann, south of Lough Neagh. Interesting sites can be found on the raised beaches at Cos. Antrim, Down, Donegal, Dublin and Louth. Stone implements at Larne form part of the 'Larnian culture'. Midden heaps contain shellfish remains. On the Louth coastline carbon-dating suggests site 4570-4000 BC.

Mesolithic axehead

Flint arrowhead

600 BC Iron-using tribes from central Europe are settling in Ireland.

The Turoe stone, County Galway

Celtic gold disc from Ireland

300 BC Celtic-speaking people take over principal centres of power and ritual used by the Neolithic farmers and their successors.

300 BC Archaeological remains: La Tène objects generally found in the northern half of Ireland. 3 great, ornamented, granite stones are near Loughrea and Ballyconnell in Co. Galway and near Athleague in Co. Roscommon. The granite, one-tonne Turoe stone, near Loughrea, is magnificently ornamented with floral and geometric patterns. The designs have s-curves and c-curves with spirals forming the 'uneasy Celtic line'. The stone must have had some special religious significance. It was found originally at the ancient enclosure of Feermore nearby. Here 80% of the bones found were of cattle. These people had large herds of cattle.

Anklet

Breast plate mount

Enamelled bit

circa 200 BC Information about settlements, rivers, islands and tribes, garnered by sailors, appears in the book on geography written by Ptolemy of Alexandria in the 2nd century. Much of the detail is obscure but the River Shannon (Senos) is noted.

A lake dwelling cranr

200 BC Houses of Gaelic society leaders are circular, wooden with thatched roofs, enclosed by banks of earth or by dry-stone walls. Called ráth, dún and lios in Irish, they give rise to the words 'rath', 'dun' and 'liss' in Irish placenames ever since. • There are also protected lake-dwellings – built on an artificial island and known as a crannóg. Finds include bones of cattle and querns for grinding corn. Excavated sites include Lagore in Co. Meath and Knockalappa in Co. Clare Probably of Iron Age origin these continued in use throughout Middle Ages.

148 BC Oak trees felled to make planks for roads across bogland in Corlea-Derryaghan in Co. Longford. Boglands have homes and grazing lands on raised islands. Roads or tracks are built of heavy, split oak beams, held in place by oak pegs through holes at the end of each beam, set transversely on a bed of birch or larch. These will support carts.

Sh decorat

Battle and conflict

300 BC Warfare between Connacht and Ulster is the theme of the *Cattle raid of Cooley* story – set in the early Iron Age but put into writing long afterwards.

200 BC Black Pig's Dyke, built from Bundoran to Strangford Lough, encloses the historical Ulster. It may have been a defensive earthwork and suggests a state of war between Ulster and its neighbours but the 'dyke' is not continuous.

100 BC A series of great roads (possibly radiating from Dublin to chief maritime landing points) were built in pre-historic times and may be from the Iron Age. They subsequently went to Waterford, the Shannon Estuary, Galway Bay, Sligo and Derry. Termed a 'slige', each was wide enough to allow two chariots to pass each other.

Rule

4000 BC After 4000 BC, Neolithic or New Stone Age people are first farmers. There is evidence of 'booleying' – the moving of cows from fertile lowlands to higher country when new grass begins to grow. Butter and cheese are made, forests cleared, animals domesticated and crops grown.

3000 BC More evidence of 'booleying' (moving cattle).

2000 BC Neolithic farmers' fields were in many places not being cultivated any more.

1860 BC Construction of Stonehenge begins in Britain.
→

1500 BC Copper extensively mined at Mount Gabriel, Co. Cork

300 BC Celtic-speaking people take over principal centres of power and ritual used by the Neolithic farmers and their successors.

300 BC By this century the Iron Age had begun in Ireland.

circa 200 BC Ptolemy of Alexandria writes about Ireland – its people and geography.

Agriculture and industry

Carbon-dating indicates bones found near Dublin are from 4340 to 3810 BC.

World events

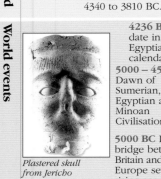

Plastered skull from Jericho

7000 BC Walled settlement at Jericho. Pottery develops. Man begins to use metals.

4236 BC First date in ancient Egyptian calendar.

3760 BC First date in Jewish calendar.

5000 – 4500 Dawn of Sumerian, Egyptian and Minoan Civilisations.

5000 BC Last land bridge between Britain and mainland Europe severed by rising sea level. Lower Mesopotamia has first settlements in fertile river valleys.

3372 BC First date in Mayan calendar.

3100 BC Menes founds 1st Dynasty in Egypt.

3000 BC Bricks first used in Egypt and Assyria

4000 BC Yang-shao rice farming culture in China.

2780 BC First pyramid is designed in Egypt.

2500 BC Early Minoan civilisation in Crete. Indus Valley civilisation in India

1000-500 BC Earlier Iron Age (Halstatt culture) in Europe.

circa 800 BC Homer writes The Iliad and The Odyssey.

580 BC Work begins on the Hanging Gardens of Babylon.

753 BC Foundation of Rome

500 BC Later Iron Age – (La Tène culture)

490 BC Persian – Greek wars

431–404 BC Peloponnesian War.

356-323 BC Alexander the Great

2000-1000 BC Bronze Age in Europe

264-146 BC Punic Wars between Rome and Carthage.

250 BC Hebrew scriptures translated into Greek.

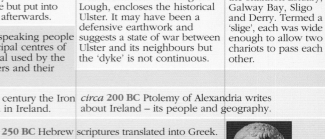

Enamelled brick lion on the walls of Babylon

218 BC Hannibal crosses Alps to invade Italy.

112 BC Parchment invented.

168 BC Roman conquest of Macedonia.

141 BC Judaea proclaimed an independent kingdom.

58-55 BC Caesar's ↑ conquest of Gaul and unsuccessful attempt to invade Britain.

54 BC Second invasion of Britai by Caesar.

51 BC Cleopa VII and Ptole XIII joint rule of Egypt.

circ 6-4 B Birth of Chris

7000 – 2000 BC Neolithic Age in Europe.

AD 100 According to legend, Tuathal seizes parts of territories that border his ancestral kingdom around Tara to form the kingdom of Meath. (*Mide* means 'middle'.) The king rules from the Irish Sea to the Shannon and takes the most fertile parts of Leinster and lands of lesser peoples. He levies on his Leinster enemies an annual *Boru Laigen* (cattle-tribute); 15000 each of cows, hogs, bed-coverings, cauldrons for beer, slave-women and maids including the Leinster king's daughter. Storytellers say the Leinster king married one of Tuathal's daughters, pretended she was dead and took the other. Both died of shame when they met and the levying of the tribute began. Tuathal is said to have instituted the Feis of Tara – a periodic assembly for business, recreational and politics. *Feis* actually means 'sleeping together'!

AD 250 Stories of Finn Mac Cool and his men are connected with all parts of Ireland, and Scotland, too. They may have originated from the Munster cycle of tales.

Ogham stone

AD 260 According to tradition, Cormac Mac Airt had a standing army called the *Fianna*, lead by Finn Mac Cool (Fionn Mac Cumhaill). Finn and his men spent their time hunting deer and boars and roaming about the countryside proving their manhood as members of a warrior-band or *fiam*.

AD 254 Suggested date for the reign of Cormac Mac Airt, traditionally believed to have founded the high-kingship of Tara.

AD 300 A rudimentary script, derived from Latin, used for brief, undated memorials to individuals, is one of earliest Irish inscriptions. Earliest manuscripts are ecclesiastical texts.

AD 300-500 Ogham inscriptions appear. These commemorate the dead and are oldest known form of the Irish language. They prove that some Irish were literate because they are based on the Latin alphabet. There are 315 inscriptions extant in Ireland, 121 in Co. Kerry, 81 in Co.Cork, 47 in Co.Waterford, 12 in Co. Kilkenny. Many have the word *mucoi*, referring to the eponymous ancestor, often a divine figure; for example, *Medussi mucoi Luga* (the stone of Medus of the people of Lug). Lug was the chief god of the people in pre-Christian times. When *mucoi* is omitted, the deceased may be Christian. Stones with *anam* (soul), *celi* (devotee) and *avi* (grandson) seem to be for Christians.

AD 300 Migration from southern Ireland, especially from Co. Waterford, to Dyfed in South Wales. Welsh stones bear ogham inscriptions –15 in Pembroke, 8 in Brecon, 7 in Carmarthen, 4 in Cardigan, 3 in Glamorgan, 2 in Denbigh, 1 in Caernarvon. As in Ireland, migrants build round wooden houses within circular enclosures.

AD 324 Traditional date in medieval annals for the fall of Eamhain Macha, ancient ritual capital of Ulster, and its conquest by descendants of Conn (called the *Uí Néill*).

AD 367 Major attack on Britain by Irish, Picts and Saxons.

AD 318 Cormac Mac Airt dies. The new king, Fiachra the Flat-headed, is a descendent of Eoghan the Great. Supposedly, his head is flat because his mother sat on a stone in the River Suir to delay his birth until after midnight so he could be King of Munster, as predicted by a druid.

AD 379 Niall of the Nine Hostages reputedly becomes King of Tara. He is an ancestor of the Uí Néill – the grandsons of Niall. The southern Uí Néill rule the Kingdom of Meath; the Northern Uí Néill will conquer Ulster. Allegedly, Niall leads raiding expeditions to Britain and Gaul to seize booty and slaves. On one occasion he is repelled in Wales by the Roman general, Stilicho.

n q r i
s c z e
f t ng u
l d g o
b h m a

← The Ogham alphabet: the marks are the earliest written Irish inscriptions

AD 450 Ogham script is still used on standing stones to commemorate the dead.

BC 463 Laoghaire sets out to attack the Leinstermen, marching between two hills, called Éire and Alba. He is supposedly killed by the sun and wind for having violated his oath.

AD 400 The principal documents from this era are the *Confession of Patrick the former slave*, the story of his life, and his *Letter to Coroticus* – an angry protest at the capture of some converts as slaves by Coroticus. Both are written in vigorous, expressive Latin.

AD 431 Mission of Palladius from Gaul is sent by the Pope to those Irish who already believe in Christ.

AD 433-4 Prosper of Aquitaine attributes conversion of Ireland to Pope Celestine.

AD 432-461 St Patrick converts Ireland to Christianity. Patrick lived originally on the west coast of Britain, his grandfather a Christian priest, his father a British/Roman official. At 16, Patrick is captured by pirates and taken to Ireland. He escapes to France and trains as a priest before returning to Britain, and then Ireland in 432.

AD 400 Christianity brings literacy, plus European (especially Latin) culture to Ireland. Not part of the Roman Empire, it now becomes part of the Roman Christian church. Many church buildings are made of wood, probably with thatched, steep-pitched roofs – like the few early stone churches built on treeless parts of western Ireland. • The first Christian missionaries may be Declan of Ciarán of Ardmore, Co. Waterford, Seir Kieran in Co. Offaly and Ailbe of Emly, Co. Tipperary.

AD 405 Niall allegedly killed on the shores of the English Channel by the King of Leinster. Nath Í becomes king of Tara and goes on piratical expeditions to Europe – is killed by lightning at the foot of the Alps. His men bring his corpse back to bury at Croghan; a pillar stone marks the grave.

AD 428 Successor of Nath Í is Laoghaire – probably a generation later than this traditional date. His reign is marked by war with Leinster on whom the midland kings levied the Boru Laigen. Unlike Nath Í, Laoghaire never goes overseas. Because of a phrophecy that he would die between Ireland and Scotland, he takes an oath never to travel by sea.

5th to 6th Century During Christian era, Ireland is united by one language and one culture, despite comprising numerous small kingdoms or tuatha, each ruled by a minor king, subservient to another more powerful 'king' above him, who in turn is under the protection of one of five provincial kings. The unit of currency is the cow.

AD 549 Outbreak of plague kills many, including monastic founders.

AD 450 Pre-christian religious practices adapt to Christianity where possible. Holy Wells are accepted for Christian uses. Wells attributed to St. Anne probably derive from Anu, the patron of fertility. Other wells named as Grania's Well were originally dedicated to the sun.
Native laws are adapted and influenced by the new religion, especially elements of the Old Testament. The status of the cleric is declared equal to the poet and seer. Ancient laws reckoned monetary value in cows and in the sét (a female slave, worth six cows). Brigit is said to found a monastery and a convent in Kildare in the 5th century. The church is attended at first by both monks and nuns. Venerated as a saint but named after the goddess of the arts, she may have been a christianisation of the goddess.

AD 500 Craft workers and scholars from all over Europe study at Irish monasteries. Later, Irish priests travel all over Europe founding schools, monasteries and cathedrals which become great centres of scholarship and religious learning. 6th-century monasteries that became famous schools include Clonmacnois on the River Shannon, founded by Ciarán, That of Clonard, Co. Meath, founded by Finnian, and Bangor, Co. Down, founded by Comgall.

AD 546 Columba becomes a monk and founds a monastery in Derry – followed by others in Kells, Swords, Lambay Island and Durrow.

AD 548 Clonmacnois ← monastery by the River Shannon founded by Ciarán.

St. Patrick

Politics, law and religion

AD 177 By tradition, Conn the Hundred-Battled became king in Tara. Legend claims he fought against Mogh, or Eoghan the Great, King of Munster and they decide to divide Ireland between them along the route of the Slige Mór – the great road from Dublin to Galway built on the Esker Riada, the post-glacial gravel mound that crosses Ireland.

AD 78-84 Agricola, Roman governor of Britain, considers conquest of Ireland.

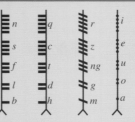

St Patrick's grave

King Cormac

circa AD 450 Eamhain Macha falls when Ulaid is invaded by the Uí Néill. Ulster people flee east of the River Bann and Lough Neagh, so Patrick the ex-slave's grave is in Downpatrick in Co. Down, although he had earlier established a church at Armagh beside Eamhain.

AD 461 One of the various dates given for the death of Patrick whose missionary activity remains the subject of controversy.

AD 503 Western Scotland is supposedly colonised by Irishmen from Antrim. Its rulers are subject to their Irish relatives who bring with them the Gaelic language and spread into the rest of Scotland. 'Scot' meant Irishman until then.

AD 519 Columba, a noble of the Uí Néill, is born in Co. Donegal.

AD 542 Enda, who founded a monastery on Aran, dies.

AD 543 Columbanus, a Leinsterman, born. Educated at Bangor monastery, he goes to France as a missionary.

People and personalities

AD 14 and **68** Cornelius Tacitus, the Roman writer, states in his Annals between 14 and 68 that the island was like Britain and was well known to merchants. He claims the Roman general, Agricola, stated that he could hold Ireland with one legion.

AD 160 Tuathal dies, according to tradition.

circa **AD 130-180** Ptolemy's account of Ireland.

AD 50 The Greek, Philemon, 50 AD, records that merchants who had visited Ireland said that the length of the island was 20 days' journey.

circa **AD 30** Christ crucified.

AD 43-77 Roman conquest of Britain.

AD 84 Agricola's Roman fleet circumnavigates Britain.

AD 80 Colosseum completed.

AD 79 Eruption of Vesuvius – Pompeii, Herculaneum and Stabiae buried.

AD 227 New Persian Empire founded.

AD 220-265 Period of the Three Kingdoms in China.

AD 235 Roman civil wars.

AD 350 Christianity reaches Ethiopia.

AD 364 Roman Empire divided.

AD 395 Partition of Eastern and Western Roman Empires.

Standing stones Waterville, County Kerry

AD 400 Irish colony is still in Wales in the fifth century.

St Patrick's shamrock represents the Trinity

AD 407 Last Roman troops leave Britain.

AD 450 Anglo-Saxons conquer Britain

AD 476 Fall of Western Roman Empire

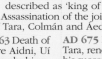

Culture and heritage

AD 575 An assembly in Drumket, now Daisy Hill near Limavady in Co. Derry, is attended by Columba from Iona. It is held by Aedh, King of the Northern Uí Néill, to decide the status of poets in Christian Ireland. Their influence is drastically curtailed for their satires are much feared by all. It is agreed that Scottish Dál Riada is to be independent of its counterpart in Ireland.

AD 600 Beginning of an important period of art and literature in Ireland.

circa AD 650 Book of Durrow, earliest of Ireland's great manuscripts, compiled.

AD 670-700 Tírechán and Muirchú produce works on St Patrick.

AD 664 Yellow plague sweeps through Ireland.

AD 700 Ireland consists of five kingdoms known as the Five Fifths of Ireland: Ulster, Meath, Leinster, Munster and Connacht. In this century Oratory of Gallerus near the harbour of Smerwick in Co. Kerry, is built. The west doorway has leaning jambs, the side walls lean inwards and shed the rain admirably. The east window is deeply splayed.

Oratory of Gallerus

Examples from the Book of Kells

AD 800s The first stone churches in many parts of Ireland are built in this century. Small, with lintelled doorways and windows and high-pitched roofs, their side-walls extended a little beyond the gables at the doorway. It is believed that in this century the first versions of the Ulster sagas are written, such as the *Cattle Raid of Cooley*. Ireland develops the first sustained vernacular literature in Europe.

AD 807 *The Book of Armagh* is begun. Scribe Ferdomhnach compiles it on the orders of the successor of Patrick. Construction of the monastery of Kells is begun.

AD 867 Johannes Scottus Eriugena publishes 6 volumes of *De divisione naturae* – disapproved by the Church.

AD 870 Ivar the Boneless, a Danish Viking, and Olaf king of Dublin capture Dumbarton in Scotland and return next year with many captives. The name Dublin derives from *Duibhlinn*, the Black Pool in the Liffey where the city was built.

AD 846 *The Book of Armagh* is completed by this date when Ferdomhnach dies. In the book are glosses on the Latin text of *Gospels* and *Acts of the Apostles*, Gaelic additions Tárecháni's Latin *Life of St Patrick* and part of *Patrick's Confession*.

Lifestyle

Battle and conflict

AD 637 An Ulaid prince, Congal Claen, banished by Domnall King of the Uí Néill, lands in Co. Down with an army of mercenaries. He is defeated in the battle of Moira. This is the end of the old independent Uliad, the kingdom of east Ulster.

AD 676
Stone fort, Grianán of Ailech near Derry – a ringfort of dry-stone wall 17ft 6ins (5.334 m) surrounded by three rings of outer defences – is destroyed by the men of the Southern Uí Néill.

AD 722 Fergal, King of Tara, invades Leinster to collect the Boru Tribute but is decisively defeated at the Hill of Allen in Co. Kildare. He and a large number of his men are killed.

AD 723 Clonmacnois plundered for the first time.

AD 738 Áed, King of Tara son of Fergal, wins a bloody victory over Leinster, in revenge for the death of his father.

AD 743 Clann Cholmáin, led by Domnall Mide, kill Áed Allán and take the overkingship of the Uí Néill.

St Kevin's church

AD 793 Vikings raid Lindisfarne.

Vikings raid Ireland

AD 800 Ireland's most famous manuscript, the Book of Kells is written. Often described as the most beautiful book in the world, it portrays the gospels in Latin using a majuscule script.

AD 840-1 Viking fleet overwinters on Lough Neagh.

AD 841 Norse Vikings build a settlement in Dublin. The Irish call the blonde-haired Norwegians *fionnghaill* (white foreigners).

AD 869 Olaf of Dublin raids Armagh and kills or captures 1,000.

AD 866 Áed Finnliath clears northern coastline of Viking bases. 867 Start of long-term struggle between Dublin Vikings (Ostmen) and their Hiberno-Viking kinsmen in York. 868 Áed Finnliath invades Brega district near Dublin and defeats Southern Uí Néill, the Leinsterman, and the Dublin Norse.

Politics, law and religion

Glendalough monastery

AD 650-750 Writing of Irish canon and vernacular law in progress.

AD 598 Kevin founds his monastery in Glendalough, Co. Wicklow, at the end of the 6th century.

circa AD 590 Columba goes to Gaul and imposes a severe monastic rule on his monks that is enforced until replaced in Europe by the more humane Rule of St Benedict.

AD 650-750 Writing of Irish canon and vernacular law in progress.

AD 664 Outcome of Synod of Whitby causes Irish clerics to withdraw from Northumbria.

AD 680 Primacy of Armagh recognises Bishop of Sletty, Co. Laois.

AD 700 The eastern Eóganacht becomes dominant in Munster. Writing of *Críth Gablach* (a law tract on status).

AD 697 Synod of Birr and the proclamation of the 'Law of the Innocents' by Abbot Adomnán of Iona, author of Life of St Columba.

8th century Viking raids attack monasteries near towns. (Ninth-century Irish metalwork has been recovered in Norway.) First raiders on the north and eastern coasts travel in long clinker-built boats, far superior to any other sea-craft in Europe then.

AD 802 Iona burned by Vikings. 806 68 members of Iona community killed by Vikings. 824 Vikings raid Skellig Michael and capture hermit, Étgal; they starve him to death. A monk on Iona is killed when he refuses to divulge to Vikings where St Columba's shrine is hidden. 825 Vikings defeat Osraige (Ossorm) but are defeated by Ulaid. Viking raids intensify. 833 Niall Laille defeats Vikings at Derry. 835 Viking raids on Dublin. 836 Viking raids penetrate deep inland. 837 Fleet of 60 Viking ships on the Liffey and Boyne; settlements established for first time. 845 Viking leader Turgesius captured in the midlands by King of Meath, Máel Sechmaill I, who had him drowned in Lough Owel in Westmeath. Forannán, abbot of Armagh, captured by Vikings. 848 Series of major Irish victories over Vikings.

AD 846-62 Reign of Máel Sechnaill I, powerful overking of the Uí Néill.

AD 858 Máel Sechnaill I becomes the first Uí Néill king to receive submission of Munster and is subsequently recognised as high-king of all Ireland.

AD 842 First reported Viking-Irish alliance.

833 New high-king, Niall Laille of the Northern Uí Néill.

AD 861 Áed Finnliath of the Northern Uí Néill plunders Meath with the Vikings of Dublin and succeeds Máel Sechnaill as high-king within a year.

AD 804 Áed Oirnide of the Uí Néill ordained overking of the Uí Néill by the Abbot of Armagh.

AD 800 The Uí Néill dominate north Leinster.

AD 820-47 Feidlimid mac Crimthainn king of Munster.

AD 879 Death of Áed Finnliath; high-kingship reverts to Southern Uí Néill king Flann Sinna.

AD 857 Cerball mac Dúnlainge of Osraige rises to prominence and is named Kiarvalr by the Vikings; his exploits pass into legend and saga.

Rule

AD 558 Traditionally, King Diarmait mac Cerbaill holds the last feis of Tara. He leaves Tara when it is cursed by St Ruadán of Lorrha because of an unjust judgment.

AD 642 The Uí Néill king, Domnall, described as 'king of Ireland', dies.

AD 604 Assassination of the joint high-kings of Tara, Colmán and Áed Sláine.

AD 663 Death of Guaire Aidni, Uí Fiachrach, king of Connacht.

AD 675 Fínanichta, King of Tara, renounces for himself and his successors the right to collect the Boru from Leinster.

AD 721-42 Cathal mac Finguine king of Munster.

AD 734 Abdication of Flaithbertach mac Loingsig. Cenél Conaill now excluded from Uí Néill overkingship.

AD 760-4 Monastic community at Clonmacnois at war with monasteries of Birr and Durrow.

AD 795 Viking raids on Iona, Rathlin, Inishmurray, and Inishbofin.

Agriculture and industry

AD 612 Columban leaves St Gallen in Switzerland after a dispute with his disciple, Gall. He travels to Bobbio in Italy where he dies in 615 after a dispute with the Pope.

AD 622 Kevin, founder of Glendalough monastery, dies.

AD 598 Aedh, high-king of the Uí Néill, is killed when he collects the Boru Tribute in Leinster.

circa AD 590 Columbanus disputes with the bishops in Gaul and incurs the ill-will of the king. He settles in Italy at Bobbio.

AD 737 Áed Adlán of Tara and Cathal of Munster proclaim the 'Law of Patrick' and acknowledge primacy of Armagh.

AD 725 Uí Briúin dynasty dominant in Connacht.

AD 750 Completion of Irish canon law compilation Collectio canonum Hibernensis and of secular law corpus Senchas Már.

circa AD 770 Culdee, from Céile Dé ('God's partner') start to reform church.

circa AD 780 Uí Briúin gain control of Bréifne (Co. Leitrim).

AD 793 Artrí mac Cathail ordained king of Munster.

The small fortified skip-camp (Longphort) of Dublin on the banks of the River Liffey is sized by Olaf, a Dane. Becomes a centre for trade with the Isle of Man, West Scotland, Northern England and Europe. The Danes are described by the Irish as (black foreigners).

Armagh comes under Uí Néill control. **AD 750-850**

AD 872 Modwen, an Irish woman healer whose convent had been destroyed by Vikings, is invited to England by Alfred the Great, to cure him of a disease called 'the evil ficus'.

AD 853

People and personalities

Currach: wicker and hide boat

AD 558 Brendan founds a monastery at Clonfert, Co. Galway. A navigator, he reputedly sails to America in a frail, hide-covered sail-boat.

AD 563 Columba goes to Iona in the Hebrides with 12 companions to evangelise Scotland.

←AD 597 St Columba dies.

AD 635 Columba's disciple in Iona, Aidan, goes to Northumberland to found a monastery, Lindisfarne or Holy Island.

AD 784 Monk and astronomer from Aghaboe, Co. Laois, dies in Wurzburg. Fergal's studies taught that the earth was round.

AD 847 Joannes Scottus Eriugena, an Irish monk and intellectual is at the court of Charles the Bald in France. He translates into Latin the works of Dionysius the Areopagite and of Maximus Confessor.

AD 844 Scotland unified after defeating the Picts.

AD 871-899 Alfred the Great king of Wessex.

World events

AD 622 Height of Mayan civilisation in Mexico

AD 632 Death of Muhammad

AD 672-735 The Venerable Bede: His writings an important source of history.

AD 618-907 Tang dynasty in China.

AD 711 The Moors (Muslim Arabs) invade Spain.

AD 732 Block printing in China for Buddhist texts.

AD 704 Death of St Adomnán, 9th abbot of Iona.

AD 750-1258 Foundation of Abbasid dynasty.

AD 757-796 Offa, King of Mercia, builds Offa's dyke to keep the Welsh out.

AD 833 Observatory built in Baghdad.

AD 805 Aachen cathedral.

AD 800 Charlemagne crowned Holy Roman Emperor of the West by Pope Leo III in Rome.

AD 861 Vikings discover Iceland: settle there in 874.

AD 885 Vikings in Paris.

AD 896 Mexican

AD 856-875 Mayan Viking attacks civilisation on Britain. ending.

AD 895-901 *Three-Part Life of St Patrick* composed. The apostle of Ireland, Patrick, is presented as travelling all Ireland. This work originated in Armagh and its claims to church primacy are based on this.

AD 900 *Sanas Cormaic* (Cormac's Glossary), the first comparative dictionary in Europe, is written in Cashel in this century, reputedly by Cormac mac Cuilemmáin, king-bishop of Cashel, killed in battle 908.

AD 922
Vikings found port and city of Limerick.There are fleets of Vikings for the next decade in Lough Foyle, Lough Neagh, Strangford Lough, Carlingford Lough, Lough Erne and Lough Corrib.

AD 900 Most people were farmers. Brats (woollen cloaks) are made from the good quality wool their sheep produce. The Irish travel long distances in stormy seas in currachs – round boats made of wicker and covered with animal hides.

AD 902 Dublin Vikings defeated; survivors seem to have left Ireland.

AD 906 Munster from Limerick to Gowran is plundered by Flann Sinna, King of Meath, and the Leinstermen. Cormac Mac Cuilenmáin, king-bishop of Cashel, allies himself against them with the Abbot of Scattery Island, on the Shannon.

AD 908
Cormac Mac Cuilenmáin killed in the battle of Ballaghmoon, Carlow, in a dispute about monastic jurisdiction but also because of the threat he posed to Uí Néill hegemony.

AD 914 Viking fleets around the Munster coasts follow the death of Cormac mac Cullenan of Cashel at the Battle of Ballymoon. Vikings seize Waterford which becomes an important settlement, trading with Europe for 700 years.

AD 917 Return of Vikings to Dublin led by Sitric Gale. A Gaelic account says: 'Immense floods and countless sea-vomitings of ships, so that there was not a harbour nor port nor strongpoint in Munster without a Danish or foreign fleet'. Vikings settle on River Lee marsh; it becomes Cork city. Uí Néill of Meath and Ulster with the men of Munster and Leinster join forces to try to stop Vikings' return but fail.
921 Godfrid arrives as King of Dublin. 32 Viking ships on Lough Foyle; Armagh attacked but its churches spared.

AD 900 Descendants of Ulster's Niall of the Nine Hostages claim to be kings of all Ireland. Their court is at Tara in Meath.

AD 900 This is the high point of the Viking or Ostmen's power until checked by the ancestors of the O'Briens of the Dál gCais in Clare.

AD 919 Niall Húndub, the Black-kneed, King of Tara, tries to expel Dublin Vikings but is defeated and killed, the first high-king to die at Vikings' hands.

AD 920 Sitric leaves Dublin to become King of York after defeat by new high-king, Donnchad Donn.

AD 927 Hiberno-Vikings, expelled from York join their kinfolk in Ireland.

AD 988
Saltair na Rann (Psalter of Stanzas), 162 stanzas of biblical history composed in Gaelic.

AD 989
Sitric Silkleand, King of Dublin, mints first Irish coins, silver pennies and mainly imitations of English coins. Some are called 'Sihtric' or even 'Aethelred'.

AD 950 Close of the second period of Viking raids.

AD 967
Mahon and his brother, Brian, go to Cashel, from where the Eóganacht dynasty rule Munster. Ivar, King of Limerick, with Eóganacht allies confronts them. His forces are defeated at Sologhead near Tipperary.

AD980
The new high-king defeats the Ostmen at Tara and captures Dublin after a 3-day siege. His men loot the city and he frees many captives, probably slaves. Dublin had a flourishing slave-trade with cities like Bristol and Chester.

AD 982
Mael Sechnaill II raids Thomond and fells the sacred tree on Mághhair where the Dál gCais kings were inaugurated. This insult was a prelude to years of skirmishing and plundering between the two.

AD 937 Hiberno-Norse ruler of Dublin and York, Olaf son of Godfrid, defeated by Anglo-Saxons and Athelstan at battle of Brunanburh.

AD 941 Murkartagh of the Leather Cloaks, son of Niall glúndub (the Black-kneed), compaigns in Munster against Cellachán king of Cashel.

AD 995
Máel Sechnaill II once more loots Dublin and takes two prized objects, the ring of Thor and the sword of Carlus. (*See* 1029).

Coin issued by King Sitric of Dublin

AD 999
Sitric, the Dublin Ostmen's king, and Maelmora, King of Leinster, resent Brian Boru's authority. Brian marches against them and defeats them with the aid of Máel Sechnaill at Glenmáma near Newcastle, Co. Dublin. Brian and Máel Sechnaill agree never to invade one another's territory.

AD 916 The high-king, Flann Sinna, dies and is buried at Clonmacnois, where he had commissioned the 'Cross of the Scriptures'. Succeeded by Niall Húndub of Northern Uí Néill, ancestor of the O'Neills of Ulster.

Cross of the Scriptures

AD 944 Dublin sacked by the men of Leinster and the Uí Néill, under the new high-king, Congalach of Knowth. In aftermath, Olaf Cuarán becomes king of Dublin; later marries Gormfhlaith, an Irish woman.

AD 963 Mahon, brother of Brian Boru, becomes king of all Munster.

AD 956-80 Domnall ua Néill overking of the Uí Néill after Congolach is slain by Dublin Norse.

AD 976 Mahon is murdered by the Eóganacht king and Brian succeeds.

AD 976-1014
←Brian Boru king of Munster, and latterly of Ireland.

AD 981 Mael Sechnaill II becomes overking of the Uí Néill.

AD 989
Sitric Silkleand begins his reign as King of Dublin.

AD 997
Brian Boru and Máel Sechnaill II divide Ireland between them on the traditonal division of Mogha's Half and Conn's Half, where the boundary is a line from Dublin to Oarinbridge, Co. Galway.

AD932
China: wood-block printing for mass production of classic books.

AD 939
Japanese civil wars start.

AD 941 Brian Boru, son of Kennedy (Cennétig) king of the Dál gCais in Thomond that is now Co. Clare, is born in Kincora by the Shannon, his family's residence.

AD 981 Olaf (Cuarán) son of Sitric, former King of Dublin, dies in Iona monastery, where he had retired after defeat at Tara.

AD 982 Viking Eric the Red visits Greenland.

AD 986
Viking settlements in Greenland.

1007 *Book of Kells* stolen but recovered, minus its ornamental cover, three months later.→

1013 Dublin Ostmen and Maelmora, King of Leinster, revolt against Brian. Brian and Murrough, his son, lead two armies to Dublin ravaging Leinster on the way. The attempt to punish the Ostmen of Dublin fails due to lack of provisions.

1088
Donal O'Loughlin of the Northern Uí Néill line claims to be high-king and raids Thomond where he destroys Kincora. Muirchertach leads his army north in retaliation. Afterwards he ackowledges his rival as high king.

1002 Brian Boru sets out to depose Máel Sechnaill in spite of the treaty between them. With the aid of his allies and former enemies, they invade Meath but Máel Sechnaill submits to Brian who is now the first effective High King of Ireland.

Brian Boru↓

1014 Dublin Ostmen and their Leinster Irish allies seek aid abroad. Ostmen from the Isle of Man, the Scottish isles and England come to Dublin. Brian Boru with Irish allies and the Limerick and Waterford Ostmen come to Dublin. In an homeric encounter the foreign Ostmen are defeated by King Brian Boru at Clontarf where Brian is killed.

1005 Brian Boru acknowledges the position of Armagh in the Irish church. A scribe describes him as 'Imperator Scottorum' (Emperor of the Irish) in an entry in the *Book of Armagh* marking the occasion.

1028 Sitric, King of Dublin, goes on pilgrimage to Rome and founds Christ Church cathedral on his return. Dímán, first bishop of Dublin, consecrated at Canterbury.

1074 Dúnán, Bishop of Dublin, dies. His successor, Patrick, had been a monk at Worcester and is consecrated at Canterbury by Lanfranc who claims to be primate of Ireland, York and the rest of England.

1096
Bishop Samuel O'hAingli founds the parish of St. Michan, Dublin. Malchus, first Bishop of Waterford, consecrated at Canterbury.

1002-14
Brian Boru reigns as king.

1046
O'Connor family dominate in Connacht.

1052 Diarmait Mac Maelnamó of Leinster becomes first native Irish king of Dublin.

1072
Diarmait Mac Maelnamó, King of Leinster is slain by Conor O'Melaghlin, King of Meath. Turlough O'Brian becomes high-king of Ireland 'with opposition'.

1086
Turlough O'Brien dies at Kincora and his son, Muirchertach succeeds him.

1022 Máel Sechnaill of Meath, Brian Boru's successor, dies. This starts the era of the 'kings with opposition'. There is continual internecine warfare for the kingship among the ruling families. Donnchad, son of Brian, claims to be his father's successor but Northern provinces never acknowledge him as such.

1086-1119
Muirchertach O'Brien king of Munster and claimant to the kingship of Ireland (1093-1114).

1064
Turlough O'Brien wrests the kingship of Munster from his uncle, Donnchadh, with the help of Diarmait Mac Maelnamo of Leinster. He forces all except Ulster to recognise him. Donnchad goes to Rome on pilgrimage and dies there.

1075
Turlough O'Brien installs his son Muirchertach as king of Dublin.

1000 Brian Boru marries Gormlaith, the mother of Sitric, King of Dublin, who was also sister of Maelmora of Leinster. Brian Boru's daughter marries Sitric.

1085
Donngus, Bishop of Dublin, consecrated at Canterbury.

1029 Olaf son of Sitric and King of Dublin kidnapped by O'Regan. His ransom, the highest on record, is 1,200 cows, 120 British horses, 60 ounces of gold with the 'sword of Carlus'.

circa 1098
Muirchertach O'Brien gives a present of great oak trees to King William Rufus to construct the roof of Westminster Hall.

circa 1045
Chinese use movable type for printing.

1071 Creation of Bayeaux tapestry.

1066
Battle of Hastings – Norman conquest of Britain.

1087
Omar Khayyám writing in Persia.

1000 Viking sighting of North America.

1044 Invention of gunpowder in China.

1069-1072
Famine in Egypt.

1086 Start of Domesday Book in England

1096-1270 The Crusades.

1100 This is a century of violent war when Ireland becomes 'a trembling sod'. Meanwhile, the country is absorbed into European life by the reform of the church and by foreign invasion.

1101 Muirchertach O'Brien goes north with a large force and wrecks Grianán of Ailech, the symbolic home of the Northern Uí Néill. Each fighting man takes away a stone from the great pile.

1115
Donnchad Mac Murrough killed in battle by Donal son of Muirchertach O'Brien and the Ostmen of Dublin. He is buried with his dog. Trying to become more powerful, Turlough O'Connor, King of Connacht, divides Meath in two between two O'Melaghlins. One kills the other.

1111 Synod of Rath Breasail presided over by Muirchertach O'Brien with Gilbert of Limerick as papal legate. Two provinces created, based on political division of Conn's Half and Mogha's Half. In the northern half is Armagh with 12 bishops and in the south, Cashel with 11 bishops. Limerick and Waterford cities included but not yet Dublin.

1116
Malchus is first Bishop of Cashel according to the acts of the Synod of Rath Breasail.

1101 Muirchertach O'Brien gives the royal capital of Munster on the Rock of Cashel ↑to the church. Synod of Cashel discusses simony, the church's freedom from taxation, clerical celibacy, marriage law. There are too many Irish bishops and their power is weak.

1106-56 Turlough O'Connor king of Connacht and claimant to the 'high-kingship' of Ireland.

1114 Muirchertach O'Brien falls seriously ill and power shifts to O'Connor of Connacht.

1118
Turlough O'Connor divides Munster in two between an O'Brien and a McCarthy. He hurls the O'Brien residence, Kincora, into the Shannon.

1105 Cellach, succeeds as Abbot of Armagh, although he is a layman. He ordains himself a priest.

1119
Muirchertach O'Brien dies in the monastery of Lismore after retiring there to take clerical orders.

1106 On Easter Sunday Maelmuirr, the principal scribe of the *Book of the Dun Cow*, is killed at a church door in Clonmacnois by Irish raiders.

1106 The Bishop of Armagh dies; Cellach succeeds him and unites abbacy and bishopric. A layman, he ordains himself a priest.

1106 Gilbert, first Bishop of the Ostmanic city of Limerick, consecrated.

1110 Dermot Mac Murrough son of Donnchad the King of Leinster born.

Culture & heritage / Lifestyle

1123 Turlough O'Connor presents to the church the processional Cross of Cong. →

1126 Turlough O'Connor sets up camp in North Tipperary to send raiders south, south-west and south-east.

1145 More war and raids by Turlough O'Connor.

circa **1170** At Clonfert the Irish Romanesque cathedral is built by Conor O'Kelly – its west doorway still survives intact. A small church in the Irish Romanesque style is built in Tuam. It is restored after an 18th-century fire but the six-ordered Irish Romanesque arch and one window have survived. Irish Romanesque churches are built throughout the country. The architectural style is typical in this era of church reform and Anglo-Norman conquest. The cathedral at Killaloe with its Irish Romanesque doorway is built by Donal Mór O'Brien.

1176 Donal More O'Brien has Limerick cathedral built. It is transitional between Irish Romanesque and Gothic. Additions were made in the 15th century. Original choir-stalls have the only surviving misericords in Ireland. In 1892 the west Irish Romanesque door was damaged by restorers.

1185 First Anglo-Norman coins minted by Prince John, silver farthings and halfpennies. The former have 'Iohannes Dominus' (John Lord) on and the latter have 'Iohannes' inscribed on them. Prince John erects motte-and-baileys at Tibberaghney near Carrick-on-Suir, Ardfinnan and Lismore and grants land in North Tipperary and part of Limerick to Theobald Walter, the ancestor of the Butlers.

1188 Charter granted to Cork by Prince John as Lord of Ireland.

Battle and conflict

1134 Dermot Mac Murrough allies himself with the Dublin Ostmen and raids Kilkenny and the Waterford Ostmen.

1137 Dermot Murrough and the Ostmen of Dublin and Wexford with a fleet of 200 Ostmanic ships, besiege Waterford city. Dermot and Murrough O'Melaghlin make a treaty. Dermot agrees to help O'Melaghlin, if he is in danger from O'Connor. The Meath king agrees to allow him to hold Offaly in peace.

1132 Turlough O'Connor raids Munster from boats on the Shannon.

River Shannon and Limerick castle ↓

1141 Dermot Mac Murrough's brother 'removes' 41 potential rivals of Dermot in Leinster.

1150 The last Ostmanic coins minted in Dublin.

1150 O'Loughlin raids the midlands.

1151 Once more Turlough O'Connor with Dermot Mac Murrough raids O'Briens and defeats them. 7,000 Munstermen killed in this battle, at Móin Mór.

1154 Tiernan O'Rourke and others plunder Dermot Mac Murrough's territory.

1170-1200 Motte-and-baileys built wherever the Anglo-Normans penetrate at this time. They are earthwork fortifications: a semi-conical hillock crowned by a wooden tower and a lower elliptical raised mound containing living quarters, stores and stables. These are the first Norman 'castles' that were built.

1169 Wexford town is captured by Combro-Norman knights and archers, including Maurice FitzGerald and Robert FitzStephen.

1170 In May a small force arrives and is joined later by Strongbow. They capture Waterford from the Ostmen. Dermot McMurrough captures Dublin with Strongbow's aid. A siege by Rory O'Connor fails. The invaders have the two major seaports in Ireland.

1177 The present Co. Cork is occupied from this year onwards by Richard de Cogan, Robert FitzStephen and others. The custody of Waterford city is given to Robert le Poer whose family hold land later in the county. Prince John, Henry's son, is appointed Lord of Ireland at the Council of Oxford but remains in England. Hugh de Lacy is appointed procurator general of Ireland. He restores homes and land to the people of Meath who had fled in 1174. He covers his lands with motte-and-baileys, the first at Trim at a ford of the River Boyne.

1174 Strongbow tries to take Munster but is defeated in a battle at Thurles. Rory O'Connor makes a hosting across the Shannon and devastates Meath.

1177-8 John de Courcy invades Ulster and captures the territory east of the River Bann.

1185 Cork city declared a dependency of the Crown.

Politics, law and religion

1127 The Leinstermen depose Conor O'Connor but a king of a rival tuath is imposed on them. Cormac McCarthy driven into the monastery of Lismore and Munster divided in three. Turlough O'Connor's men travel on the Shannon and raid the surrounding countryside.

1138 Turlough O'Connor with Tiernan O'Rourke raids Meath but is aided by Dermot Mac Murrough. The armies retire without fighting.

1152 Christian O'Conarchy, Bishop of Lismore and Cardinal Paparo, papal legate attend the Synod of Kells. The Irish church is divided into four provinces with archbishops in Armagh, Dublin, Cashel and Tuam. The Archbishop of Armagh, Gelasius, was to be primate of Ireland. Laws against simony, robbery, usury, sexual misconduct and Irish marriage customs.

1162 Lorcán O'Toole Archbishop of Dublin.

1170 A bishops' synod at Armagh states that God is punishing the Irish people for buying English children as slaves. However, the Irish church reformers welcome the invaders as allies.

1172 Henry II tells a synod of prelates in Cashel that he wishes to regulate discipline in the church. In Anglo-Norman Ireland the parish-system is developed. Parishes are sometimes based on old territorial units but generally are based on the manor as a parish with the manor-lord as patron.

1139 Malachy visits Clairvaux and is much impressed by the Cistercians. In his lifetime Cistercian abbeys are founded in Mellifont, Bective, Balltinglass, Monasteranenagh. Some more are founded before the Norman invasion. There were 41 houses of the Canons Regular of Saint Augustine in Ireland during Malachy's life.

1142 Foundation of the first Cistercian house in Ireland (at Mellifont).

1136 Consecration of Cormac's Chapel at Cashel. →

1165 Ostmen from Dublin and other cities go to help King Henry II in his expedition in Wales.

1166-7 Dermot goes to Bristol and then France to ask King Henry II at Acquitane for aid to regain his kingdom. He promises to acknowledge him as overlord. Henry gives leave to recruit his subjects for this purpose. In Wales Dermot recruits and promises his daughter to Richard de Clare, 'Strongbow'. He returns to Ireland with a small group of Flemings from South Wales.

1166 Death of Muirchertach Mac Lochlainn, 'high-king' of Ireland Tiernan O'Rourke responds by going with a large force of Irish through Meath to Dublin to receive the submission of the Ostmen. They ally themselves with him to raid Leinster. Dermot Mac Murrough is forsaken by his allies and flees abroad.

1172 Henry assures the Irish rulers at Cashel of his protection but he nonetheless divides the country among his knights. He also grants Dublin to the Bristol men. Meath is given to Hugh de Lacy to keep Strongbow in check.

↓ *Henry II*

Rule

1126 Dermot Mac Murrough becomes king of his sub-kingdom (Uí Chennselaig). Turlough O'Connor makes his son, Conor, King of Leinster and Dublin.

1136 Turlough O'Connor blinds his son, Alsh, thus making him ineligible for kingship. Niall of the Clann Sinnaich succeeds Muirchertach but is expelled.

1143 Turlough's son killed by the Meathmen. Then Turlough divides the lands between Dermot Mac Murrough and Tiernan O'Rourke.

1147-8 Muirchertach O'Loughlin, king in the north-east, makes all Ulster subject to him.

1171 On Dermot Mac Murrough's death Strongbow claims his kingdom. This is contrary to Irish law, but legal in English practice. Henry II is concerned that his knights might establish a kingdom in Ireland, so he decides to come and overawe them with a great army. Dermot Mac Carthy, King of Desmond, meets him at Waterford and submits to him. Henry goes to Lismore where he meets churchmen and then to Cashel where Donal O'Brien submits. In Dublin he receives some Irish princelings who also submit to him. Rory O'Connor and the northern leaders do not come.

1175 Three ambassadors are sent to England by King Rory O'Connor to make a treaty with Henry at Windsor. Rory as a vassal of Henry II is to remain King of Connacht and of wherever the Normans have not settled.

1180 Donal Mór O'Brien establishes an abbey of Cistercians, Holy Cross, 4 miles (6.5 km) south-west of Thurles. Still a religious house in the 18th century, it is restored as a parish church in the 1970s.

1185 Prince John arrives in Waterford as Lord of Ireland with Gerald de Barry, historian better known as Giraldus Cambrensis, Theobald Walter, Philip of Worcester and others. He goes westwards taking over the Suir valley. He antagonises many of the Gaelic Irish and the established settlers.

Agriculture and industry

1120 Turlough O'Connor and Donal O'Loughlin of Ailech expelled from Meath. Murrough O'Melaghlin divides the province in four.

1122 Malachy of Armagh, dedicated reformer, goes to Lismore and is taught there by Malchus.

1124 Malachy Bishop of Down and Connor.

1144 At the request of the Irish clergy, led by Gelasius, the Bishop in Armagh, Turlough frees his son, Rory, whom he had imprisoned. He also declares 'a perfect peace'.

1128 Turlough O'Connor raids Uí Chennselaig and goes back by Dublin taking rustled cattle. He has as an ally, Tiernan O'Rourke, an evil choice.

People and personalities

1121 Donal O'Loughlin dies in the monastery of Derry after retiring from his kingship. Gregory consecrated as Bishop of Dublin in Canterbury but not allowed to take possession of his See. Celsus resents the foreign connection.

1127 Malachy, expelled from Down and Connor, goes to Lismore. Cormac McCarthy, King of Munster, expelled by Turlough O'Connor. He goes to Cashel.

1129 Cellach dies and is succeeded by another member of the Clann Sinaich, Muirchertach.

1142 Murrough O'Melaghlin is taken prisoner by Turlough O'Connor and he gives Meath to his son.

1148 Malachy dies and is buried in Clairvaux.

1137 Malachy breaks the claim that the Clann Sinnaich has a hereditary right to the church in Armagh. Succeeded by Gelasius.

1152 Tiernan O'Rourke is deprived of some of his territory by Turlough O'Connor aided by Dermot Mac Murrough, who then abducts O'Rourke's wife, Devorgilla, and her cattle and property with her full consent. She leaves him later.

1156 Turlough O'Connor dies. He was arguably the most innovative claimant to the high-kingship since Brian Boru.

↑ *Strongbow's tomb*

↓ *Marriage of Strongbow to Aoife*

1176 Strongbow dies and William FitzAudelm is appointed 'procurator' of Ireland in his stead.

1177-8 John de Courcy invades Ulster and his victory is ensured by the chronic disunity of the Ulster peoples. He holds the country by dotting it with motte-and-bailey forts, ten in all. He also has three castles of stone built, especially at Carrickfergus. John de Courcy was a founder of abbeys and monasteries in his territory, six in all.

1170 Strongbow marries Aoife MacMurrough.

1186 Hugh de Lacy murdered.

1180 Hugh de Lacy marries Rory O'Connor's daughter, which increases his influence. Henry II, being suspicious of him, dismisses him but soon afterwards reinstates him.

World events

Start of Gothic architecture. **1138**   **1147-1149** Second Crusade.   **1151** End of Mexican Toltec Empire.   **1156-1185** Civil wars in Japan.   **1161** Explosives first used in China.

↑*A chieftain's feast*

1199 liberties of Bristol
nted to Cork city.

1197 rince John grants
narter to Limerick.

more Castle, Waterford ↓

1200 Colony settles down but complete political and cultural conquest of Ireland had been thwarted. The colonists outside Dublin gradually become Hibernicised. • King John's castle built in Limerick. Some of the curtain-walls with a gate-house and angle towers survive. • Start of Classical Irish period in literature, lasting until 1600.

↓*St. Patrick's Cathedral, Dublin*

1229 A new charter for Dublin with a mayoralty.

↑*Carrickfergus Castle*

1200-20 The era of castle-building. At Carlow a castle is built to guard a ford on the River Barrow. In Carrickfergus a castle forms part of the stone wall that encloses the large courtyard or bawn. In Trim the castle is in the centre of the bawn.

1195 The McCarthys and O'Briens joined by Cathal Crobderg in campaign against Normans.

1196 O'Neills, under Aedh Méith, begin to gain dominance in mid-Ulster.

1197 John de Courcy attempts to expand west of the Bann into Derry and Tyrone.

1210 Munster is made a shire.

1213 St Patrick's becomes Dublin's second cathedral.

1202 Limerick city reserved to the Crown and the natives are driven outside the walls into the 'Cantred of the Ostmen'.

1203 William de Burgo invades Connacht, builds castle at Meclick, plunders the Cistercian abbey at Abbeyknockmoy and founds Athassel Abbey in Co, Tipperary.

1209 On Easter Sunday many Dublin people go to Cullenswood, where they are attacked by the O'Byrnes and the O'Tooles from the mountains who kill 300 men, women and children.

1224 William Marshal II, the justiciar, wages war against Hugh de Lacy and wastes all of Meath.

1227 Aedh O'Connor plunders and burns the town of Athlone. He thus forfeits his land. In May all Connacht is granted to Richard de Burgo and a large army of settlers overrun Connacht.

1224 First Irish Dominican houses in Dublin and Drogheda

←*Holy Cross, Tipperary*

1219 Archbishop O'Lonergan orders that Munster be put under interdict and the justiciar excommunicated unless the matter is settled.

1190 At Abbeyknockmoy, Co. Galway, Cathal Crobderg O'Connor brother of King Rory founds a monastery for St. Malachy canonised.

1218 Archbishop Donat O'Lonergan of Cashel charges that de Marisco had dispossessed him of the new vill of Cashel. This was part of a new royal policy of removing Irishmen from positions of influence in the church.

1222 Pope Honorius orders the archbishop to lift the interdict. But he also orders that royal policy towards the native Irish should change.

1225 St Lorcán O'Toole cannonised by Pope Honorius III.

1210
King John arrives on 20th June to deal with some of his subjects, especially the de Braoses and de Lacys. He stays nine weeks and visits Inistioge, Kilkenny, Naas and New Ross where a wooden bridge is built. On 28th June he is in Dublin.
John meets the King of Connacht, Cathal Crobderg, at Kells and goes to Carrickfergus. Hugh de Lacy burns his own castles in the king's path and flees to Scotland. King John returns to Dublin on 18th August.
During his time in Ireland he confiscates the lands of William de Braose, expells the de Lacys and takes hostages from Earl William Marshal, the heir of Strongbow's lordship. John also seizes the principal castles of Ulster and Meath. He leaves Ireland 24th August.

1202 Cathal Crobderg O'Connor becomes King of Connacht after killing his cousin Cathal Carrach aided by John de Courcy and Hugh de Lacy the younger. His cousin is aided by William de Burgo.

1227
Stephen of Lexington sent on visitation of the 34 Irish Cistercian abbeys where rules of choir, silence and of communal meals are often not observed. Stephen rules that only those with knowledge of Latin or French should be admitted.

1216
John de Courcy, former 'Prince of Ulster' dies, as does William Marshal, Lord of Leinster.

1215 Cathal Crobderg holds Connacht at 300 marks a year and receives a confirmatory charter of all the land of Connacht except Athlone. Geoffrey de Marisco appointed justiciar.

188 evorgilla, ife of Tiernan 'Rourke tires to ellifont.

1205 Hugh de Lacy the younger having invaded Ulster and defeated him receives John de Courcy's forfeited land and becomes Earl of Ulster.

1207 Strongbow's successor as Lord of Leinster, William Marshal, comes to Ireland to expand colony.

1208 King John's fallen favourite William de Braose, Lord of Limerick, flees to Ireland, welcomed by Walter de Lacy, Lord of Meath, and Marshal, Lord of Leinster.

1223 Archbishop O'Lonergan resigns

1224 Cathal Crobderg O'Connor dies in the Abbey of Knockmoy where he had retired.

1227 Hugh de Lacy the younger restored to the Carldom of Ulster.

1193 Devorgilla O'Rourke dies at Mellifont.

1198 Death of Rory O'Connor, last high-king of Ireland.

1194 Donal Mór O'Brien, king of Thomond, dies.

1206 Mongol Empire founded
1206 Inca dynasty founded
1210 Franciscan order founded

Famine in Egypt.1202

1215 Dominican order founded

1228-1229 Sixth Crusade

92 Third Crusade

1202-1204 Fourth Crusade

1217-1219 Fifth Crusade

1232 Galway castle built by de Burgo. • Chancery of Ireland set up. • Co. Kerry formed from shire of Munster.

circa 1254 Cos. Limerick and Tipperary formed. • Castle built at Roscommon.

1242 Cork city granted a charter by Henry III.

1236 Loughrea castle built by de Burgo

1245 Sligo Castle built by Maurice FitzGerald.

1235 Cos. Dublin, Waterford, Munster (Cork), Kerry, Limerick and Uriel (Louth) are in existence.

1265 Long narrative poem in Norman-French describes building of walls of New Ross by citizens.

1261 Cos. Dublin, Waterford, Munster (Cork), Kerry, Limerick, Uriel, Connacht and Roscommon are in existence.

1270-78 Walls of Galway built by the de Burgos.↓

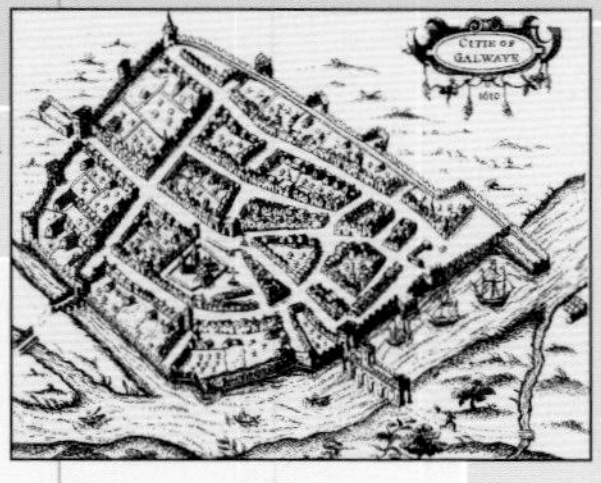

1230 First Irish Francisian houses founded at Youghal and Cork.

1234 Earl Richard Marshal at war with Henry III, is critical of invasion of Connacht. Richard de Burgo and other enemies arrange to meet him for talks on the Curragh of Kildare. He is attacked and dies from his wounds.

1262 Battle of Callan: John FitzThomas of Desmond and his heir defeated and killed by Finghin MacCarthy, himself slain later that year.

1252
Justiciar, John FitzGeoffrey, campaigns against Brian O'Neill in Ulster.

1260 Battle of Down.

1241 Brian O'Neill brings the power of the Mac Lochlainas to an end at battle of Caiméirge.

1257
Death of Maurice FitzGerald; his lordship of Sligo ravaged by Gofraid O'Donnell, king of Tír Conaill after victory in Battle of Credran. Normans in Thomond defeated by Conor O'Brien and his son, Tadhg.

1268 Bishops of Lismore and Waterford ordered by papal legate to excommunicate mayor and citizens of Waterford for forbidding public whipping.

1254 Ten of the twenty three Irish dioceses have foreign bishops and the primate is an Italian.

1264 One of the earliest recorded Irish Parliaments meet at Castledermot, Co. Kildare.

1266 Mayor and bailiffs ordered to prevent public whipping in the streets of lay people condemned in church courts in Dublin.

1235 Since 1228 de Burgo has attempted to subdue Connacht; he succeeds this year. O'Connors are granted the five King's cantreds; they continue electing a King of Connacht.

1243 Ulster becomes a possession of the crown.

1245 Last of the sons of William Marshall dies without male heir. Leinster partitioned between heiresses.

1254 Henry III appoints his eldest son, Edward, as Lord of Ireland.

1258 Meeting at Caol-Uisce on the Erne between Aodh son of O'Connor, Tadhg son of O'Brien, and Brian O'Neill, self-styled 'King

1241 Walter de Lacy, Lord of Meath, dies without male heir: Meath partitioned.

1243 Richard de Burgo dies in Poitou on active service. • Death of Hugh de Lacy

1245 Felim O'Conor serves Henry III in Welsh campaign.

1230 Aedh Méith O'Neill dies. Felin O'Connor installed by de Burgo in Connacht.

1237 De Burgo begins to organise his lordship. He rewards his allies with land-grants.

1255 Aedh son of Felin O'Conor forms an alliance with Brian O'Neill.

1260 Defeat and death of Brian O'Neill. at Battle of Down.

1249 Aedh, son of Felin O'Conor begins career of opposition to colonists.

1232 Earliest known use of rockets in war between Chinese and Mongols.

1248-1270 Seventh Crusade led by Louis IX of France

1248 Building of Cologne Cathedral begun

1264 Major outbreak of civil strife between the Geraldine and de Burgh factions.

1263 Earldom of Ulster bestowed on Walter de Burgh, lord of Connacht.

1260 Mongol leader Kublai is elected khan

1278 D'Ufford, justiciar, spends, £3,200 on massive Roscommon castle: two storeys, with round towers, twin-towered gate building and southern gateway.

1284 Stone walls built around Cork city.

1295
The deeds of Piers Bermingham described in a contemporary ballad *Ever be rode about With strength to hunt them out.*

1292
Custody of rents, homages, and services of all Crown tenants English and Irish in the Decies and Desmond granted to Thomas Fitz Maurice of Desmond.

1267 Riot among Irish students in Oxford.

1299
Edward II orders that base coinage should not be used in Ireland. Export from Ireland of good coin or silver plates forbidden.

1274 First major outbreak of war by the Irish of Leinster since invasion.

1286 Richard de Brugh, the 'Red Earl' of Ulster, campaigns in Connacht and Ulster for first time.

1270 Aodh O'Conor victorious in battle of Áth-in-chip; destroys ←Roscommon, Rindown and other English castles in Connacht.

1294
Another outbreak of strife between de Burghs and Geraldines.

1276 Irish of Leinster again defeat government forces in Glenmalure.

1295
Large army leaves Ireland to support King Edward I against the Scots.

1272 Cistercians given Hore Abbey, Cashel. Benedictines expelled because Archbishop McCarvill dreams they plan his murder. 10,000 marks offered to king to grant English citizenship to Gaelic Irish. First Irish Carmelite houses founded (Ardee and Leighlinbridge).

1297
First real parliament summoned by justiciar – archbishops, bishops, abbots, priors, earls, barons, 'chief people'. He orders sheriffs and seneschals to have honest knights elected. In Wogan's parliament first comprehensive legislation since 1169 enacted. Englishmen forbidden to dress as Irishmen and, without justiciar's licence, no-one to lead out armed men in 'the land of peace'. Cos. Meath and Kildare constituted.

1282
First Irish Augustinian friary in Dublin.

1291
A riot in Cork between Gaelic and Anglo-Irish Franciscans. Sixteen friars are killed and many wounded.

1265 Felin O'Conor, king of Connacht, dies; succeeded by son Aodh.

1283 Aodh Buidhe O'Néill killed. Succeeded by nephew, Donal son of Brian.

1282 Mac Murchads, king of Leinster, and his brother, murdered by justiciar.

1263 Irish, possibly Aedh O'Connor and others, attempt to get King Hoakon of Norway to accept kingship of Ireland. Aodh Buidhe becomes king of Tír Eoghain.

1299
Year of bumper harvests. Wages rise for labourers because of need for many workers.

1260 Collapse of attempt to revive high-kingship after Brian O'Neill killed at Battle of Down.

1262 Richard de la Rochelle comes to Ireland as justiciar and begins the building of a castle at Roscommon.

1277 Thomas de Clare murders Brian Rus O'Brien, king of Thomond.

1276
Hereditary lordship of all Thomond granted to Thomas de Clare.

1287
Series of deaths among the FitzGeralds leaves John FitzThomas head of the Leinster Geraldines, later 1st Earl of Kildare.

1271 Death of Walter de Burgh, earl of Ulster and Lord of Connacht.

1295
Sir John Wogan appointed justiciar.

1274 Aodh O'Connor, the last great king of Connacht, dies.

↑*Castle of the Geraldines*

Culture & heritage

1311 Papacy grants permission for a university for Dublin.

1306 Co. Carlow constituted following death without heirs of Roger Bigod, earl of Norfolk, and Lord of Carlow. Cos. Kilkenny and Wexford are palatinates that become counties.

1316-1317 Years of great famine.

1316 The walls of Cork city are repaired and strengthened.

1319 At Kilcullen a stone bridge built over the Liffey.

1320 Stone bridge erected over the Barrow at Leighlinbridge. • St. Nicholas' church built in Galway city.

1383 The plague returns.

Lifestyle

1301 Another large Irish army serves in Scotland.

1316 Bruce marches his army southwards and they win two victories, one over Roger Mortimer in Meath and the other over the Earls of Carrick and Kildare and Maurice Fitz Gerald with their forces at Ardscull near Athy.

1327 Epidemic of small pox.

1330 Maurice FitzGerald, is asked to aid the Viceroy. He succeeds but then exacts 'coyne and livery' on the settlers, i.e. he quarters his fighting men on them. This custom had been common among the Gaelic Irish but is now used by the government.

1332 In Connacht the power of the Crown is weakened badly and constables are no longer kept in the castles of Roscommon and Raindown.

1348 The Black Death, bubonic plague, spreads throughout Ireland. It is not known how many die but it reduces the population severely.

1349 There is a severe shortage of workmen and to attract labourers the Statute of Labourers is extended to Ireland from England. This deals with payment for ploughmen, carters, threshers, servants and the like.

1353-1357 The justiciar, Thomas de Rokeby, campaigns against O'Byrnes, O'Tooles, and other Irish of Leinster.

1369 Beginning of unsuccessful military campaigns against the Irish by William of Windsor.

1377 Art McMurrough Kavanagh burns Carlow town in retaliation when his black rent to stay out of the settlers' lands is stopped. He demands 80 marks but receives 40 marks when he meets the justiciar, Ormond, and promises aid to the king for a year against Irish rebels.

1383 Niall Mór Ó'Neill active against the English settlers in east Ulster.

↓ *Art McMurrough meeting troops*

Supply ships bringing food for Richard's army →

Battle and conflict

1300 Money for the Scottish war is sought but no budget as such is presented. It is suggested to the justiciar, John Wogan, that he visit communities in the country and persuade them to contribute.

1303 Richard de Burgh campaigns in Scotland with Edward I.

1308 Castlekevin, Co. Wicklow, burned by the O'Tooles.

1316 Battle of Athenry; rebellious Irish chiefs of Connacht defeated and killed including Felin O'Conor, king of Connacht. Perhaps the bloodiest battle in Ireland since the Anglo-Norman invasion. Carrickfergus Castle surrendered to Edward Bruce after a long siege. Robert Bruce arrives in Ireland with a large army to aid his brother.

1315 Edward Bruce, brother of Robert Bruce King of Scotland, invades Ireland at the invitation of the Gaelic chiefs who want him as their king. His principal supporter is Donal O'Neill of Tyrone. Their armies overrun eastern Ulster where the descendants of the settlers live. They burn Ardee and Dundalk in Co. Louth. Richard de Burgo marches northwards but is routed at Connor, Co. Antrim. Death, famine and ruin are left behind everywhere.

← *Seal of Athenry*

1317 Edward and Robert Bruce fail to take Dublin, whose citizens burn the suburbs. Citizens of Dublin arrest Richard de Burgh, earl of Ulster, fearing that he supports Bruce, his son-in-law. The Scots army marches south as far as Castleconnell, Co. Limerick, hoping to join forces with the Irish, but the O'Briens fail to unite behind them and their starving army retreat north.

1329 Sir John Bermingham, the victor of Faughart, ambushed and slain with relatives and retinue by Gernons and Savages near Ardee. In Munster the Barrys and Roches in Co. Cork murder Lord Philip Hodnet and 140 retainers.

1333 The Earl of Ulster is murdered by relatives including his uncle-in-law on the way to Mass in Carrickfergus. His people murder 300 that they suspect of being involved in the murders. Although the slain earl leaves a 14 year old daughter, his relatives in Ulster and Connacht seize her vast properties. In Mayo the occupier is known as Mac Liam Íochtair and in Galway, Mac Liam Uachtair (Lower Fitz William and Upper Fitz William respectively). The murder of the Earl of Ulster and the Bruce invasion mark the end of the first era of English occupation of Ireland.

1344-1346 Sir Ralph Ufford, appointed Lord Justice, seizes the Earl of Desmond's estates, hangs some of his knights and jails the Earl of Kildare. He dies suddenly in 1346 before he can do more harm.

1341 Sir John Morris is appointed justiciar. He takes back all the lands and privileges that the king and his father had granted and reclaims all debts that had been cancelled. His actions lead to a crisis in relations between Edward III and his Anglo-Irish subjects.

1378 The O'Briens are in arms and have to be bought off with 100 marks from looting the Leinster counties. • Cork city burned by the Gaelic Irish.

Politics, law and religion

1300 City and borough representatives in parliament for the first time. Only the king's coinage is to be used in Ireland.

1307 Since 1295 Wogan had held courts in the cities and thirty-one towns in Ireland. The cases tried were civil and criminal.

1310 Parliament at Kilkenny bans Irishmen from Anglo-Irish monasteries.

1315 Franciscans are often supporters of Bruce. Disciplining of the rebel friars is urged.

1318 Bruce tries to invade the south of Ireland but is brought to battle at Faughart near Dundalk where his army is defeated and he falls in the fray. • The commander of the Anglo-Irish forces, John de Bermingham, is created earl of Louth. • The Bruce expedition to Ireland inflicts plague, famine and slaughter on the country. • Battle of Dysert O'Dea: Richard de Clare defeated and killed by O'Brien, ending English settlement in Thormond.

1324 Disputes between Gaelic and Anglo-Irish friars among the Franciscans result in an order that both nationalities be mixed in all friaries.

1333 From this date onward more than half the dioceses had Anglo-Irish bishops.

1340 There are 35 Franciscan, 25 Dominican, 16 Carmelite and 11 Augustinian friaries in Ireland. Franciscans have only 2 houses in Connacht and 3 in eastern Ulster at this time.

1342 The Earls of Desmond and Kildare convene a parliament of their own in Kilkenny. A remonstrance is drawn up to the king complaining of the conduct and fraud of English officials. They blame their incompetence for losses of land. Their requests are granted.

1351 Parliament at Dublin enacts laws to prevent further Gaelicisation of colonists.

1360 Government council meeting at Kilkenny asks Edward III to send a powerful English lord to govern Ireland.

1366 Parliament at Kilkenny before Prince Lionel codifies the defensive legislation of the previous fifty years, prohibiting *inter alia* the adoption of the Irish language by the colonists. The 'statutes of Kilkenny', however, fail in their purpose.

1370 Franciscans take over the former Carthusian house at Abbey, Co. Galway.

1361 Lionel. third son of King Edward III, who is married to the heiress of the Earl of Ulster, is sent to Ireland as viceroy. He assumes the titles of Earl of Ulster and Lord of Connacht. He fails to solve the difficulties of the colony by force.

1380 Edmund Mortimer, Earl of March and heir to the de Burgo lands, arrives as Lord Lieutenant and devastates Ulster. However peace does not come to Ireland. The rule of law is breaking down.

Rule

1317 Donal O'Neill sends a Remonstrance of the Irish Princes to the pope about the treatment of the Gaelic people. English/Anglo-Irish could kill anyone of them on sight. He asks for the papal recognition of Edward Bruce as King of Ireland. Edward II suggests to the pope that the appointment of an Irishman as bishop among 'the beastlike and untaught' could threaten his people.

1318-1360 Episcopacy of Richard de Ledrede, the Bishop of Ossory, who forbids his clergy to sing love-poems on holy-days. One stanza goes:
Alas, how shall I sing?
Lost is my enjoyment.
How shall I with that old man
live and lose my lover,
Sweetest of all things.
(Mod. Eng.)

1325 Death of Donol O'Neill, king of Ulster; succeeded by Henry of the Clandeboye branch.

1327 Donal Mc Murrough inaugurated as king of Leinster.

A royal ordinance from Edward III declares that all Irish, whether of Gaelic or English descent, who hold public office in Ireland should be dismissed and their posts filled with English-born men who have property in England.

1342 A royal

1368 Absentee lords ordered to return and defend their lands in Ireland.

1384 Kingdom of Connacht divided between O'Connor Don and O'Connor Roe.

1375 Art McMurrough Kavanagh elected King of Leinster by the Gaelic Irish, but described as 'captain of his nation' by the rulers of the country. He holds sway in the wooded hills of Wicklow.

Agriculture and industry

1307 King Edward I dies. His reign since 1272 is the high-water mark in English rule. The Knights Templar are suppressed and their property sequestrated by royal command.

1310 Felin O'Conor installed as king of Connacht following traditional inauguration rite.

1318 Central government is weakened resulting in general disorder growing year by year. From about this time the government have to pay yearly black rents as appeasement money for the safety of settlers.

1321 Epidemic of cattle murrain in Irish herds.

1325 Cattle murrain epidemic still active.

1328 Corn crop damaged by great thunderstorms.

1331 Sir Anthony Lucy, justiciar, has Sir William Bermingham and the Earl of Desmond arrested. Both are suspected of

1335 The justiciar, Darcy, and the earls of Ormond and Desmond campaign with King Edward III↓ in Scotland.

1332 Bermingham is hanged but Desmond is released. Richard Fitz Ralph of Dundalk appointed Chancellor of Oxford university.

1358 Aodh Mór O'Neill extends his power throughout Ulster.

1356 Death of Maurice Fitz Thomas, 1st earl of Desmond.

1357 Art McMurrough Kavanagh born.

1361 Lionel moves the Irish exchequer from Dublin to Carlow.

1380 From now onwards trade between Galway, Portugal and Spain develops.

1367 Gerald Fitz Maurice Fitzgerald, third earl of Desmond, appointed justiciar. Known as 'gearóid Iarla' he was an accomplished Gaelic poet.

1386 Richard II appoints Robert de Vere, Earl of Oxford as Lord Lieutenant. and makes him 'duke of Ireland'. He was to lead 500 men-at-arms and 1,000 archers to Ireland. A dispute between the king and parliament causes the king to postpone the expedition. He needed Oxford by his side in England.

People and personalities

1302 Elizabeth, daughter of Richard de Burgh, earl of Ulster, marries Robert Bruce, future king of Scots.

1303 Death of Nicholas Mac Maol Íosar, last native Irish archbishop of Armagh before the Reformation.

1305 Death of Bernardus de Gordan whose book *Lily of Medicine* was used by the O'Hickeys, the physicians of the O'Briens. Sir Pirrs de Bermingham invites the O'Conor Falys to a feast in Carbury Castle, Co. Kildare and massacres them.

1306 Robert Bruce, now king of Scotland, seeks refuge on Rathlin island. • Roger Mortimer marries granddaughter of Geoffrey de Geneville and becomes Lord of Trim.

1316 John FitzGerald created Earl of Kildare

1317 Robert returns to Scotland.

1315 Edmund Butler is appointed justiciar and tries to unite the de Burgos, le Poers and the FitzGeralds against Bruce. He is created Earl of Carrick.

1327 Robert Bruce arrives in Ulster, his real intentions unknown.

1324 Dame Alice Kyteler charged in Kilkenny by Bishop Richard de Ledrede with heresy, idolatry and sorcery. She escapes being burnt at the stake but not her maid, Petronilla.

1326 Death of Richard de Burgh, the 'Red Earl' of Ulster; suceeded by his young grandson, William the 'Brown Earl'.

1329 Maurice FitzGerald is created 1st Earl of Desmond.

1328 Adam Duff O'Toole burned at the stake at le Hogges near Dublin for heresy and blasphemy. William de Burgh, earl of Ulster, arrives in Ulster along with a dying Robert Bruce. James Butler created 1st Earl of Ormond.

1330 Roger Mortimer, lord of Trim, hanged at Tyburn after governing England badly since the accession of Edward III.

1333 John Darcy appointed justiciar. He releases the Earl of Desmond from jail.

1341 Elizabeth de Burgh, heiress to earldom of Ulster and lordship of Connacht marries Edward III's son, Lionel.

1346 Earl of Kildare is released from imprisonment and earl of Desmond submits and goes to England to defend himself against charges of rebellion. Richard Fitz Ralph becomes archbishop of Armagh.

1347 The Earl of Kildare joins Edward III at the siege of Calais. Desmond is appointed Lord Justice for life. There are no further efforts to break the power of the Earls of Kildare, Desmond and Ormond.

1377 Art McMurrough Kavanagh marries Elizabeth le Veele – her property in Co. Carlow is confiscated for violation of the Statutes of Kilkenny.

1385 Richard II creates Robert de Vere, 'marquis of Dublin'.

World events

1317 France adopts Salic law, excluding women from succession to the throne.

1325 Traditional date for foundation of Tenochtitlán (Mexico City) by the Aztecs.

1337 Beginning of 'The Hundred Years' War' between England and France (ends 1453)

1347 Black Death (bubonic plague) reaches Cyprus from eastern Asia.

1348 Black Death reaches England.

1360 Death of Richard FitzRalph, archbishop of Armagh; later cannonized as St Richard of Dundalk.

1358 Revolt of French peasants.

1381 Peasant

1364 Ming dynasty founded.

387 Niall Mór Ó'Neill holds celebration of aelic culture at Eamhain Macha (Navan Fort), ancient capital of Ireland.

1389 To restore order in Ireland the justiciar, the Bishop of Meath, appoints Sir Thomas de Burgo 'keeper of Connacht' and deputy justiciary, the Earl of Ormond as 'keeper and governor' of Cos. Tipperary and Kilkenny and many other such posts to appease noble law-breakers and rebels.

1387 Disputes and open warfare between the Earls of Ormond and Desmond.

1394 Richard II decides to come to Ireland. With 34,000 men he arrives in Waterford and Art McMurrough Kavanagh burns New Ross in an act of contempt. Richard's army on the way to Dublin is harassed from the woods of Leighlin by McMurrough Kavanagh's forces.

1395 Seventy-five Irish chiefs submit near Carlow and at Drogheda.

1399 Richard II returns to Waterford and leads his army to punish McMurrough Kavanagh into the Wicklow fastnesses. Here his men are harassed as they struggle through woods, hills and bogs in the inclement weather. Their supplies are cut off. They arrive in disarray at the coast near Arklow. Richard leaves Ireland in haste without his army and dies in unknown circumstances. He had been replaced by Henry IV. • Art McMurrough's raids become so frequent that he is compensated for the loss of his wife's lands.

1388 English Statute of Labourers fixing wages adopted.

1388 Earl of Kildare appointed to arbitrate between Ormond and Desmond.

Henry IV. 1399

1391-93 James Butler, 3rd Earl of Ormond and fluent speaker of the Irish language, acquires the Liberty or Palatinate of Kilkenny and many lands and lordships of Hugh Dispenser. Kilkenny is henceforth the chief residence of the Ormond earls.

1390 Stanley arrests Aodh Óg, the son of O'Neill of Tyrone, who is pushing settlers out of Ulster. He demands hostages for O'Neill's behaviour before releasing his son.

revolt in England.

1396 Charter granted to Galway by Richard II.

1395 Richard II describes people living in Ireland as English subjects (loyalists), Irish rebels (rebellious settlers) and Irish savages (Gaelic Irish).

1391 Charges are made that many English who hold office in Ireland are absentees and have sent deputies in their places.

1405 First historical reference to whiskey: an Irish lord dies from excess consumption.

1400 John Stanley, Lord lieutenant, campaigns Irish of Meath, Leinster and Munster.

Richard II's fleet leaving Ireland ↑

1401 Art McMurrough raids Wexford.

1402 John Drake, Mayor of Dublin, leads an army to Bray and kills 500 of the O'Byrnes, allies of Art McMurrough.

1405 Art McMurrough overruns Co. Wexford and burns Carlow and Castledermot.

1407 Art McMurrough goes into Co. Kilkenny as far as Callan where the Lord Deputy, Sir Stephen le Scrope, defeats him in a pitched battle.

1413 Art McMurrough once more overruns Co. Wexford.

1416 Art McMurrough is faced with a hosting of Wexfordmen whom he defeats on their own soil and gives hostages for future good behaviour.

1445 Irish Franciscan province have a native Irish provincial for the first time, William O'Reilly.

1426 Killeenbrenan, Co. Mayo, is the centre of the unique Irish and Connacht Franciscan movement, the Third Order Regular.

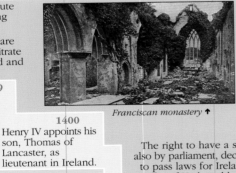
Franciscan monastery ↑

1400 Henry IV appoints his son, Thomas of Lancaster, as lieutenant in Ireland.

1395 Submission of chiefs includes Art McMurrough and his allies, O'Byrne and O'Nolan. Later in Dublin Richard knights O'Neill of Ulster, McMurrough Kavanagh of Leinster, O'Brien of Thomond and O'Connor of Connacht.

1402 Death of Niall Óg O'Neill, king of Ulster. Succession dispute follows.

1416 Art McMurrough dies on New Year's Eve.

1417 John Talbot, Lord Furneval, a military man, arrives as Lord Deputy.

1398 Death of Roger Mortimer, the king's cousin and heir, in war against Leinster Irish.

1396 Ottoman Turks and conquer Bulgaria.

1400s Inca and Aztec empire

1415 Henry V invades France and beats the French at Agincourt.

1430 Parliament awards grant towards cost of building castles in Cos. Louth, Meath, Dublin and Kildare.

1433 Gaelic bardic convention held by Máiréad O'Carroll, wife of O'Connor Faly.

1435 Irish poets and musicians banned on the Isle of Man.

1446 The term 'Pale' used for first time to describe Cos. Louth, Meath, Dublin and Kildare.

1439-1480 Outbreak of plague in Dublin.

1449 Disorder at harvest time when soldiers with their families and friends go into the countryside eating and drinking freely. They rob peasants and often kill workers. An Act of Parliament is passed to stop this.

1446 By a charter of Henry VI the Guild of the art of Barbers is established in Dublin city to practise 'chirurgery'.

1417 John Talbot traverses the land to subdue all disorder but departs leaving the Pale under further attack.

1414-47 Prolonged struggle between the factions of James Butler, fourth earl of Ormond, and John Talbot, earl of Shrewsbury, for control of royal government in Ireland.

1446 Earls of Ormond and Desmond at War.

1423 The Ulster Irish lords raid and loot Cos. Louth and Meath and force the people to pay black rent.

1445 Irish Franciscan province have a native Irish provincial for the first time, William O'Reilly.

1449 The right to have a separate coinage is granted also by parliament, declared to be the only agency to pass laws for Ireland. • Richard Plantagenet, Duke of York and heir to the throne appointed Lord Lieutenant. He acts very well while in Ireland.

1402 Death of Niall Óg O'Neill, king of Ulster. Succession dispute follows.

1422 Niall Garbh O'Donnell succeeds to kingship of Tír Conaill and becomes most powerful of the gaelic lords because of intermecine wars of the O'Neills.

1429 Niall Garbh O'Donnell visits English court.

1426 Callhach O'Connor Faly begins successful rise to power in borders of Leinster.

1431 Joan of Arc burned at the stake. Henry VII of England crowned King of France.

1446 Denis Fernandez discovers Cape Verde and Senegal.

---

circa 1450 Castle built by Edmund mac Richard Butler to protect river-traffic at Carrick-on-Suir.

1452 Drought and heat are so great in summer that the Shannon can be crossed on foot.

1461-1483 Brass half-farthings are minted inscribed 'Patrik' with branch and crown and farthings with 'Patricius' and mitred head on the reverse.

Co. Carlow from Carlow to Leighlinbridge and Co. Kildare from Calverstown to Carlow are cleared of rebels, but owners and tenants do not return.

1453 Wars of the Roses: Earls of Kildare and Desmond side with the House of York and the Earl of Ormond with the Lancastrians.

1461 Battle of Towton Field; afterwards Earl of Ormond is taken prisoner and beheaded. Yorkist victory paves the way for a restoration of Geraldine influence.

1462 John Butler, Earl of Ormond, arrives in Waterford and with his cousin, Edmund mac Richard Butler of Desmond, is defeated by the Desmond army at Piltown, Co. Kilkenny – only Wars of the Roses battle fought in Ireland. Edmund mac Richard ransomed for the *Psalter of Cashel* and the *Book of Carrick*.

1459-60 Parliament meeting at Drogheda upholds authority of Duke of York against Henry VI, and English Act of Attainder – also declares Irish legislature independent of English parliament.

1467-8 Edward IV appoints Tiptoft, earl of Worcester, Lord Deputy in place of Thomas FitzGerald, earl of Desmond. Tiptoft has earls of Desmond and Kildare attainted for treason, felony and alliance with the Irish. Kildare flees to England but Desmond comes to Tiptoft at Drogheda and is tried and beheaded. This embitters the Desmonds against English rule.

1463 Thomas FitzGerald, Earl of Desmond and Lord Deputy. King Edward IV sends gifts to Henry O'Neill, acknowledged as high-king by O'Brien.

Kildare has been in charge of Irish administration in Dublin almost continuously since 1470. Duke of Suffolk appointed Lord Lieutenant now but never comes to Ireland – Kildare acts as his deputy. Thomas, 7th earl of Kildare, dies; succeeded by his son Gerald, known as Gearóid Mór.

1458 Calbhach O'Connor Faly dies.

1459-60 Duke of York's second visit to Ireland.

1451 Richard Plantagenet returns to England.

1455-85 English Wars of the Roses.

1453 Fall of Constantinople to Turks (end of Byzantine Empire)

1454 Printing with movable type perfected in Germany.

1467 Beginning of over one hundred years of civil war in Japan.

1465 In the Pale, English law is paramount.

1470 People of Saggart, Co. Dublin, put themselves under the protection of the O'Tooles as a safeguard against other Wicklow raiding clans.

1471 Justiciar is given a retinue of 80 archers to protect people of Dublin, Meath, Louth and Kildare.

1471 Saggart burned by the O'Tooles and the O'Byrnes.

1474 Guild of St George established by parliament; a force of 120 mounted archers, 40 horsemen and 40 pages paid by a grant of customs. It is commanded by the Lord Deputy and 12 honourable persons of the Pale. In Ulster 900 Scots (McDonnells) arrive.

1465 Thomas, Earl of Desmond, Lord deputy, has an act of parliament passed to found a university in Droghedra. It fails for lack of funds. Irish government bans foreigners fishing off her coasts.

1465 The Irish Parliament passes a law that every person within the Pale should bear an English name and dress in the English manner. It is declared lawful to decapitate a thief who is not 'English' unless accompanied by an 'Englishman'.

1474 The king is requested to send back to Ireland all landowners of Irish birth upon pain of forfeiture. This could greatly increase the revenue.

1470 Earl of Kildare elected justiciar and Tiptoft, Earl of Worcester, executed by Lancastrians.

1470 Earl of Kildare elected justiciar and Tiptoft, Earl of Worcester, executed by Lancastrians.

1477 The Earl of Kildare visits England and returns with 200 archers. Deaths of earls of Ormond and Desmond, the latter by his own kin.

1478 Grey leaves Ireland and eventually Kildare is appointed Lord Deputy.

1462 Earls of Ormond become absentees in England from this time until 1515.

Portuguese ships

1473 Great fire destroys Galway city.

1479 A law is prepared to stop summoning of Irish men to England.

1478 Lord Henry Grey is appointed Lord Deputy and summons a parliament to meet at Trim. No-one attends and Grey is even deprived of the use of the Great Seal. • Octavianus del Palatio, an Italian, becomes Archbishop of Armagh.

1479 Grey leaves Ireland and eventually Kildare is appointed Lord Deputy.

1488 A long poem is sent to the Archbishop of Dublin from Waterford city, praising the loyalty of the city and remonstrating with Dublin for accepting Lambert Simnel, pretender to the throne.

1483-85 Pennies, groats and half-groats minted. Three-crown design (England, Ireland, Scotland) first used.

1480 1487 First record of use of firearms in Ireland, by forces of Ardh Ruadh O'Donnell.

1485-1508 Pennies, groats and half-groats minted. Three crowns on some of them. FitzGerald arms (Kildare, Desmond) on one grout coin.

1488 King Henry VII permits his deputies in Ireland to grant 'English law and liberty' to any fit person who is barred by the Statutes of Kilkenny. In this year Cormac McCarthy, Lord of Muskerry in Co. Cork, receives this grant.

Beyond the Pale
The term for being sent beyond a boundary in Ireland; four counties over which English jurisdiction was established.

1483-85 Reign of Richard III

1483 Attempt made to check power of the Earl of Kildare. Earl of Desmond has gone over to the Irish. Ormond is absent so Kildare is only powerful nobleman in Ireland supporting Crown interests. Richard III tells Kildare that he intends visiting Ireland and appoints him Lord Deputy for a year. Kildare is requested to come to England.

1485-1508 Reign of Henry VII

1487 Coronation of royal pretender, Lambert Simnel, Christchurch Cathedral, Dublin, by the Bishop of Meath; witnessed by Earl of Kildare and the Archbishop of Dublin.

1487 Simnel is refused entry to Waterford city. • After defeat, Kildare and others receive pardons and take oath of allegiance to Henry. • James Butler of Paulstown describes himself in his will as 'principal captain of my nation', the Gaelic chiefs' term. He is deputy of the Earl of Ormond, an absentee in England.

1484 Kildare goes to England. • An Irish bishop is sent from England to the Earl of Desmond stating that his father had been 'extorciously slain and murdred' and the king deplored it. He is urged to take oath of allegiance and asked to dress and act like an Englishman.

1485 The Earl of Kildare retained as Lord Deputy.

1478 Spanish Inquisition.

1482 Portuguese explore Congo estuary.

1488 Diaz rounds Cape of Good Hope.

Culture & heritage

1500 This is the last century of the trained Gaelic poets. Their patrons are gradually being defeated. The poets of the northern half of the land of Ireland engage in controversy with the southerners about which part of Ireland is superior. A poet sums it up: 'Lewy, Teig and Torna,/ Noble poets of our country;/ Hounds they are of much knowledge;/ Fighting over an empty kennel'.

Lifestyle

1500 A printing press to produce a Gaelic Bible is assembled in Dublin but nothing comes of the scheme. • Throughout the century tower-houses are built, often single-towered, four-floored residences of the landed gentry with windows only on top floor. Many are in areas where the old Gaelic Irish hold power. They are the beginning of stone-built domestic architecture in Ireland.

1509 For the first time coinage bearing a harp is minted: pennies, halfpennies, groats and half-groats.

↑British advance

←Earl of Kildare

1504 Earl of Kildare's army along with the English of the Pale and O'Donnell defeat the forces of Ulick McWilliam Burke and O'Brien at Knockdoe, Co. Galway. This is a first step in halting the turbulence in Ireland.

1551 *The Book of Common Prayer* is printed in Dublin, the first ever printed in Ireland.

1548-53 Inauguration of garrison policy to surround the Pale with fortified positions; pursued by successive governors, Sir Edward Bellingham, Sir Anthony St Leger, and Sir James Croft.

English settlers are introduced who build farmsteads of a kind not seen before in Ireland. The families of O'Connors, Dempseys, Dunnes, O'Mores and Delaneys are expelled to the hills and bogs where they live with their movable property.

1547-1553 Reign of Edward VI. A shilling, dated and with a harp, is minted.

1556 Tyrconnell, O'Donnell's country, is invaded unsuccessfully by Seán O'Neill, Conn's son.

1553-54 Reign of Mary I. Pennies, groats, shillings with harp have head of Mary minted. After 1552 heads of both Mary and Philip appear.

1558-1603 Reign of Elizabeth I. Groats, pennies, threepences, sixpences and shillings minted. Copper halfpennies (1601-2); harps on all coins and three harps on a 1561 silver shilling.

156
The Tudor Manor House in Carrick-on-Suir built by Thomas, Earl of Ormond. Only Irish example of Tudor long gallery and of bricks, wide glazed windows and indoor sewage disposal.

1565 The last battle to settle noblemen's private quarrels in Ireland takes place at Affane in Co. Waterford.

Battle and conflict

1500 This is the era of the Tudor Reconquest of Ireland by military means.

1510 Kildare marches through much of Munster along with O'Connell but is defeated by O'Brien and the earl of Desmond near Limerick city.

1512 Connacht is invaded by the Great Earl when he captures Roscommon and then plunders McDonnells in the Glens of Antrim.

1521 In a war between two McCarthy chiefs and the Earl of Desmond, Surrey makes peace between them.

1522 A war is waged by Conn O'Neill of Tyrone against the O'Donnells of Tyrconnell (Donegal) claiming overlordship. It ends in a rout when the O'Neills' camp is raided at night. Hostilities continue for years despite the efforts of the Earl of Kildare, a cousin of Conn O'Neill.

1534 Kildare is put in the Tower of London. When Thomas hears a rumour of his execution, he rebels but fails to take Dublin Castle. His enemy, Archbishop Alen, flees but is killed by Thomas' men after he dismisses him. This earns him excommunication.

1535 Maynooth Castle bombarded by the Lord Deputy, Sir William Skeffington who captures it. The survivors are put to death despite a promise of mercy. Rebellion is crushed and Thomas and five uncles are taken to London. Lord Leonard Grey takes charge of the army in Ireland.

↓English artillery and cavalry

1557-8 Establishment of a military 'plantation' in Laois-Offaly; murder of Matthew O'Neill, baron of Dungannon by order of his half-brother, Seán (Shane); launching of a military campaign in Ulster to uphold 'surrender and re-grant' arrangements.

1561 Earl of Sussex invades Tyrone but defeated by Seán O'Neill, who goes to London on the Queen's invitation.

↑English cavalry **1569**
James FitzMaurice FitzGerald, cousin of Desmond, organises the Geraldine League in the south of Ireland in defence of the lands and the Catholicism of all the landowners. Sir Henry Sydney visits Munster, proclaims the leaders and acts with brutality.

1569 Elizabeth I excommunicated by the pope. Military aid is sought from Catholic Spain and the pope to save Catholic landowners' property.

Politics, law and religion

1494-5 Poynings' Law' makes all past legislation of English parliament applicable to Ireland, and requires king's approval for all future summons of Anglo-Irish parliament and contents of its legislation.

1508 Ninety new houses of the Franciscans, the Dominicans, Carmelites and Augustinians friars have been founded since 1400.

1516 Ardh Dubh O'Donnell attends council at Dublin.

1524 Royal commission resolves differences between Ormond and Kildare and restores Kildare to the office of Lord Deputy. He is directed to arrest the Earl of Desmond, his kinsman, who eludes his efforts to capture him.

1541 A parliament in Dublin is the first to be attended by many Gaelic chiefs. Henry VIII creates Conn O'Neill Earl of Tyrone, Mac William Burke Earl of Clanrickard, O'Brien Earl of Thomond.

1552 Archbishop Dowdall of Armagh opposes the new Edwardian forms of Protestant worship and is deposed by the new Lord Deputy.

1560 The Protestant religion is restored at a parliament in Dublin. The Act of Supremacy, that the monarch is supreme governor of the church on earth, and the Act of Uniformity, the compulsory use of the Book of Common Prayer, are made obligatory for public office-holders. Fines are to be levied on those not attending Sunday service (recusants).

1551 Sir Anthony St Leger introduces the new Protestant forms of worship in Dublin that come with the reign of Edward VI. Archbishop Browne fully supports him.

Rule

← 1509-1547 The reign of Henry VIII.

1520 Kildare, known as Gearóid Óg, is replaced as Lord Deputy. He has restored more order in the country than has been there for years. Cardinal Wolsey and others intrigue against him. He is suspected of purloining Crown revenues. • His successor the Earl of Surrey sets out to punish Conn O'Neill of Tyrone for an invasion of Meath. He receives the submission of O'Neill who receives a chain of gold from Henry VIII.

1521 Surrey advises the king to confiscate lands in Ireland and plant them with English to restore order. Henry VIII considers a policy of surrender and re-grant of land a better method of dealing with the problem.

1536 Parliament pass an act making Henry VIII the supreme spiritual Head of the Church in Ireland. All government office-holders are obliged to take an oath recognising this royal supremacy. All monasteries are suppressed. Monastery lands are taken willingly by noblemen and landowners but the doctrines of the Reformation are not preached outside Dublin. It is largely an exchange of land-ownership. There are few conversions to the new religions. The Archbishop of Dublin, Browné as a former friar, burns the *bachall osa* (Jesus' staff), the supposed crozier of Patrick, in the street.

1541 Henry VIII is proclaimed king of Ireland at an Irish parliament called in Dublin. He claims the position as head of the Church in Ireland, even though the vast majority of Irish are Roman Catholics. • The king henceforth not to be known as the Lord, but the King of Ireland.

1547-1553 Reign of Edward VI

1553 **1553-54** Death of Edward VI; Reign of accession of Mary I. Mary I.

1558-1603 ↑Reign of Elizabeth I.

Agriculture and industry

1500 The plantation of land by English settlers begins.

1529 Appointment of Sir William Skeffington as royal commissioner.

1548 Plans for plantation continue.

1540 Sir Anthony St Leger is appointed Lord Deputy. His policy is to press chiefs to conform by 'small gifts, honest persuasions and nothing taking of them' and not to use 'great rigour'.

1541 Edmund Butler created Baron of Dunboyne.

1556 King's County and Queen's County formed out of Offaly and Laois for the first plantation. English settlers are introduced who bring new husbandry methods and build farmsteads of a kind not seen before in Ireland.

People and personalities

1491 Another pretender to the English throne, Perkin Warbeck, arrives in Cork. He is accepted by the people there and supported by the Earl of Desmond but not by Kildare. He fails in his attempt.

1499 Perkin Warbeck is hanged at Tyburn with John Walter, Mayor of Cork.

1496 The Earl of Kildare sent back to Ireland as Lord Lieutenant.

1498 Cathal Mac Manus, dean of Lough Erne, chief compiler of the Annals of Ulster, dies. One of his 12 children marries Bishop of Kilmore's daughter.

1494-5 In the wake of Anglo-Irish support for Perkin Warbeck, Henry VII dismisses Kildare (1492) and sends Sir Edward Poynings as Lord Deputy.

Perkin Warbeck

1521 Surrey is collecting evidence, especially from Piers Roe, Earl of Ormond, against Kildare but this ceases when the Roe marries Elizabeth Grey, a relative of Henry VIII. Surrey returns to England.

1532 Kildare, in England again, secures the Lord Deputyship.

1533-4 Lord Deputy Kildare summoned to court and leaves his son Lord Offaly (Silken Thomas) as vice-deputy.

1537 All six FitzGeralds of Kildare are tried for high treason, condemned and hanged at Tyburn. Young Garret, brother of Silken Thomas, is spirited abroad for his safety and lives in Rome with his kinsman, Cardinal Pole.

1534 Henry VIII begins reconquest and then attempts to enforce the Reformation.

1530 Earl of Kildare exiled in England, returns to Ireland and campaigns with Skeffington.

1546 James, Earl of Ormond dies, poisoned at a London banquet. His son Thomas Butler aged fourteen becomes Earl of Ormond.

1548 O'Connor of Offaly and O'More of Lewis are forced into submission and sent to England.

1550 Richard Butler, nephew of the Earl of Ormond is created Viscount Mountgarret.

1554 Queen Mary restores to Garret FitzGerald the title of Earl of Kildare, the 11th Earl.

1556-64 Thomas Radcliffe, earl of Sussex, serves as governor in Ireland.

1551 The first ever printing of *Book of Common Prayer* in Ireland.

1559 Thomas Butler, Earl of Ormond and Queen's favourite, created Lord Treasurer of Ireland. • Conn O'Neill dies – by English law his title should go to Matthew, his heir. In Irish law the title goes to Seán, Conn's second son, who is elected by the seniors of the family.

1562 Seán O'Neill returns home with the Queen's pardon but carries on as before.

1563 Adam Loftus consecrated as archbishop of Armagh. Later transferred to Dublin.

1565 Earls of Ormond and Desmond, are summoned to London and Desmond is held in the Tower for a while.

1565-71 Sir Henry Sidney serves for his first period as governor of Ireland.

1567 Seán O'Neill flees after a defeat by the O'Donnells to the McDonnells of Antrim and is murdered by them. The Earl of Desmond and his brother are arrested by Sir Henry Sidney and lodged in the Tower.

1568 Hugh O'Neill, son of Matthew, made baron of Dungannon.

World

1497 John Cabot discovers Newfoundland.

1492 Christopher Columbus discovers America.

circa 1503-06 Leonardo da Vinci paints Mona Lisa.

1502 War between France and Spain.

1501-04 Michelangelo creates *David*.

1505 Mozambique founded by Portuguese.

1507 World map produced by Waldeseemüller.

1520 Cortés conquest of Mexico.

1517 Ottomans conquer Egypt. Beginning of reformation.

1521 Spanish overthrow Aztec empire.

1509 Watch invented in Nurenberg.

1519-21 Magellan's expedition circumnavigates the world.

1527 Sack of Rome by Charles V.

1544 Treaty of Crépy between France and Spain.

1549 Introduction of uniform Protestant service in England with Edward VI's Book of Common Prayer. In Japan, St Francis Xavier introduces Christianity.

1559 Tobacco enters Europe.

1562 Beginning of slave trade.

1562-98 French Wars of Religion.

1576 Connacht and the present Co. Clare shired.

1579 Charter of Galway city confirmed by Elizabeth I. The mayor is Admiral of Galway Bay and the Aran Islands.

1583 Co. Longford constituted.

1570 The Ards peninsula in Co. Down colonised by Englishmen who receive government grants.

1576 The Guild of Barbers unite with the Dublin surgeons by royal charter.

1585-7 Grantees of Munster Plantation lands assume possession of their properties; Perrott experiences increasing difficulty in dealing with his English Protestant officials who consider him excessively lenient in this treatment of Catholic recusants.

1587 Butter is the staple food of the Irish fighting man

1570 James FitzMaurice FitzGerald in Munster wages war against the government.

1572 Sir John Perrott and Sir Edward Fitton regain authority as presidents respectively of Munster and Connacht by bringing rebels to surrender.

1582-3 Systematic suppression of rebel forces in Leinster and Munster.

1573 James FitzMaurice FitzGerald surrenders after a campaign by Perrot and goes to France.

1575 Essex campaigns further in Ulster, forcing Turlough O'Neill into submission and massacring the Rathlin islanders.

1579 The pope fits out three ships with 700 Italian soldiers to invade Ireland commanded by an English venturer. It never reaches Ireland. James FitzMaurice FitzGerald arrives in Smerwick in Kerry with 80 Spaniards, a Jesuit and a papal delegate. He goes northwards and is killed at Castleconnell, Co. Limerick in a skirmish with the Burkes, old enemies of his family.

1580 The lands of the Desmonds are invaded by several armies commanded by Englishmen and an Irish one by the Earl of Ormond. Desmond has to join the ragged rebellion that is in progress. All Desmond's lands and castles are ravaged. The rebellion in Munster is joined by a second revolt in Leinster led by James Eustace, Viscount Baltinglass, and Feagh Mac Hugh O'Byrne and supported by discontented Palesmen who profess themselves free from allegiance to a Protestant monarch. Arthur Lord Grey de Wilton is appointed governor to deal with the dual revolt and his army is defeated at Glenmalure in Wicklow but he ousts the Continental force from Smerwick. • Lord Grey of Wilton besieges the garrison at Smerwick by land and Admiral Winter by sea. The garrison surrenders and all are butchered. In Grey's army Hugh O'Neill, Baron of Dungannon the heir of Matthew, serves at the siege.

↑*English troops leave Dublin castle*

1584 Provincial councils reconstituted in Munster and Connacht.

1585 The lands of the Earl of Desmond and 140 of his family and followers, a million acres in all, are confiscated by the Irish parliament. A commission in England devises a scheme for distribution of the confiscated Munster property and establishment of a plantation. The president of Connacht devises the Composition of Connacht. • Hugh O'Neill, Baron of Dungannon, attends this parliament and is recognised as Earl of Tyrone.

1569-71 Meeting of parliament in Dublin declares the entire lordship of Tyrone forfeit to the Crown; appointment of first provincial presidents in Connacht and in Munster; launch of private colonization ventures in Munster and in Ulster; outburst of local revolts in Munster, Leinster and Connacht against government policy.

Sir Henry Sidney being greeted by the citizens of Dublin on his victorious return from campaigns against the Gaelic Irish↓

Hugh O'Neill→

1577 Sir Henry Sidney causes uproar in Dublin and the Pale by imposing a tax without consent of the Irish Parliament. He has to compromise.

1571-5 Sir William FitzWilliam serves for his first period as governor of Ireland.

1575-8 Sir Henry Sidney serves for second period as governor of Ireland.

1588-94 Sir William FitzWilliam serves as governor for the second time.

1586 A proclamation in England invites gentlemen to undertake the plantation of Munster. 86 families come. Overlarge, unwieldy lots sell cheaply at a few pence an acre (0.4046 ha). Among the planters are Walter Raleigh and Edmund Spenser, the poet. Eochaidh Ó hEodhusa appointed file to Maguire of Fermanagh.

1576 Sidney launches an apparently conciliatory policy and brings private colonization to a close. The Earl of Essex, the last of the private colonizers, dies in Dublin.

1581 Ormond finally recovers his family's lands in Ormond, north Tipperary, from the O'Kennedys. • The Earl of Desmond and his family are fugitives in Munster, they and their followers hide in the woods and hills.

1584-8 Sir John Perrott serves as governor of Ireland.

1583 Earl of Ormond appointed Lord General of the royal forces in Munster. Of the three great Irish families, Ormond survived in power and profited from the rebellions. Gerald, Earl of Desmond, was murdered in Glenageenta in Co. Kerry; young Kildare was powerless.

1573 The Earl of Desmond and his brother are released. The 'undertaker' of the plantation in the Ards peninsula, Thomas Smith, is killed. Walter Devereux, Earl of Essex, is 'undertaker' to plant Co. Antrim. He treats the inhabitants with brutality but fails and returns to Dublin.

1580-98 Edmund Spenser in Munster.

1582 Lord Grey is recalled to England.

1587 Hugh O'Neill, Earl of Tyrone, receives his inheritance from the Queen. He gives back 240 acres on a strategic ford on River Blackwater in Co. Tyrone to build a fort at Portmore. He brings English captains to train Irishmen as soldiers in the Queen's service – nicknamed 'the butter captains'; butter was the staple food of the Irish fighting man in Elizabethan times.

1571 Sidney appoints Presidents of Connacht and Munster. The latter is Sir John Perrot. Sir Richard Bingham and Sir Edward Fitton aim to pacify Connacht.

1575 Sir James Fitz Maurice FitzGerald departs from Ireland to seek Catholic support in Continental Europe for continued opposition to the government.

1578 Sidney surrenders his position as governor and leaves Ireland in the belief that his government has been undermined by lawyers in the Pale.

1584 Walter Raleigh attempts to found colony of Virginia

1588 Defeat of Spanish Armada.

1571 Battle of Lepanto.

1577-80 Francis Drake ciircumnavigates the world.

1580 Spain occupies Portugal

1589 Early ballet in France.

1592 Trinity College founded in Dublin on site of the dissolved priory of All Hallows.

1596 Edmund Spenser completes *A View of the Present State of Ireland.*

1600 *The Annals of the Four Masters* record a chronology of Irish history from now-lost manuscripts.

1604 Derry given its first city charter.

1610-30 Geoffrey Keating works on *Foras Feasa ar Éirinn.*

1606 Co. Wicklow formed from parts of Cos. Dublin, Kildare and Carlow. Foundation of St Anthony's Franciscan College, Louvain.

1610 *Desiderius* by Flaithrí Ó Maolchonaire.

1611 First printed catholic book in Irish, a catechism, printed in Antwerp and edited by the Franciscan, Bonaventure Ó hEodhasa, *An Teagasg Críosdaidhe.* The work had existed for some time in manuscript.

1612 Publication of Sir John Davies, *A Discovery of the True Causes Why Ireland was never entirely subdued*

1611 First public house licence granted in Ireland.

1594 Enniskillen Castle captured by English but its subsequent siege by Hugh O'Donnell forces the Lord Deputy to send a relief force. This is intercepted and defeated by Maguire in the battle of 'the Ford of the Biscuits'.↓

1600 Grim-looking tower-houses are no longer built by the rural gentry; they are replaced in the first half of the century by large windowed, oblong, three-storeyed turreted 'mansion-houses'.

1610 Land in Ulster granted to 'undertakers'. The plantation counties formed in 1585 are now administered as such for the first time.

1613 James I grants Derry and large estates to London merchants, hence the name 'Londonderry'. • Coleraine was granted to the Honourable Irish Society. • Sir John Perrot had built the first town houses with oaken frames prefabricated in London.

1603-25 Reign of James I: Shillings and sixpences minted – head of James and a crowned harp on each coin.

1608 Revolt of Sir Cahir O'Doherty.

1607 Confiscation of Donegal and Tyrone.

1592 Red Hugh O'Donnell seeks to expel all English officials from the lordship of Tyrconnell and with Hugh Maguire opposes the imposition of Composition arrangements on their respective territories.

1598 Hugh O'Neill defeats Sir Henry Bagenal at the Battle of the Yellow Ford, Co. Tyrone – the greatest overthrow of the English yet. Rebellion extends into Munster and the plantation is overthrown.

Siege of Kinsale

1601 Spanish fleet captures Kinsale. North side is blockaded by Sir George Carew and Lord Mountjoy. O'Donnell marches there and counter-blockades government forces. He is joined by O'Neill. Attack to trap government troops between the town and Irish positions fails. O'Neill goes back to Ulster; O'Donnell to Spain for military aid.

1595 Army of 3,000 troops is sent from England. Monaghan town is relieved but Tyrone defeats relieving party. 9-year rebellion begins, led by Hugh O'Neill, Earl of Tyrone, and Hugh O'Donnell of Tyrconnell – they begin negotiations for support from Spain.

1605-99 The reconquest of Ireland by the Tudors and their successors is consolidated.

1596 O'Neill insists in all negotiations that liberty of religion be a condition of peace. Fiach MacHugh O'Byrne rebels in Wicklow.

1599 Ballyshannon Castle besieged but English have to retire. Desmond lands in Munster are in the hands of rebels. Robert Devereux, earl of Essex, appointed to suppress rebellion. Dissipates his energies and agrees on truce with Tyrone.

1600 Lord Mountjoy appointed Lord Deputy and brings the largest English army to Ireland so far. • Sir John Dowcra seizes Derry and fortifies it, taking stone from a monastery and churches. Clay walls are stone faced with masonry. Mountjoy sites forts on perimeter of Ulster to hem in rebels. He raids rebel territory and destroys wheat crop. • Hugh O'Donnell campaigns in Connacht. • Sir George Carew begins to regain Munster.

1597 A sortie into Ulster is defeated but Portmore is regained and garrisoned.

1595-99 Hugh O'Donnell makes cattle-raids into Connacht.

1593-4 Opposition to government intervention in Ulster intensifies but Tyrone remains loyal even though his brothers have engaged in rebellion.

1603 All Irish city authorities obliged to insist on those in public office taking the Oaths of Supremacy and Uniformity. The recusancy laws are also enforced. Towns seek formal acceptance of Catholic worship.

1613-15 Meeting of Irish parliament, which endorses the plantation scheme in Ulster, and provides increased representation of settler population in future parliaments. Meeting of Convocation of the state church adopts 104 articles of faith.

1608 A commission appointed by the English government to survey six Ulster counties of Cavan, Fermanagh, Tyrone, Donegal, Derry and Armagh.

1603 Death of Elizabeth; accession of James I of England (James VI of Scotland).

1606 Government attempts to dismember Ulster lordships through judicial investigation.

1591 Hugh O'Neill elopes with Mabel Bagenal, sister to Henry Bagenal, the senior English official serving in Ulster; FitzWilliam seeks to impose a Composition of the McMahon lordship.

1605 Sir Arthur Chichester appointed as governor; proclamation declaring all persons in Ireland to be free subjects of the king; proclamation expels Jesuits and seminary priests from Ireland; pressure on Dublin merchant community to conform in religion.

1592 Red Hugh O'Donnell, kidnapped by government agents in 1587, escapes from Dublin castle and returns to Ulster with a bitter hatred of the English. He is inaugurated by his clan as lord of Tyrounell.

1605 Plans for the plantation of Clandeboye and the Ards set in train.

1609-10 Government proceeds with scheme for plantation of the six Ulster counties; grantees begin to arrive.

1601 O'Donnell dies in Samancas.

1602 Order restored to Munster by George Carew, president of that province; Mountjoy continues to penetrate the province of Ulster.

1603 O'Neill surrenders and is pardoned.

1596 Fiach MacHugh O'Byrne rebels in Wicklow.

1600 Hugh O'Neill visits Munster in Spring but returns to Ulster on hearing that Lord Mountjoy is Lord Deputy.

1607 O'Neill, O'Donnell and their friends under suspicion. They flee abroad. Their departure is known as the 'flight of the earls'.

1599 Giordano Bruno burned at the stake for heretical theory of the universe

1605 Gunpowder plot in English parliament.

1600 East India Company formed.

1594 Shakespeare's *Romeo and Juliet* written. Globe theatre built.

1602 Dutch East India Company founded.

1611 Authorized version of the Bible.

1610 Galileo uses telescope.

1598 Edict of Nantes ends civil wars in France.

1604 French East India Company founded.

1613 Russian Romanov dynasty founded.

1570 1577 1584 1590 1600 1608

Culture and heritage

1616 *Desiderius* (Gaelic translation by a Franciscan, Flaithrì Conroy, of a pious work) published in Louvain.

1618 *A Mirror of the Sacrament of Repentance* by the friar, Aodh Mac Aingil, published in Louvain.

1619 Publication in Dublin of book by Dermot O'Meara (a member of a family of physicians to the Earl of Ormond) *Hippocraticam Febrium Etiologium et Prognosim* (Description & Prognosis of Fevers) the first Latin work published in Ireland.

1632 Friars in Donegal begin collating the annals of Ireland. *The Annals of the Four Masters* is compiled to preserve Irish records of Ireland for very uncertain future years.

1634 Dr Geoffrey Keating completes first history of Ireland in manuscript – not printed until 1809 but copied continually.

1637 Because of its archiepiscopal status the title and dignity of city conferred on Cashel but not on Tuam and Armagh. Dublin's first theatre opens in St Werburgh's street.

1639 *Catechismus* by Theobald Stapleton OSF published in Brussels. He criticises the Gaelic poets, saying the common people act like jackdaws who try to recite the *Lord's Prayer* and *Creed* in Latin.

1646 Publication of Sir John Temple's *The Irish Rebellion*.

1650 *Parlaimint Chlainne Tomáis* (Parliament of Clan Thomas) completed.

1653 Surveys commence for Cromwellian plantation. • William Petty directs the Down Survey to map Irish lands and the Civil Survey which details the title of every landowner in Ireland.

1665 Mayor of Dublin becomes Lord Mayor.

1664-5 Sir James Ware's major works published in Dublin.

1667 Royal College of Physicians founded.

Lifestyle

1615 The Lynch Catholic school in Galway city closed by government.

1628 Undertakers in the Ulster plantation permitted to retain 'natives' as tenants.

1634 Citizens' obligation in Irish towns to hold archery practice is no longer compulsory.

1652 Some Confederate soldiers join European armies, or are held in camps to be sent to the Spanish army; others enslaved in the West Indies.

1653 All Catholic landowners and suspect gentry ordered beyond the River Shannon.

Sir Phelim O'Neill →

Propogandists make the most of atrocities associated with the 1641 rising. Two examples of their art above and above left

↓ Siege of Wexford

Battle and conflict

1646 Peace declared between Ormond and the Confederates in the Spring. General Owen Roe O'Neill defeats Anglo-Scotch parliamentary army at Benburb, Co. Tyrone.

1641 Rebellion in Ulster of the dispossessed Irish, led by Sir Phelim O'Neill.

1643 Truce between Confederates and Royalists in November.

1644 The Earl of Inchiquin, Murrough the Burner O'Brien, captures Cork city and banishes Irish inhabitants.

1644-5 Ireland in chaos; Archbishop Rinuccini arrives from the Papacy to provide direction to the rising.

1642 Scots Covenanter army under Robert Monro lands in Ulster (April); Owen Roe O'Neill arrives from the Spanish Netherlands to form an Ulster Catholic army (July); civil war between king and parliament commences in England. Rebellion of Catholic gentry. There are four warring parties in Ireland divided on religious grounds: the Ulster Gaelic Catholics, the Anglo-Irish Catholics of the rest of Ireland, the royalist Protestant party and the English Parliamentarian Puritans' supporters. This is a religious war from the beginning.

1647 Earl of Inchiquin, a supporter of English Parliamentarians, captures many Munster Confederate towns.

1649 Cromwell leads New Model Army to suppress the Irish. His swift, ruthless campaign means one third of the Irish population die. • The Confederates use troops to defend cities, not to fight pitched battles.

1649 Ormond and Confederates sign a treaty and Rinuccini returns to Rome. Cromwell picks off the garrisons serially. The eastern coastline is cleared first. Drogheda is captured and the garrison massacred. Wexford suffers a similar fate. Cromwell fails to capture Waterford and Clonmel but Kilkenny surrenders to him.

1650 In the spring Cromwell takes Clonmel. When he returns to England, Waterford and Limerick are besieged and captured by Cromwell's deputy, Henry Ireton.

1650-52 Cromwellian conquest continues.

1649 Roman Catholic worship is forbidden. Priests are killed or sent to other colonies. Some go into hiding and hold secret Catholic services.

↓ Castle of Limerick

↓ Owen Roe O'Neill

Oliver Cromwell

1641 Irish Catholic clergy in Europe are the strength behind the great rebellion – Ireland's part in the Thirty Years' War and as such a religious war.

1642 English parliament seeks suppression of the Irish rising through the 'Adventurers Act' • Catholic Confederacy assembles at Kilkenny. The aim of the Confederation of Kilkenny is 'unanimous for God and Motherland'. This assembly is dominated by the relatives of the Earl of Ormond, leader of the Royalist Protestants.

1646 Rinuccini condemns the Ormond Peace and in a synod at Waterford excommunicates all who supported it.

1648 Truce declared between Inchiquin and the Confederation. Rinuccini excommunicates all who support the truce; he sees Irish as 'Barbarians but good Catholics'.

1652 The 'Act for Settling Ireland' plans scheme to pay Cromwell's soldiers – and those who invested in the war – with Irish land.

Siege of Limerick

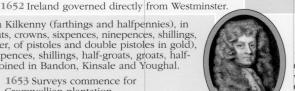
City of Limerick ↑

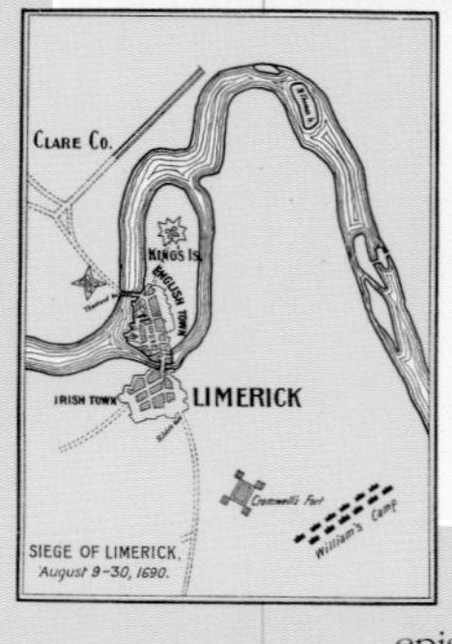

Politics, law and religion

1622 Comprehensive survey of the Irish church and government and of all plantations established in Ireland.

1625 More tolerance is shown to Catholics. James Ussher appointed archbishop of Armagh.

1631 Abbots appointed for some abbeys in Ireland. Thus begins weak Catholic Counter-Reformation in a country where there had been no real Protestant Reformation.

1634-5 Irish parliament convened; Wentworth reveals his intention to proceed with a plantation of Connacht and to disregard the Graces.

1629 Government temporarily in control of Viscount Loftus and the earl of Cork, who attempt suppression of Catholic worship in Dublin.

1639 Scots Covenanters oppose extension of an episcopal form of church government to Scotland; Wentworth seeks to have Scots settlers in Ulster swear their allegiance to the king.

1640 Wentworth (now earl of Strafford) convenes Irish parliament; this resists him once he has left the country, remonstrating against his rule.

Earl of Stafford

1625 Death of James I.

1625-49 Reign of Charles I: Minted coins look English but bear the crowned harp.

1628 Charles I offers 'Graces' to his Irish subjects in return for subsidies. This provides for the tacit toleration of Catholicism in Ireland, thus vexing his Protestant subjects. Fifty-one 'Graces' granted by Charles I to Irish Catholic landowners, who are the vast majority still in Ireland.

Rule

1633 Thomas Wentworth, later Earl of Strafford, is Lord Deputy. He sets out to increase royal revenues in Ireland.

1640 Wentworth recalled and tried for various aspects of his rule in Ireland.

1643 Overtures proceed between the Confederacy and the king.

1661 Reconstitution of an episcopal state church in Ireland.

1662 Act of Settlement: the new regime accepts Cromwellian land settlement in general. Court of Claims to examine claims to land.

1663 Closure of court of claims for Irish lands, its business unfinished.

1652 Ireland governed directly from Westminster.

1665 'Act of Explanation' obliges Cromwellian grantees to surrender one-third of their lands to provide for 'innocents' who have been dispossessed.

Agriculture and industry

1635 The title of the Crown is found to lands in Counties Roscommon, Sligo and Mayo. This reverted to the crown from the de Burgo title of 1333.

1621 Grants of land given to planters for Counties Leitrim, Westmeath and north-west Wexford, for King's County (Offaly) and Queen's County (Laois).

1636 Crown title found also in Co. Galway.

1628 Undertakers in the Ulster plantation permitted to retain 'natives' as tenants.

1641 Wentworth executed 12th May.

1642-9 'Siege Money' minted in Kilkenny (farthings and halfpennies), in Cork, ('Inchiquin Money' of groats, crowns, sixpences, ninepences, shillings, half-crowns and crowns; of silver, of pistoles and double pistoles in gold), Dublin ('Ormond Money' of sixpences, shillings, half-groats, groats, half-crowns, crowns). Money also coined in Bandon, Kinsale and Youghal.

1653 Surveys commence for Cromwellian plantation.

1649 Two thirds of Irish lands are confiscated and given to English landowners and farmers.

1643 The Earl of Ormond, whose numerous Catholic relatives dominate the Confederation, is appointed Lord Lieutenant.

1647 General Jones of the English Parliamentary party arrives in Dublin; Ormond vacates for him.

1662 Duke of Ormond ←appointed governor of Ireland.

1660 Restoration of Charles II; declares he will uphold the Cromwellian conquest and restore property to 'innocent papists'.

1654 Former Catholic landowners and retainers ordered to leave for Galway and Mayo by 1st May. Countryside is left to the workers, tradesmen and new planters.

People and personalities

1616 Death in Rome of Hugh O'Neill, earl of Tyrone.

1620 Known as the 'Eagle of Doctors', Owen O'Shiel, chief of medical faculty in Royal Hospital of Malines, returns to Ireland and settles in Dublin.

1645 Lord Glamorgan makes secret treaty with the Confederates on behalf of the king.

1650 Ormond leaves for France in December.

1649 Death of General Owen Roe O'Neill.

1655 Cromwell's son Henry arrives to take charge of army in Ireland.

1658 Death of Oliver Cromwell.

1662 1663 Irish cattle Irish wool-exports exports and general forbidden. trade with England and the colonies restricted by Act of the English Parliament.

World events

1616 Japan evicts Christian missionaries.

1618-48 Thirty years war.

1620 Landing of the pilgrims from *Mayflower*.

1621 Slide rule invented.

1635 Treaty of Prague.

1637 Invention of barometer.

1632 Taj Mahal building begins.

1643 *circa 1649* Taj Mahal completed.

1644 End of Ming dynasty.

1642 Civil war in England between Roundheads and Cavaliers.

1648 Expansion of Atlantic slave trade.

1652 Cape Town founded.

1656 1656 First Pendulum Villmergen war clock invented. in Switzerland.

1665 1666 Isaac Newton announces Spirit level Law of Gravity. invented.

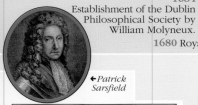
← *Patrick Sarsfield*

BATTLE OF AUGHRIM July 12, 1691.
← *Battle of Aughrim*

↓*James II landing at Kinsale*

↓*Battle of the Boyne*

1684 Establishment of the Dublin Philosophical Society by William Molyneux.

1680 Royal Hospital of Kilmainham founded

1687 Guild of Barbers enlarged by entry of apothecaries and periwig makers.

1689-94 Reign of William and Mary. Copper halfpennies with heads and crowned harp minted.

1685-89 Reign of James II. Crowned harp and king's head on coins 1685-8. 'Gun-money' minted in Dublin 1689-90; silver sixpences, shillings, crowns, half-crowns and few gold coins. Pewter groats, halfpennies and pence. King's head, crowned harp, month and year on coins. Brass siege money in Limerick 1691 – farthings and halfpennies.

1694-1702 Reign of William III. Copper halfpennies with head and crowned harp minted.

1692 Charter given to College of Physicians: full power and authority given to examine all persons engaged in midwifery.

1689 James II lands in Ireland with a French army, calling on Roman Catholic Irish to rebel in his support. Army besieges Protestant garrison at Derry. During 105 days' siege, 15,000 people starve to death before the English fleet comes to the rescue.

1691 In the Battle of Aughrim, Co. Galway, Irish Jacobites defeated. • The second Siege of Limerick ends in defeat for the Jacobites. A treaty is signed by General Ginkel and Patrick Sarsfield, giving guarantees to those who remain in Ireland and allowing over 10,000 soldiers to emigrate and serve in the Irish Brigade of the French Army. The victory of William of Orange is the final act in the reconquest of Ireland.

1690 William III arrives near Carrickfergus; defeats James' forces at the Battle of the Boyne. James flees to France and William takes Dublin. Sieges of Athlone and Limerick fail but Williamite courts in Dublin commence hearings against those who fought William III.

1701 Archbishop Marrh's library built, the first public library in Ireland.

1703 *A Supplement to the New Testament* by Dublin's Nahum Tate published, a metrical version of the psalms. He is author of *While shepherds watched their flocks by night. Parlaimint na mBan* (Parliament of Women) composed.

1712 Foundation stone of Trinity College library laid.

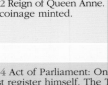
Captain Lemuel Gulliver

1715 The Apprentice Boys Club founded in Derry by Colonel Mitchelbourne, governor during the siege.

1710 The medical school of Trinity College, Dublin, is founded. A laboratory, anatomical theatre and physic garden (herb garden) are provided.

1702 Reign of Queen Anne. No coinage minted.

1725 Establishment of the the Grand Lodge of the Masons in Dublin.

1726 Dean Jonathan Swift's *Gulliver's Travels* published.

1731 Westport House designed by Richard Cassels with alterations by James Wyatt, built for the Marquess of Sligo.

1741 Newry ship canal completed above the town. • The first public performance conducted by George Frederick Handel of his *Messiah* in the New Music Hall, Dublin.

Charter of incorporation granted to the Rotunda Maternity Hospital in Dublin by George II. Bartholomew Mosse, aided by parliamentary grant and money from lotteries and public amusements, plans this hospital.

1729 Dean Swift's *Modest Proposa* published, suggesting that instead of being allowed to die of starvation, the children of the poor Catholics should be fattened as food for the rich. New parliament building commenced at College Green.

1737 *The Belfast News Letter* first published, the oldest newspaper in Ireland.

1759 The Guinness Brewery is founded in St James's Street in Dublin where 2.5 million pints of stout are still brewed daily. The thick black stout becomes world famous and very much a part of the Irish heritage. It is served in taverns and pubs which were often the scene of impromptu music playing.

1727-60 Reign of George II: Copper halfpence minted every year from 1736 bearing king's head and crowned harp. 1737, 1738, 1744, 1760 farthings with same design as halfpence.

1722-24 Coins with the King's head with Lady Ireland and harp on the reverse are under-weight and largely rejected.

1745 Building of Leinster House begins.

1750 The Dublin Society founded.

1752 This was the first year when the Gregorian Calendar replaced the Julian, 'losing' 11 days.

1751 Rotunda Hospital built.

1756 Charter of incorporation granted to the Rotunda Maternity Hospital in Dublin by George II.

1757 Dean Swift's money used to found St Patrick's Hospital for Imbeciles, the first such institution in Ireland.

1739-1741 Major Irish famine. 400,000 die.

1704 Act of Parliament: One Catholic priest allowed for each parish but must register himself. The Test Act becomes law to keep all Catholics and Dissenters from holding any public office. They are denied positions in public life and Catholics are made poor and ignorant, with no right to public office or influence in Irish society. Election to parliament is denied them unless they take an oath at variance with their beliefs. They, the majority of the population, become the victims of total discrimination. Protestants fear another revolt against their hegemony in the country.

1719 Toleration Act is passed for Protestant Dissenters but not for Catholics.

1720 The power of the Irish Parliament, already limited by Poynings Law (1492), is now further limited by a declaration of the British Parliament (the 6th of George I) that it can legislate for Ireland.

1728 The few Catholic freeholders, who still held the franchise, are deprived of it by the Irish Parliament.

1753 College of Physicians refuse to licence physics engaged in midwifery.

1715 William Conolly elected speaker of the Irish House of Commons.

1714-27 Reign of George I.

1727-60 Reign of George II.

1714 William Wood buys from the Duchess of Kendal royal patent to mint copper halfpence and farthings, for £10,000.

1733 Appointment of Nioclas O'Domhnaill, friar and former Professor of Philosophy in Louvain as Guardian of Adare Friary Co. Limerick. • A Gaelic poet, he presided over the Croom Poetry School.

1738 Death of Turlough Carolan, harpist and composer.

1728 Death of Aogán Ó Rathaille, poet.

← **1724** Jonathan Swift, Dean of St. Patrick's Cathedral in Dublin, writes the *Drapier's Letters*, an anonymous attack on the grant to William Wood of the

1713 Jonathan Swift becomes dean of St. Patrick's.

1759 Arthur Guinness acquires brewery at St James's gate, Dublin.

1750 The Dublin Society, the predecessor of the Royal Dublin Society, is founded to encourage good horticulture, agriculture and animal breeding.

1756 The construction of the Grand Canal from Dublin to the Shannon and the Barrow begins.

1745 Dean Swift dies.

1747 First visit to Ireland of John Wesley.

1669 Oliver Plunkett consecrated in Ghent as Catholic archbishop of Armagh.

1670 Synod of Catholic bishops meets in Dublin.

1673 Catholic bishops and members of religious orders banished; Catholic schools closed.

1671 Direct imports from the colonies forbidden.

1681 Oliver Plunkett found guilty and hanged at Tyburn, mainly on the evidence of Florence McMoyer, custodian of the *Book of Armagh* which he pawns to go to London. He never redeems it.

1679 Oliver Plunkett, Archbishop of Armagh, arrested but acquitted when put on trial in Dublin; sent to London for retrial.

1678 So-called Popish Plot, fabricated by Titus Oates in England, brings Catholics under suspicion of treason. Further moves against Catholic public worship in Ireland.

1686 Payments made to Catholic bishops at wish of King James II.

1685-89 Reign of James II

1688 King James II, rejected by the English Parliament, is supported in Ireland by the Catholic gentry who had lost land and status.

1689 Catholic 'parliament' underway in Dublin.

1689-94 Reign of William and Mary.

1695 Penal Acts of the Irish Parliament against Catholics concerning education, arms-bearing and ownership of a horse worth more than £5.

1697 Act of Parliament banishing Catholic clergy.

1699 Laws against the Irish woollen trade passed in English and Irish Parliaments.

1694-1702 Reign of William III.

1699 Laws against the Irish woollen trade passed in English and Irish Parliaments.

1680 Invention of the match. Abolition of death penalty for witches in France.

1685 Revocation of Edict of Nantes.

1685-1750 Johann Sebastian Bach.

1688 Birth of a son to James II's wife; 'invitation' to Prince William of Orange and his wife Mary (James II's daughter) to accept the throne of England; flight of James II to France.

1687 Richard Talbot, earl of Tyrconnell, appointed Lord Deputy of Ireland, sets about replacing Protestant officials with Catholics.

1692 Sir Patrick Dun is first president of College of Physicians.

1698 Death of Daíbhí Ó Bruadair, poet.

1702 Queen Anne.

1701 James II dies, after fleeing back to France from Ireland.

1712 Steam engine invented.

1701-13 War of the Spanish Succession.

1692 Witch trials in Salem, Massachusetts.

1728 Danish explorer Bering discovers Straits.

1719 Defoe writes *Robinson Crusoe*.

1740-48 War of Austrian Succession.

1752 Chinese invade and conquer Tibet.

1741 Bering discovers Alaska.

1756 Treaty of Versailles. *Black Hole of Calcutta*: Nawab of Bengal captures Calcutta and imprisons 146 in small room – most die.

1748 Pompeii excavated.

1700s Agricultural revolution in Britain and Europe.

1670 Palace of Versailles built.

Culture and heritage

1761 Newry ship canal completed below the town.

1760-1896 Coins
Reign of George III: Unofficial coinage (copper farthings and halfpence) bearing words *Voce Populi* and king's head struck from button maker dies in 1760. • Halfpennies from London mint 1766, 69, 74-6, 81-2 with king's head and crowned harp and from similar coins Soho mint. 1805. 'union penny' 1789 with Lady Ireland shaking hand of Brittania and 1805, pennies from Soho mint. • Bank of Ireland tokens issued: 1804 (six shillings), 1895 (fivepences, tenpences, six shillings), 1813 (tenpences), 1808 (thirty pences) Castlecomer token (five shillings and five pence counterstamped on Spanish-American dollar. King's head and on reverse e.g. 'BANK OF IRELAND TOKEN TEN PENCE' • Regal copper issue: Farthings 1896 from the Soho (Birmingham) mint with king's head and crowned harp.

1770 Oliver Goldsmith's poem *The Deserted Village* published in London. It is a nostalgic evocation of a countryside where a landlord preferred grazing lands to people tilling the land.

1775 Richard Brinsley Sheridan, who was born in Dublin, writes the play *The Rivals*, staged at Covent Garden, London.

1773 Oliver Goldsmith's comedy, *She Stoops to Conquer* published.

circa **1780** James Wyatt designs town of Westport with its tree-lined mall.

1780 *Cúirt an Mheán Oíche* (The Midnight Court) composed by Brian Merriman.

1781 Gandon's Custom House begins construction in Dublin.

1784
College of Surgeons granted a charter. The Society of Surgeons is formed by those dissatisfied with the Guild of Barbers in 1780.

1786 ↑ Building of the Four Courts begins. Designed by Gandon.

1785 Royal Irish Academy founded in Dublin by Lord Charlemont, commander of the Volunteers.

1787 Romanesque cathedral in Tuam burned.

1791 Wolfe Tone's *Argument on behalf of the Catholics of Ireland.*

1800 *Castle Rackrent* by Maria Edgeworth published.

1795 St. Patrick's College in Maynooth opens, financed by British government.

1792 A great harp festival held in the Linenhall Library, Belfast, includes Art O'Neill (1727-1816), the blind wandering harper. Young Edward Bunting sets out to record the harpers' music and preserves about 300 airs for posterity.

1793 Catholics first allowed into Trinity College, Dublin.

1802 Parliament House becomes headquarters of Bank of Ireland.

1797 Orange Lodge formed in Dublin.

1789 Charlotte Brooke's translations of Gaelic poems *Reliques of Irish Poetry* published.

Lifestyle

1775 Dublin citizens gather at City Hall to urge peace with American colonies.

1779 Irish volunteers parade on College Green, Dublin, demanding reduction of trade restrictions.

1782 Catholic colleges reopen, using English language.

A great harp festival is held in 1792

1791
Grand Canal reaches Athy on the Barrow. Passengers and goods transported.

1792
Catholics allowed to practise law and have own schools without local Protestant Bishop's permission.

1795 St. Patrick's College in Maynooth opens, financed by British government.

1796 Local yeomary corps established throughout Ireland for service in own area.

The French at Bantry Bay

1798 Lord Edward → Fitzgerald, senior officer in Ireland, captured and mortally wounded four days before the planned date of rebellion.

Harsh treatment of suspects led to the 1798 rebellion

Battle and conflict

1776 Outbreak of the American Civil War: Troops sent from Ireland to America.

1778
Protestant volunteer corps founded to defend the country

1769
Outbreak of 'Hearts of Steel' violence in Ulster.

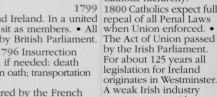

1784 Sectarian clashes in Co. Armagh lead to formation of Protestant Peep o'Day Boys and Catholic Defenders.

1772 Relief Act allows Catholics to lease bogland.

1774 Edmund Burke elected MP for Bristol.

1776
Draconian anti-Whiteboy Act passed.

1768 Octennial Act limiting duration of Irish parliaments.

1766 Second Whiteboy Act against assemblies.

1798
Irish Rebellion. Uprisings in May and June ferociously suppressed. In Co. Wexford, first action is at Oulart Hill, where Fr. John Murphy leads United Irishmen. Rebels fail to hold New Ross after taking it and are defeated at Battle of Vinegar Hill. • Presbyterians United Irishmen, led by Henry Joy McCracken defeated in their only battle in Antrim town. Co. Down rebels, led by Henry Munroe, defeated at Ballynahinch. • A French expedition fails; too small and too late, it lands in the West of Ireland in August – defeated 8th September at Ballinamuck, Co. Leitrim. French survivors taken prisoner and the Irish hanged or murdered. • Catholic bishops and parish priests oppose rising but some Wexford priests lead it. Fierce sectarian feelings in Wexford: some Protestant gentlemen lead rebels.

1762 Leasing of land causes bloodshed and disorder. Enclosures are so resented in Co. Tipperary that a secret society, the Whiteboys, is founded and spreads through the southern counties. The Whiteboys counter the enclosures by levelling fences, murdering opponents, burning houses, and marching around at night intimidating enemies.

Dublin Volunteers salute the statue of William III

1795
Militia units formed throughout Ireland for service within the country. • Orange Order founded following Battle of the Diamond in Co. Armagh after Protestant/Catholic fight at Loughgall, Co. Armagh.

1796
Tone, a brevet-officer in the French Army, persuades French to send expedition to Ireland; it arrives in December – soldiers cannot land in Bantry Bay due to storms.

1794
United Irishmen suppressed so decide on armed revolution.

1797
General Lake begins repressive anti-insurgency measures, including hanging of William Orr, United Irish leader, in Carrickfergus.

1793
Volunteers suppressed and arms movements restricted.

1798 Catholic bishops and parish priests oppose rising but some Wexford priests lead it. Fierce sectarian feelings in Wexford: some Protestant gentlemen lead rebels.

1804 Foundation of Irish Christian Brothers in Waterford city by Edmund Rice.

1796 Local yeomary corps established throughout Ireland for service in own area.

1795 Orange Order founded.

Politics, law and religion

1762 Whiteboys wage campaign against paying tithes to the Established Church of Ireland. This is a wholly Catholic society condemned by the priests who were often little heeded.

1763 Irish Parliament passes law against assemblies, the first so-called Whiteboy Act. A harsh regime of hangings begins.

1778 The leaders of the Protestant volunteer corps decide to free their parliament from the control of the English Parliament. • Relief Act allows Catholics leasehold and inheritance rights.

1775 Irish House of Commons approves the sending of 4,000 troops to America. Henry Grattan makes his maiden speech.

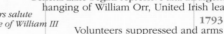

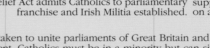

1793
Relief Act admits Catholics to parliamentary franchise and Irish Militia established.

1794 United Irishmen suppressed so decide on armed revolution.

1801 No repeal of the last Penal Laws in spite of promise made to the Catholic hierarchy.

1799
First steps taken to unite parliaments of Great Britain and Ireland. In a united parliament, Catholics must be in a minority but can sit as members. • All secret societies except Masonic Lodges banned by British Parliament.

1800 Catholics expect full repeal of all Penal Laws when Union enforced. • The Act of Union passed by the Irish Parliament. For about 125 years all legislation for Ireland originates in Westminster. A weak Irish industry must compete with mighty industrial revolution in Great Britain.

Rule

1783 Convention of Volunteers led by Henry Flood meets at Rodunda, Dublin, to press (unsuccessfully) for further parliamentary reform.

1796 Insurrection Act to apply military law, if needed: death penalty for administering an oath; transportation for taking one.

1791 Inspired by the French Revolution, the society of the United Irishman is founded in Belfast by Theobald Wolfe Tone, to seek legislative reforms.

Irish House of Commons

1782 Volunteers call for legislative independence at Dungannon convention; Rockingham government in Britain brings administration favourable to Irish claims; Relief Acts allow Catholics to own freehold outside parliamentary boroughs and gives access to educational rights; repeal of 'Sixth of George I' and amendment of Poynings' Law. This effectively gives legislative independence to Irish parliament, known popularly as Grattan's Parliament.

1792 Wolfe Tone appointed secretary of the Catholic committee. They meet in 'Back Lane Parliament' to draw up petition to king.

1797 Last general election to the Irish Parliament.

1800 Daniel O'Connell.

1760-1896 Reign of George III

1762-72 Viceroyalty of Townshend.

1780 Dissenters freed from the Test Act that had debarred them from public bodies.

Agriculture and industry

1804 Grand Canal reaches the Shannon.

1791 Grand Canal reaches Athy on the Barrow. Passengers and goods transported.

1762 Landlords begin to lease land to tenants or farmers to have it enclosed. Pattern of fields created on Irish landscape.

1780 Colonial trade opened to Irish goods, following Volunteers' campaign.

1783 Linen production

People and personalities

1766
Fr. Nicholas Sheehy hanged in Clonmel for a Whiteboy crime, probably an injustice.

1785
First Irish airman, Richard Crosbie, travels from Ranelagh Gardens, Dublin, to Clontarf island in ten minutes.

1784
Death of Eoghan Rua Ó Súilleabháin, Irish poet.

Lord Edward Fitzgerald

1798
Wolfe Tone, leader of the Society of United Irishmen, captured and commits suicide. • Lord Edward Fitzgerald, senior officer in Ireland is killed.

1803 Attempted rebellion of Robert Emmet in Dublin. He is tried and hanged.

1801 Act of Union unites Great Britain and Ireland.

World events

1770
Boston Massacre: British troops fire on mob in Boston.

1770-1827 Ludwig van Beethoven

1776
American Declaration of Independence.

1762 Britain declares war on Spain. • Treaty of St Petersburg.

1773 Boston Tea Party

1771 Discovery of Oxygen.

1764 Spinning Jenny invented.

1767 Townshend Acts: tax imposed on various imports into North America.

1788
Convicts first transported to Australia.

1791 Bill of Rights: first 10 amendments to US Constitution. • In France the Guillotine is invented.

1799 Discovery of Rosetta Stone enables understanding of Egyptian hieroglyphics.

1797 French invasion of Wales, Great Britain.

1803 War between England and France.

1804 Napoleon declares himself Emperor.

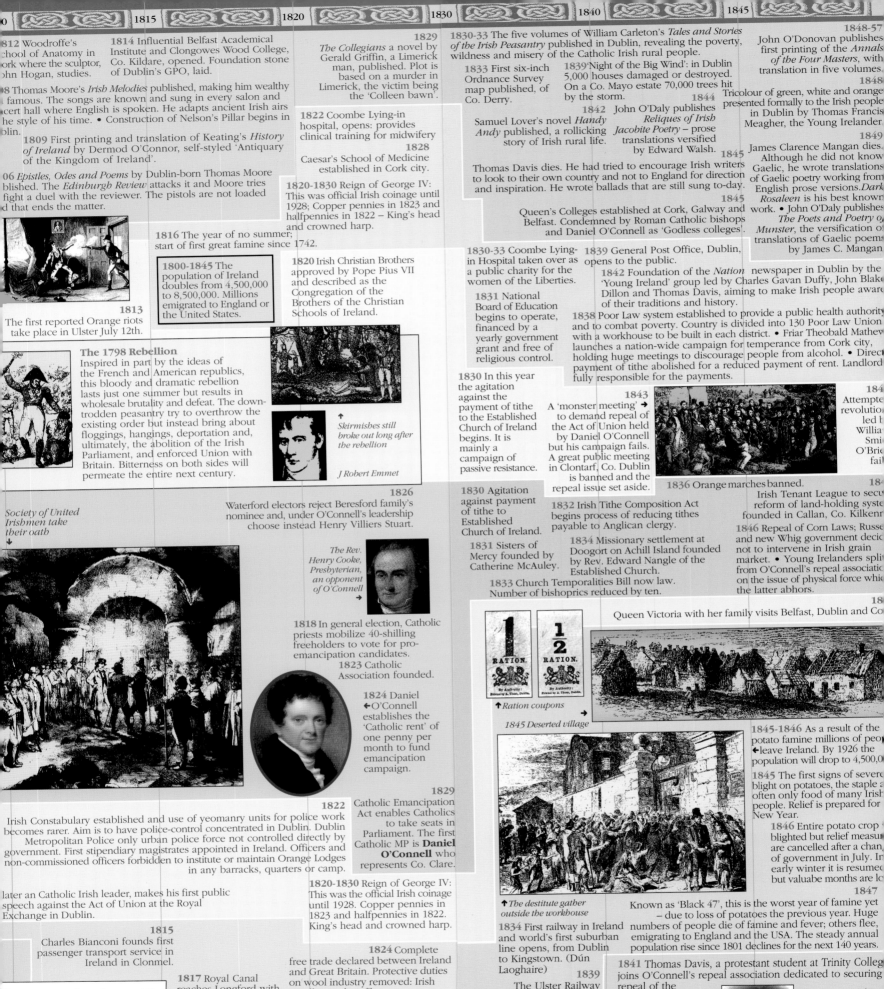

1812 Woodroffe's school of Anatomy in Cork where the sculptor, John Hogan, studies.

1814 Influential Belfast Academical Institute and Clongowes Wood College, Co. Kildare, opened. Foundation stone of Dublin's GPO, laid.

1808 Thomas Moore's *Irish Melodies* published, making him wealthy & famous. The songs are known and sung in every salon and concert hall where English is spoken. He adapts ancient Irish airs to the style of his time. • Construction of Nelson's Pillar begins in Dublin.

1809 First printing and translation of Keating's *History of Ireland* by Dermod O'Connor, self-styled 'Antiquary of the Kingdom of Ireland'.

1806 *Epistles, Odes and Poems* by Dublin-born Thomas Moore published. The *Edinburgh Review* attacks it and Moore tries to fight a duel with the reviewer. The pistols are not loaded and that ends the matter.

1816 The year of no summer; start of first great famine since 1742.

1800-1845 The population of Ireland doubles from 4,500,000 to 8,500,000. Millions emigrated to England or the United States.

1813 The first reported Orange riots take place in Ulster July 12th.

The 1798 Rebellion
Inspired in part by the ideas of the French and American republics, this bloody and dramatic rebellion lasts just one summer but results in wholesale brutality and defeat. The down-trodden peasantry try to overthrow the existing order but instead bring about floggings, hangings, deportation and, ultimately, the abolition of the Irish Parliament, and enforced Union with Britain. Bitterness on both sides will permeate the entire next century.

Skirmishes still broke out long after the rebellion

J Robert Emmet

Society of United Irishmen take their oath ↓

1826 Waterford electors reject Beresford family's nominee and, under O'Connell's leadership choose instead Henry Villiers Stuart.

The Rev. Henry Cooke, Presbyterian, an opponent of O'Connell →

1818 In general election, Catholic priests mobilize 40-shilling freeholders to vote for pro-emancipation candidates.

1823 Catholic Association founded.

1824 Daniel ←O'Connell establishes the 'Catholic rent' of one penny per month to fund emancipation campaign.

1822 Irish Constabulary established and use of yeomanry units for police work becomes rarer. Aim is to have police-control concentrated in Dublin. Dublin Metropolitan Police only urban police force not controlled directly by government. First stipendiary magistrates appointed in Ireland. Officers and non-commissioned officers forbidden to institute or maintain Orange Lodges in any barracks, quarters or camp.

1829 Catholic Emancipation Act enables Catholics to take seats in Parliament. The first Catholic MP is **Daniel O'Connell** who represents Co. Clare.

…later an Catholic Irish leader, makes his first public speech against the Act of Union at the Royal Exchange in Dublin.

1815 Charles Bianconi founds first passenger transport service in Ireland in Clonmel.

1817 Royal Canal reaches Longford with passenger and goods transport services.

1817 William Sadler crosses the Irish Sea in a balloon from Drumcondra to Anglesea in Wales.

1824 Complete free trade declared between Ireland and Great Britain. Protective duties on wool industry removed: Irish woollen trade suffers.

1820 Death of Henry Grattan.

1829 First Catholic MP: Daniel O'Connell, represents Co. Clare.

1820-1830 Reign of George IV: This was the official Irish coinage until 1928. Copper pennies in 1823 and halfpennies in 1822. King's head and crowned harp.

1825 Stevenson's locomotive The Rocket pulls the first public train.

1812 Napoleon invades Russia.

1815 Battle of Waterloo.

1829 *The Collegians* a novel by Gerald Griffin, a Limerick man, published. Plot is based on a murder in Limerick, the victim being the 'Colleen bawn'.

1822 Coombe Lying-in hospital, opens: provides clinical training for midwifery

1828 Caesar's School of Medicine established in Cork city.

1820-1830 Reign of George IV: This was official Irish coinage until 1928; Copper pennies in 1823 and halfpennies in 1822 – King's head and crowned harp.

1820 Irish Christian Brothers approved by Pope Pius VII and described as the Congregation of the Brothers of the Christian Schools of Ireland.

1830-33 Coombe Lying-in Hospital taken over as a public charity for the women of the Liberties.

1831 National Board of Education begins to operate, financed by a yearly government grant and free of religious control.

1830 In this year the agitation against the payment of tithe to the Established Church of Ireland begins. It is mainly a campaign of passive resistance.

1830 Agitation against payment of tithe to Established Church of Ireland.

1831 Sisters of Mercy founded by Catherine McAuley.

1832 Irish Tithe Composition Act begins process of reducing tithes payable to Anglican clergy.

1834 Missionary settlement at Doogort on Achill Island founded by Rev. Edward Nangle of the Established Church.

1833 Church Temporalities Bill now law. Number of bishoprics reduced by ten.

1834 First railway in Ireland and world's first suburban line opens, from Dublin to Kingstown. (Dún Laoghaire)

1839 The Ulster Railway Company opens line from Belfast to Lisburn.

1837 Humphrey O'Sullivan, the diarist, dies.

1840 Daniel O'Connell → first Catholic Lord Mayor of Dublin after Municipal Reform Act.

1837-1901 Queen Victoria's reign.

1833 Slavery abolished in British colonies.

1830 William IV of England.

1830-33 The five volumes of William Carleton's *Tales and Stories of the Irish Peasantry* published in Dublin, revealing the poverty, wildness and misery of the Catholic Irish rural people.

1833 First six-inch Ordnance Survey map published, of Co. Derry.

1839 'Night of the Big Wind': in Dublin 5,000 houses damaged or destroyed. On a Co. Mayo estate 70,000 trees hit by the storm.

1842 Samuel Lover's novel *Handy Andy* published, a rollicking story of Irish rural life.

1844 John O'Daly publishes *Reliques of Irish Jacobite Poetry* – prose translations versified by Edward Walsh.

Thomas Davis dies. He had tried to encourage Irish writers to look to their own country and not to England for direction and inspiration. He wrote ballads that are still sung to-day.

1845 Queen's Colleges established at Cork, Galway and Belfast. Condemned by Roman Catholic bishops and Daniel O'Connell as 'Godless colleges'.

1839 General Post Office, Dublin, opens to the public.

1842 Foundation of the *Nation* newspaper in Dublin by the 'Young Ireland' group led by Charles Gavan Duffy, John Blake Dillon and Thomas Davis, aiming to make Irish people aware of their traditions and history.

1838 Poor Law system established to provide a public health authority and to combat poverty. Country is divided into 130 Poor Law Unions with a workhouse to be built in each district. • Friar Theobald Mathew launches a nation-wide campaign for temperance from Cork city, holding huge meetings to discourage people from alcohol. • Direct payment of tithe abolished for a reduced payment of rent. Landlord fully responsible for the payments.

1843 A 'monster meeting' → to demand repeal of the Act of Union held by Daniel O'Connell but his campaign fails. A great public meeting in Clontarf, Co. Dublin is banned and the repeal issue set aside.

1836 Orange marches banned.

1845 Deserted village

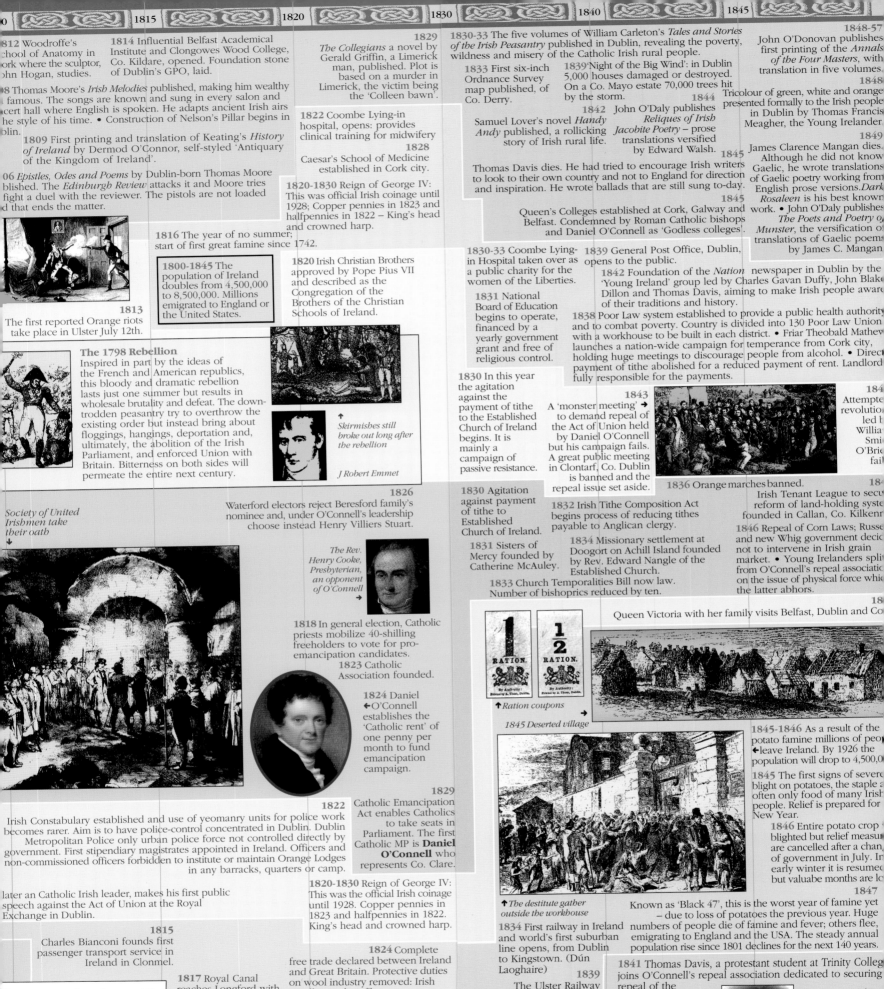

↑*Ration coupons*

↑*The destitute gather outside the workhouse*

1841 Thomas Davis, a protestant student at Trinity College joins O'Connell's repeal association dedicated to securing repeal of the Act of Union.

1848-57 John O'Donovan publishes first printing of the *Annals of the Four Masters*, with translation in five volumes.

1848 Tricolour of green, white and orange presented formally to the Irish people in Dublin by Thomas Francis Meagher, the Young Irelander.

1849 James Clarence Mangan dies. Although he did not know Gaelic, he wrote translations of Gaelic poetry working from English prose versions. *Dark Rosaleen* is his best known work. • John O'Daly publishes *The Poets and Poetry of Munster*, the versification of translations of Gaelic poems by James C. Mangan.

184. Attempted revolution led by William Smith O'Brien fails.

Irish Tenant League to secure reform of land-holding system founded in Callan, Co. Kilkenny.

1846 Repeal of Corn Laws; Russell and new Whig government decide not to intervene in Irish grain market. • Young Irelanders split from O'Connell's repeal association on the issue of physical force which the latter abhors.

18.. Queen Victoria with her family visits Belfast, Dublin and Co...

1845-1846 As a result of the potato famine millions of people ←leave Ireland. By 1926 the population will drop to 4,500,000.

1845 The first signs of severe blight on potatoes, the staple and often only food of many Irish people. Relief is prepared for New Year.

1846 Entire potato crop is blighted but relief measures are cancelled after a change of government in July. In early winter it is resumed but valuable months are lost.

1847 Known as 'Black 47', this is the worst year of famine yet – due to loss of potatoes the previous year. Huge numbers of people die of famine and fever; others flee, emigrating to England and the USA. The steady annual population rise since 1801 declines for the next 140 years.

1847 Daniel O'Connell dies in Genoa on the way to Rome.

18.. Californian gold rush.

184. Revolutions: in France, Italy, Germany, Ireland, and Hungary.

Culture and heritage

1853 *Grammatica Celtica* by Johann Casper Zeuss published in Germany. Zeuss traces the form, grammar and syntax of the earliest form of Gaelic. His sources are the glosses in manuscripts written by Irish monks.

↓ *Comedy melodrama by Boucicault*

1858 *The Irish Times* becomes a daily newspaper.

1860 Publication of William Carleton's Collected Works *Traits and Stories of the Irish Peasantry*, 1830. • Dionysius Lardner Boucicault's play *The Colleen Bawn* produced.

1861 Limerick St. John's RC cathedral completed. • *Manuscript Materials for Irish History*, a monumental work, published for Eugene O'Curry.

1864 Official opening of the National Gallery of Ireland in Dublin. • First Dublin Horse Show organised by Royal Agricultural Society.

1865 Samuel Fergusson's *Lays of the Western Gael* published. His poetry is heavily influenced by old Gaelic poetry.

1869 P.W. Joyce's *The Origin and History of Irish Place-Names* published.

1873 Eugene O'Curry's *Manners and Customs of the Ancient Irish* published.

1875 Production of Dion L. Boucicault's melodrama, *The Shaughrawn*.

1876 Society for the Preservation of the Irish language founded in Dublin.

1879 Publication in book-form of *Knocknagow or the Homes of Tipperary* by Charles J. Kickham, a regional novel. • Publication of Standish James O'Grady's 'History of Ireland: The heroic Period', a popular narration of the old Gaelic sagas.

1880 Trinity Hall → restored to Trinity College.

18[..] *Poems and Ballads of Young Irela[nd]* published; includes poems ← W. B.Yeats, T. W. Rollestan, Pádr[..] Colum, Katharine Tynan. This w[as] the beginning of the great litera[ry] revival, called the *Celtic Twilig[ht]*.

Lifestyle

1850 Synod of Roman Catholics prelates resolve to establish a Catholic University in Dublin. John Henry (later Cardinal) Newman chosen as Rector.

1854 Work on Catholic University begun but a charter is refused. Students are few and Newman's Oxford attitudes unhelpful to those who hanker for a Louvain in Ireland. Only its Medical School in Cecilia St at the Apothecaries' Hall survives and prospers until the foundation of the National University 1904.

1858 Medical Act recognises the following qualifications in Ireland: Licence and fellowship of Colleges of Surgeons and Physicians, Licence of the Apothecaries' Hall, Licence in Medicine and M.S. of Trinity College Dublin, the Queen's University Belfast.

1855 Stamp duty on newspapers abolished, making them accessible to more people.

1876 Women allowed to register as physicians.

1873 Religious tests for entry to Trinity College Dublin abolished.

1875 Irish team, playing first rugby international against England, defeated at Kennington Oval, London before a crowd of 3,000.

Trinity College Founded 1581 by Queen Elizabeth I • Famous graduates include Samuel Beckett, Edmund Burke, Oliver Goldsmith, Bram Stoker, Jonathan Swift, JM Synge, Wolfe Tone • Its fine architecture was used as the setting for the film, Educating Rita. • Its famous library has a collection of 3 million books: 200,000 are in the old library, including the medieval masterpieces, the *Book of Kells* and *Book of Durrow*.

1879 Mass meeting at Irishtown, Co. Mayo, organized by Davitt, leads to widespread agitation by tenants for greater rights. Irish National Land League is founded with Parnell as President.

1880 The Irish Rugby Football Union founded.

At Birr in Co. Offaly first All-Ireland hurling final play[ed] Tipperary (Thurles) defeat Galway (Meelick). First Gae[lic] Football All-Ireland in Dublin. Limerick (the Commercia[ls]) defeat Dundalk (the Young Ireland[s]).

1884 Gaelic Athletic Association founded

1886 After Home Rule debate, riots in Belfast begin on the docks and spread in the city – last three months.

1887 *The Times* publishes forged documents purporting to show Parnell's support for the Phoenix Park murders.

Battle and conflict

1857 Sectarian riots stirred up by Rev. Hugh Hanna ('Roaring Hanna'), and Rev. Thomas Drew against Catholics in Belfast: some deaths and injuries.

1859 Sectarian riots in Belfast.

1861 Funeral in Dublin of the *Young Irelander* Terence Bellew McManus becomes occasion of major Fenian demonstration.

1867 Fenian rising 5th March: isolated incidents in Dublin City, Cos. Cork, Limerick, Tipperary, Clare and Louth. Heavy snowstorm disrupts plans and rising fails. • Fenian bombing at Clerkenwell prison, London, kills several.

1882 Lord Frederick Cavendish and Thomas Burke brutally murdered in Phoenix Park, Dublin, by the 'Invincibles' who use surgical knives.

1875 Charles Stewart Parnell elected at Meath by-election.

1885 Irish Loyal and Patriotic Union founded (1891: Irish Unionist Alliance). Ashbourne Land Act allows for easier purchase by tenants of their holdings, through government loans.

1886 Lord Randolph Churchill reveals his intention to play the 'orange card' in opposing Gladstone's Plans for Home Rule.

1886 Gladstone introduces first Irish Home Rule Bill: it is defeated.

← **1889** The forger of the Parnell documents exposed.

Politics, law and religion

1856 'Phoenix Society' (a precursor of the Fenian movement) founded at Skibbereen by Jeremiah O'Donovan Rossa, who is soon joined from his exile in France by James Stephens.

1858 The IRB, Irish Republican Brotherhood, founded in Dublin by James Stepehens.• Irish Americans found the Fenian Brotherhood whose aim is to bring about an Irish Republic, if necessary by force.

1864 Archbishop Cullen of Dublin issues St Patrick's Day pastoral condemning Ferians.

1866 Archbishop Paul Cullen → of Dublin, the first Irish Cardinal, strengthens ties with Rome and authority of hierarchy in Ireland.

1867 The Irish RC hierarchy condemns Fenians as anticlerical.

1871 Isaac Butt elected MP for Limerick.

1868 Campaign begins for amnesty for Fenian prisoners.

1878 Fenian 'New Departure' initiated by Davitt and Devoy.

Three 'Manchester Martyrs', Fenians who killed a policeman while trying to rescue comrades, hanged in public in November. **1867**

1869 The Irish Church Act now law: Church of Ireland as a State institution disestablished.

1874 Butt's Home Rule motion defeated in House of Commons. Campaign of parliamentary 'obstruction'.

Charles Stewart Parnell 1846-1891

Irish nationalist and Home Rule leader, Parnell was born into a Protestant landlord family in County Wicklow. He was a man of great determination, vigour and formidable strength of character.

He became President of the Nationalist Party in 1877, was arrested and imprisoned in 1881 and released in 1882.

He transformed the Home Rulers into the Irish Parliamentary Party. He channelled idealism into practical politics and a disciplined, well-organised party emerged under his jurisdiction – but his being cited in a divorce case in 1889, after his long-term association with Kitty O'Shea was exposed, led in due course to his political downfall.

Agriculture

1850 Passenger services on the Royal and Grand Canals cease.

1851 Railway from Dublin reaches Galway.

1852 Railway lines from Dublin to Belfast, and Limerick to Waterford, completed.

1852 Submarine cable from Howth to Holyhead completed – the first telephone link between Ireland and Great Britain.

1855 Dublin to Belfast railway line open for traffic.

1862 Harland & Wolf shipyard opens in Belfast.

1866 First submarine cable link between Ireland and Newfoundland completed. The Irish station at Valentia remains in service for a century.

1872 Gladstone → makes his first speech to House of Commons on subject of Irish Home Rule. • Ballot Act introduces secret voting in parliamentary elections.

Apparitions on gable-end of chapel reported in Knock, Co. Mayo. Over twenty said to have witnessed them. Knock a place of pilgrimage for devout Irish Catholics ever since. **1879**

1882 Kilmainham Treaty between Charles Stewart Parnell and W.E. Gladstone; The 1881 Land Act to be amended and arrears of rent dealt with by the government.• Edward McCabe, Archbishop of Dublin, created Cardinal.

Katharine (Kitty) O'Shea ↓

1890 After O'Shea divorce case Gladstone threatens to resign if Parnell remains leader.
← Parnell denounced and repudiated.

People and

1856 George Bernard Shaw born: Author and playwright (1856-1950) →

1862 Thomas Francis Meagher, one of the 1848 rebels, Brigadier-General of the Irish Brigade in American Civil War, leads his men in the Battles of Bull Run, Antietam Creek and Fredericksburg.

1860 Roderic O'Connor, Ireland's greatest Impressionist painter, born in Co. Roscommon.

1865 W B Yeats born: Irish poet, → leader of Celtic revival and founder of Abbey Theatre in Dublin. (1865-1939)

1867 Brigadier Thomas Francis Meagher drowned in River Missouri in unexplained circumstances.

1854 Oscar Wilde → born: Author and playwright (1854-1900)

1873 Home Rule League founded after conference at Rotunda, Dublin.

Evictions of starving families continued through the century →

1870 First Irish Land Act recognizing tenant rights.

1877 Michael Davitt released from Dartmoor prison; returns to Ireland.

1879 Irish Land League formed →

1880 A land agent in Co. Mayo, named Capt. Boycott, is ostracised by local community and his name is added to English language. • Series of bad harvests continues. Many evictions of tenant farmers unable to pay rent.

World

1854 USA treaty with China.

1854-56 Crimean War.

1857 Indian Mutiny.

1860 Garibaldi conquers Naples and Sicily.

1861 Italy (bar Rome and Venice) united.

1863 Lincoln abolishes slavery.

1865 Abraham Lincoln USA President assassinated.

1866 Austro-Prussian War.

1869 Disestablishment Act ends Irish Church.

1868-78 Ten Years War: Spain/Cuba

1871 German Empire declared. • Trade unions legal in Britain.

1873 First Republic in Spain.

1876 Battle of Little Big Horn.

1877 Russia and Turkey at war.

1879 Zulu War.

1877 Parnell elected president of Home Rule Confederation of Great Britain.

1880 Parnell elected chairman of Irish Parliamentary Party.

1881-1894 Alexander III Tsar of Russia

1882 British occupy Cairo • Triple Alliance: Germany, Austria and Italy.

1885 Louis Pasteur injects against rabies.

1888 William II German Emperor.

1895 Oscar Wilde's *The Importance of Being Earnest* first performed. • Wilde later found guilty of homosexual acts and given 2 years' imprisonment.

1893 *The Celtic Twilight* by W. B. Yeats, published in London. • Foundation of the Gaelic League to revive the Gaelic language. Two books of translations from Gaelic by Dr. Douglas Hyde are published: *Love-Songs of Connacht* and *Songs Ascribed to Raftery*.

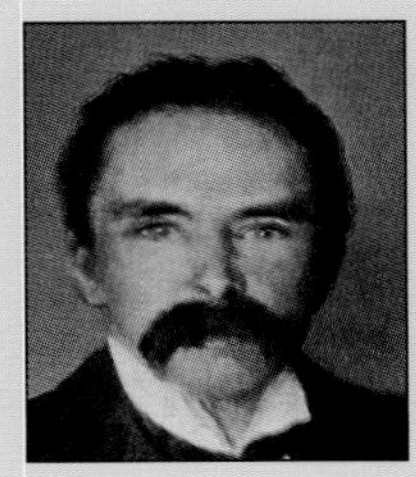

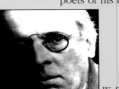

Dr Douglas Hyde ←

1899
The Irish Literary Theatre's first production of Yeats' *Countess Kathleen and the Heather Field* by Edward Martyn. This group was created by W. B. Yeats, Lady Augusta Gregory, George Moore and Edward Martyn. • Publication begins of the *United Irishman* edited by Arthur Griffith and of *An Claidheamb Soluis* edited by Eoin MacNeill. • Building begins of St. Anne's Cathedral (Church of Ireland) in Belfast. • Canon Patrick Sheehan's first novel: *My New Curate* published, a humorous, gentle evocation of the life of Irish Catholic priests.

1900 First publication by Irish Texts Society: *Poems of Keating*.

1903 P.W. Joyce's *A Social History of Ancient Ireland* Vol. I published. Pádraic Colum's play *Broken Soil*, a presentation of Irish rural life, produced by the Irish Literary Society • *Poets and Dreamers* by Lady Gregory.

1902
National Theatre Society produces W.B. Yeats's *Cathleen ní Houlihan* and G.W. Russell's *Deirdre*. AE (his pen-name) is a painter, mystic and great influence on young poets of his time.

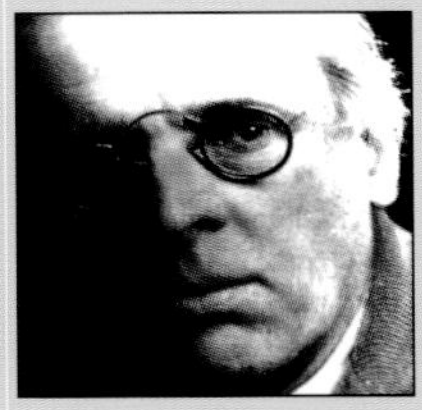

W. B. Yeates ←

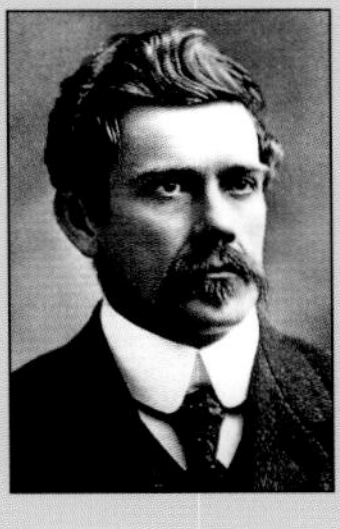

←*John M Synge*

1909
Volta the first cinema in Dublin, opens.

1905 First edition of the *Irish Independent* on 2 January – owned and edited by William Martin Murphy.

1909
Old Irish Folk Music and Songs by P. W. Joyce.

1908
National University of Ireland founded. • Patrick Pearse's school, *Scoil Énna* opens in Cullenswood House, Ramelagh.

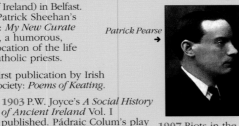

Patrick Pearse →

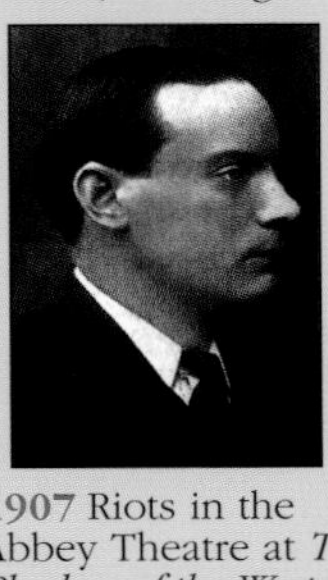

1907 Riots in the Abbey Theatre at *The Playboy of the Western World* by John M. Synge. • *Chamber Music*, a volume of poems by James Joyce, published in Dublin.

1904 Abbey Theatre opens on the 27 December with *On Baile's Strand* by W.B. Yeats and *Spreading the News* by Lady Gregory. • *Dubliners* published, short stories by James Joyce.*John Bull's Other Island* by G. B. Shaw.

1894 Ireland's rugby team win first Triple crown, playing in Belfast against Wales. Score: a penalty goal to nil.

1907 Dockers' strike and riots in Belfast.

1911-14 George Moore writes *Hail and Farewell* – Vols. 1-3 – roguish account of the greater figures in the Irish Literary Revival whom he knew in Dublin.

1911 Countess Marckievicz founds *Cumann na mBan*. the Irish women's revolutionary movement. National Insurance introduced.

1915
Irish Republican Brotherhood reorganized and Military Council formed.

1914
Employers' Federation fails to break the ITGWU. By February there is a gradual return to work. It is the first test of the union.

1913
Strike of city tram-workers, members of the Irish Transport & General Workers' Union, begins 26th August. Dockers' strike causes the Employers' Federation to lock out all members of ITGWU. Workers and their families face starvation. Food sent by trade unions in England. • Ulster Volunteer Force founded to oppose imposition of Irish Home Rule by United Kingdom parliament. • Irish Volunteers founded 25 November at a meeting in the Rotunda Rink to support Home Rule and counter Ulster Volunteers. • Irish Citizens' Army founded by James Larkin and James Connolly to protect workers against police.

1914
'The Curragh Mutiny': 57 British officers, including Major-General Sir Hubert Gough, threaten in March to resign if ordered to march against Ulster Volunteer Force. • At Larne 10,000 guns and 3,000,000 rounds of ammunition from Germany are landed for the Ulster Volunteer Force. • At Howth Harbour 1,000 guns and 30,000 rounds of ammunition from Germany landed; that evening British troops kill 3 people and wound 37. Searches do not reveal where arms are hidden.

1915
The *Lusitania* sunk off the coast of Cork by German submarine. 1000 perish.

1917
Ineffectual Irish Convention; reorganization of Sinn Féin and Irish Volunteers. • Remaining men interned in Fromgoch camp are released. • Thomas Ashe, a veteran of 1916, dies in Mountjoy Jail from force feeding when on hunger strike.

1916 *Literature in Ireland* published: the work of Thomas McDonagh (an executed rebel leader) on Gaelic influence on Anglo-Irish literature. • *Portrait of the Artist as a Young Man* by James Joyce published.

1917 Ineffectual Irish Convention; reorganization of Sinn Féin and Irish Volunteers.

1919
Shipyard, gas, electric workers strike.

1916 Easter Rising, 24-29 April. It breaks out chiefly in Dublin and rebels occupy buildings in city centre. Area is surrounded by troops, a gunboat on the River Liffey bombards them and they surrender. • Some parts of Dublin burned and pulverised by bombardment, 56 rebels fall in action, over 100 British armed forces, 17 policemen and some 200 civilians. • Thomas Ashe with a small group of volunteers captures police barracks in County Meath, the only victory in the rising. • 16 rebel leaders shot between 3rd and 12th May. In August Sir Roger Casement is hanged in Pentonville Prison for treason. This treatment of the Sinn Féin leaders turns Irish opinion against the British completely. Before Christmas 600 men of 863 are released from internment camp at Fromgoch in Wales.

1919-1921
The IRA, led by Michael Collins, receives money from supporters in the USA which help fund three years of fighting. Soldiers' barracks bombed and railways blown up. British recruit special regiments of soldiers, known as 'Black and Tans' (after the uniform they wear). Both the IRA and the 'Black and Tans' commit terrible atrocities during this 3-year period.

1919
Two RUC men are killed in County Tipperary at Soloheadbeg by Irish Volunteers acting on their own initiative.

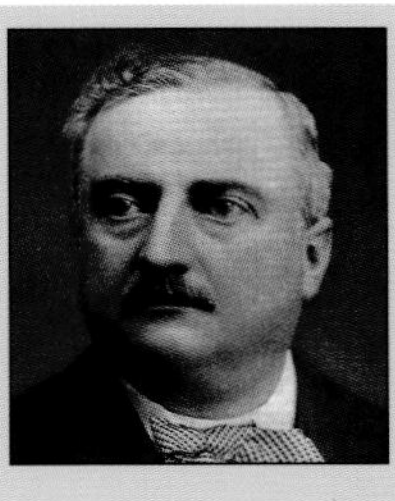

1900
←John Redmond elected chairman of Irish Parliamentary Party and United Irish League. Parmellite split brought to an end.

1904
Irish Reform Association founded to promote 'devolution'.

1903 Wyndham's Land Purchase Act. • Independent Orange Order founded by T.H. Sloan. • Formation of Griffith's National Council.

1902 Land Conference representing nationalists and landlords,

1897
First Gaelic League *Oireachtas* and First *Feis Ceoil*.

1893 Michael Logue, Archbishop of Armagh, created Cardinal.

1890 The split in the Irish Parliamentary Party leaves Parnell with 28 MPs as 45 led by Justin McCarthy withdraw support.

1909
First compulsory powers of land purchase enacted in the 'Birrell Act' • Bultner Hobson's *Fianna Éireann* founded, headed by Countess Markievicz.

1908
Foundation by James Larkin of Irish Transport and General Workers' Union • Old Age Pensions Act.

1905 Sinn Féin movement established by Arthur Griffith. Its declared aim is that the Irish are a free people and that no law should be binding on them without their consent. • Formation of Ulster Unionist Council and Irish Industrial Development Association; reorganization of Ancient Order of Hibernians, under Redmondite Board of Erin.

1912 Irish Labour Party founded in Clonmel by the Irish Trade Union Council. • Third Home Rule Bill introduced in the House of Commons in April. Edward Carson leads members of the Orange Order to sign a solemn league and covenant to oppose Home Rule.

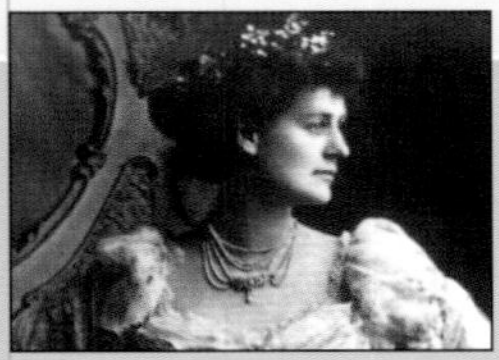

↑*Constance Gore Booth*

The ill-fated Titanic built in Belfast↓

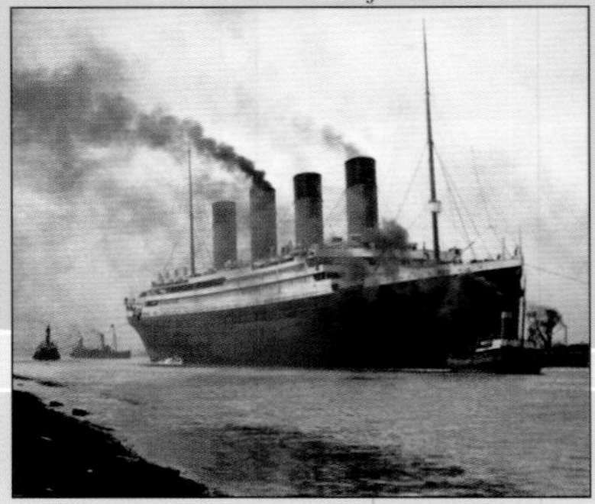

1919
Sinn Féin MPs meet in the Mansion House in Dublin on January 21st to form the first Dáil. These MPs are now called **Teachtaí Dála** (TDs). • One of them, Countess Markievicz, is first woman elected to the House of Commons. 34 members are in jail.

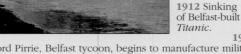

1917
Count Plunkett wins Roscommon by-election on Sinn Féin ticket. Eamon de Valera later elected for East Clare – becomes President of Sinn Féin and the Irish Volunteers.

1918 In the general election 14th December Sinn Féin wins 73 seats, Irish Party 6, Unionists 25, Independent Unionists 6. Sinn Féin MPs elected in every constituency in Ireland outside some ports of Ulster.

1912 Sinking of Belfast-built *Titanic*.

1919
Belfast shipyard engineers strike, demanding a 44-hour week. Other shipyard workers, plus gas & electric workers join in.Following take over of the gas works by the army, strike crumbles.

1917
Lord Pirrie, Belfast tycoon, begins to manufacture military aircraft. Eventually, 6 de Havilands, 100 Handley Page V/1500 and 300 Avros are built in Belfast.

1899 Department of Agriculture and Technical Instruction for Ireland established.

1893 Emigrants embarking at Queen's Town.→

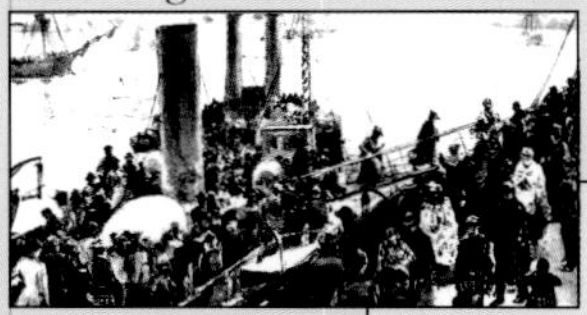

1894
Irish Agricultural Organisation Society founded by Sir Horace Plunkett, begins co-operative creamery movement. • Irish Trades Union Congress meets for first time.

Emigrants arriving at The Battery, New York →

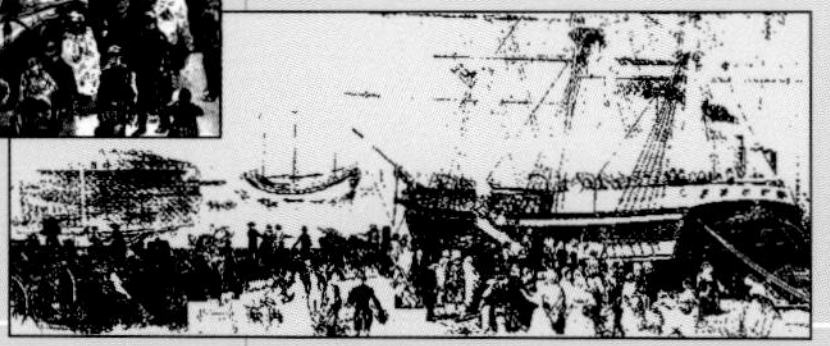

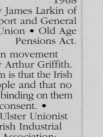

1890 Michael Collins born: Collins is elected a member of the Dáil in 1918 and a leader of the military wing of Sinn Féin (later to be called the Irish Republican Army). Collins is assassinated in 1922.

1891 Charles Stewart Parnell marries Kitty O'Shea in June but dies in Brighton, ten days after making his last speech.

1909
James Joyce manager of *Volta* cinema • Harry Ferguson travels 150 yards (137.16 m) at 4 yds (3.65 m) off the ground in an aeroplane built by himself, the first such flight in Ireland.

Ernest Shackleton
1874-1922, born Kilkee. Expeditions to Antarctic 1907-9 and 1914-16

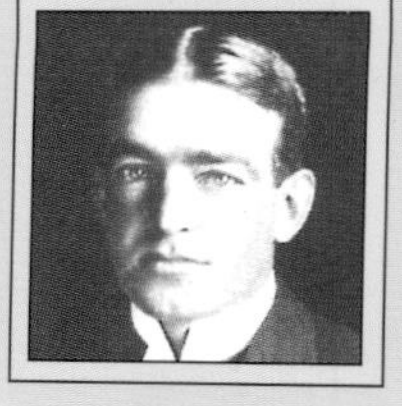

1913 Jack B. Yeats exhibits five pictures in the Armory Show, New York. Later he is first Irish artist to have a one-person show at the Tate and National Galleries, London.

1914 George Moore leaves for England disenchanted with literary pomposity.

1915 Pearse makes moving oration at funeral of O'Donovan Rossa.

1919
Michael Collins (1890-1922) elected a member of the Dáil in 1919. A future leader of the military wing of Sinn Féin (later called the Irish Republication Army), Collins is assassinated in 1922. • First transatlantic flight from Newfoundland to Clifden made by John Alcock and Arthur Whitten Brown.

1896 General Kitchener begins re-conquest of Sudan.
1901 Vacuum invented.
1903 Aeroplane invented.
1894 (-1917) Nicholas II Tsar of Russia.
1901 Commonwealth of Australia founded.
1888 and **1899-1902** Boer Wars in Africa.
1900 Boxer Rebellion in China.
1898 Spain and USA at war over Cuba.
1904-05 Russian - Japanese War.

1912 Winston Churchill visits Belfast to address the Liberal association.
1912-13 Balkan Wars
1912 First parachute descent from an aircraft.
1914-18 First World War.
1914 Opening of Panama Canal.

Culture and heritage

1922 James Joyce's *Ulysses* published in Paris. →

1923 Seán O'Casey's *The Shadow of a Gunman* produced at the Abbey.

1924 Seán O'Casey's *Juno and the Paycock* produced at the Abbey. Its success helps restore the severe financial situation of the theatre. Irish Free State's first annual grant to Abbey Theatre.

1926 2RN, predecessor of Radio Eireann and RTE, officially opened by Dr Douglas Hyde.

1929 *An tOileánach* (The Islandman) by Tomás Ó Criomhthain.

1930 Technical colleges established following Vocational Education Act.

1931 *The Irish Press* first published.

The Tailor and Ansty, racy account of Irish rural life by Eric Cross, is banned by the book-censor as obscene, without just cause. • *The Great Hunger* by Patrick Kavanagh.

1939 The publication of *Finnegan's Wake* by James Joyce

1942 1943 Irish Exhibition of Living Art.

Lifestyle

1920 Government of Ireland Act introduces partition between two Home Rule states. Riots in Derry and Belfast, revival of Ulster Volunteers, and expulsion of Catholic shipyard workers is followed by Republican 'Belfast Boycott' – reorganization of police, suspension of judical process and habeas corpus, followed by partial martial law; sporadic violence and ambushes culminate in Dublin's 'Bloody Sunday' (Nov.) and burning of central Cork (Dec.).

1925 *The Hidden Ireland* by Daniel Corkery on the hidden Gaelic culture in the 18th century published.

1928 First Irish coinage since 1823, designed by Percy Metcalfe.

1926 Population of Ireland drops to 4,500,000 - the figure back in 1800. • In Drumcollogher, Co. Limerick, 46 die in a cinema fire.

1932 All processions in Belfast banned after fights between police and workers. Both Catholics and Protestant unemployed come together to demand more money under Outdoor Relief Scheme.

1935 Importation and sale of contraceptives banned.

1940 Emergency powers introduced in Éire to combat IRA.

1942 First American troops arrive in Belfast. US naval base set up in Derry.

Battle and conflict

1921 Truce is declared in the south of Ireland.

1922 Irish regiments in British Army disband; men are advised to join Free State Army. • *Gárda Síochána* founded.

1923 First designs for new Irish paper currency by Sir John Lavery who places a portrait of his wife on the banknotes.

1924 National Army reorganization, cut-back, and mutiny.

1926 Rioting at opening of *The Plough and the Stars* by Seán O'Casey.

1927 Free State Minister for Justice, Kevin O'Higgins, assassinated.

1932 'Tariff war' provoked by De Valera's withholding land annuities from British Exchequer.

1935 Two months of violence against Catholics in Belfast begins 12 July.

1936 At end of year, General O'Duffy leads Irish Brigade to Spain to fight with the General Franco's forces and 150 republicans, led by Frank Ryan, go to support Spanish republicans.

1939-45 Ireland remains neutral during World War, although over 10,000 men and women serve in the British Armed Forces and war industries.

1941 Fierce German air-raids in Belfast and Dublin.

1939 IRA bombing campaign in Britain, and raid on Magazine Fort in Phoenix Park; Éire's declaration of neutrality implemented after outbreak of war (Sept.).

The Proclamation of Independence, 1916. The seven men whose names appear at the bottom were all executed

← *Aftermath of the Easter Rising in Dublin* ↓

1935 headlines about civil unrest

THE PROCLAMATION OF
POBLACHT NA H EIREANN.
THE PROVISIONAL GOVERNMENT
OF THE
IRISH REPUBLIC
TO THE PEOPLE OF IRELAND.

IRISH WEEKLY INDEPENDENT

WILD SCENES IN BELFAST STREETS

Six Persons Killed in Week of Terror

SHOOTINGS AND BURNINGS

TENSE ATMOSPHERE IN THE CITY

TROOPS CALLED OUT

DUNDALK CASE CONCLUDES

1943 John Andrews resigns as prime minister of Northern Ireland; succeeded by Sir Basil Brooke.

Éamon de Valera Taoiseach 1932-1948 ↓

Politics, law and religion

1933 Fianna Fáil receives over-all majority in general election. • The Fine Gael party founded. • Civil Authorities (Special Powers) Act made permanent. Oath of allegiance and right of appeal to British privy council abolished.

1938 Agreement between de Valera and Chamberlain to end tariff dispute and return 'Treaty ports' to Éire; UK guarantee to subsidize NI social welfare payments to British levels.

1922 Four republican prisoners executed by firing squad in Mountjoy. As a reprisal, Irish Free State orders jail without trial.

1922 Irish Civil War begins with the siege by the Irish Free State Army of republicans in the Four Courts and Public Record Office, Dublin. It is captured but much archive material is burned.

1930 Irish Labour Party separates from Trades Union Congress. Vocational Education Act. • Free State elected to Council of League of Nations.

1936 IFS Senate abolished; IRA proscribed by de Valera; Governor-General eliminated under Constitution (Amendment No. 27) Act; link with Crown further weakened by External Relations Act.

1940 Deaths of IRA hunger-strikers in Éire; joint Anglo-Irish military consultations; covert imposition of economic sanctions by UK against Éire. • John Charles McQuaid consecrated RC archbishop of Dublin.

1922 Anglo-Irish Treaty ratified by the Dáil in Dublin by 64 votes to 57. Elections in June confirm this. Republicans reject both votes.

1923 Cosgrave's *Cumann na nGaedheal* founded. • Free State admitted to League of Nations.

1927 Fianna Fáil enters Dáil.

1929 Proportional representation abolished in NI parliamentary elections (as in local elections, 1922); censorship of publications centralized in Free State.

1937 Referendum on a new constitution held on 14th June and accepted by majority of a small turn-out with 13% between the two sides. Laying a claim to the whole island of Ireland, it is largely de Valera's handiwork. Free State, renamed Éire, leaves Commonwealth.

1921 Northern Parliament opened by King George V in Belfast. Partition of Ireland begins and the reign of the Unionist Party in Northern Ireland that lasts until 1972.

1924 First meeting of Boundary Commission, with Eoin MacNeill representing Free State.

1925 Northern nationalists enter NI Commons; Boundary Commission collapses and partition confirmed by tripartite agreement.

1932 Fianna Fáil in government for the first time. De Valera replaces Cosgrave president of Executive Council. • Blueshirt movement founded by General O'Duffy • 31st International Eucharistic Congress held in Dublin.

Rule

1922-1927 Timothy Michael Healy Governor General.

1926 De Valera leaves Sinn Féin and founds Fianna Fáil; 'Balfour Declaration' at Imperial conference proclaims Commonwealth co-partnership.

1931 *The Irish Press* helps put Fianna Fáil in power and make them dominant Irish party. • Banning of IRA; autonomy of Free State extended by Statute of Westminster.

1932-1948 Éamon de Valera, Taoiseach.

1938-1945 Douglas Hyde First President of Ireland

Agriculture and industry

Moves to peace

1923 Republicans end hostilities in the Civil War and dump arms.

1921 On 11th October an Anglo-Irish peace conference meets in London, led by Arthur Griffith and Michael Collins. A treaty is signed by both sides in London on 6th December.

1929 A Papal Nunciature established in Dublin.

1927-1932 James McNeill Governor General.

1936 Irish Sea Airways, later called Aer Lingus, established with £100,000 authorised capital. First flight is from Dublin to Bristol. • Hydroelectric stations of 58 megawatts built at Poulaphuca and Golden Falls on the River Liffey. • Short & Harland Ltd founded to build Hereford bombers, Bristol Bombays and Sunderlands.

1938 Sydenham aerdrome built on 400 acres of land reclaimed in Belfast Lough.

1939 Four factories built to deal with the increase in pig production and processing – now 450,000 pigs per year give a sales income of £4,423,000. • The first aircraft lands at Shannon Airport.

1925 Shannon hydro-electric scheme initiated.

1923 Remaining tenanted land vested in Land Commission.

1927 60 megawatt hydroelectric station built on River Shannon at Ardnacrusha. ESB (Electricity Supply Board) founded to operate national grid.

People and personalities

1920 Hugh O'Doherty elected Derry's first Catholic mayor. Terence MacSwiney, Lord Mayor of Cork, dies on hunger strike in prison. Kevin Barry executed in Mountjoy jail.

1922 General Michael Collins, commander of the Free State Army killed in Co. Cork. Later Arthur Griffith dies suddenly of brain haemorrhage. Both were key figures in the rise of the new Ireland. • General O'Duffy appointed the first Gárda Commissioner.

1922-1932 William T. Cosgrave President of Executive Council of Irish Free State.

1923 Edward O'Brien is first Irishman to sail around the globe in his own yacht (June 1923 to June 1925). • W.B. Yeats awarded Nobel Prize for Literature.

1926 George Bernard Shaw receives Nobel Prize for literature.

1925 The Archbishop of Armagh, Rev. Patrick O'Donnell, created Cardinal.

1928 Colonel Fitzmaurice co-pilot of the *Bremen* sets out with Baron von Hünefeld and Captain Kohl from Baldonnel, Dublin, to cross Atlantic east to west. They land on an island near Labrador 1½ days later.

1929 Joseph McRory, Archbishop of Armagh, created Cardinal.

1933 General O'Duffy is first leader of Fine Gael party.

1935 Workman Clarke shipyard closes due to lack of orders.

1934 O'Duffy resigns, allows Cosgrave's instatement as Fine Gael leader. • Sir James Craig (now Lord Craigavon), PM of Northern Ireland, boasts of running 'a Protestant Parliament and a Protestant state'.

1940 Dublin Airport at Collinstown opens.

1939 Death of Yeats.

1941 James Joyce dies in Zürich.

World events

1922 Tutankhamun's tomb discovered.

1923 End of Ottoman Empire.

Wall Street crash. **1929**

1927 Lindberg flies the Atlantic.

1928 Invention of electric razor.

1930 R101 Airship disaster in France.

1932 Atom split by Cockcroft and Walton.

1930-31 Empire State Building built in New York.

1935-36 Abyssinian War.

1936-39 Spanish Civil War.

1940 Assassination of Trotsky

1939-45 Second World War

1949 *Cré na Cille* by Máirtín Ó Cadhain.

Samuel Beckett ←

1952 *Waiting for Godot* by Samuel Beckett.

1954 *The Quare Fellow* by Brendan Behan.

1961 *Ceoltóirí Chualann* founded by Seán O'Riada to promote and develop traditional Irish music.

1962 On New Year's Eve Radio Telefís Éireann goes on the air for first time. • RTE begins transmission of Gay Byrne's *Late Late Show*.

1963 Hillery's plan for universal secondary education in Republic.

From mid-60's to the 90s William Trevor writes many novels ↓

1971 Irish decimal currency is introduced.

1968 The Northern Ireland Civil Rights Association go on 'freedom march' August to highlight discrimination in public housing in Co. Tyrone. • Belfast students form 'People's Democracy'; in Derry, 'Citizens' Action Committee' formed.

1976 Movement known as the 'Peace People' established in Belfast, enjoying initial success, and Nobel Peace Prize for its leaders. • *North*, by Seamus Heaney.

1979 Relaxation of Republic's ban of contraceptives.

1947 Universal secondary schooling enacted in NI.

1952 First use of diesel locomotives in Ireland. • Despite the effective campaign to deal with TB, 6,795 new cases reported.

1970 The Ulster Defence Regiment (UDR) is formed to succeed the B-Specials.

1974 General strike organized by Ulster Workers' Council (May), brings about collapse of power-sharing executive and direct rule reimposed (May); multiple killings in Dublin explosions (May) and Guildford and Birmingham pub bombings (Nov. and Dec.). • Draconian Prevention of Terrorist Act introduced in UK in response. Provisional IRA announces ceasefire (December 22).

1948 Campaign to combat spread of tuberculosis initiated by Dr Noel Browne. Sanatoriums built – at least one in every county. • Poor Law system swept away fully by Health Service Board. Free health care is now given to all but the Mater hospital in Belfast which did not join new service on religious grounds. National Health Service introduced in NI.

1945 Angry exchange over airwaves between Churchill and de Valera over Irish neutrality in War.

Winston Churchill ←

1954 IRA raids the Gough military barracks in Armagh taking a quantity of rifles, Stenn and Brenn guns across the frontier to arm new IRA movement.

1957 Funeral in Limerick of IRA Volunteer Seán South is occasion of mass Republican demonstration.

1956-62 Border campaign by IRA.

1955 IRA campaign in Northern Ireland begins.

1960 Irish forces depart for UN service in Congo; 10 subsequently killed in ambush.

1962 IRA announces cessation of border campaign.

1964 Sinn Féin flies a tricolour in Belfast during a by-election campaign. Days and nights of violence follow its removal by policemen.

1966 Nelson's Pillar, Dublin, destroyed by Republican explosion. Major commemoration of 50th anniversary of Easter Rising. Catholic barman shot dead in Malvern Street, Belfast, by Loyalist UVF.

1972 'Direct Rule' imposed after episodes such as Derry's 'Bloody Sunday' (Jan.) in which soliders kill 13 CRA marchers, and bombing of Aldershot barracks; 11 killed in 'Bloody Friday' explosions caused by Belfast IRA (July); 'special position' of Catholic church expunged from Republic's constitution.

1979 Lord Louis Mountbatten killed in August by a bomb off Mullaghmore, Co. Sligo. • 18 soldiers killed in IRA bomb at Warrempoint (Down) on same day. • Airey Neave is killed by a car bomb outside the British House of Commons.

1946 NI National Insurance aligned with British system.

1951 Free Presbyterian church founded by Rev. Ian Kyle Paisley.

1954 Flying the Irish tricolour in Northern Ireland is made an offence. Last execution in Republic carried out in Mountjoy Jail.

1969 Serious riots in Derry and Loyalist raids in Belfast into Catholic areas cause introduction of British Army units into both cities. • Ambush by a Loyalist mob at Burntollet, Co. Derry, of People's Democracy marchers going from Belfast to Derry: 300 injured. • First in series of Belfast explosions (Mar.) and deaths in 'Troubles' (July); army drafted to NI after Protestant 'siege' of Bogside (Derry) following Apprentice Boys' parade (Aug.); reform of central and local franchise in NI (Dec.).

1975 Miami showband massacre by Loyalists (July).

1945 Congress of Irish Unions formed after split in Trades Union Congress. • De Valera visits German Representative to extend formal condolences on death of Hitler.

1952 Founding of Bord Fáilte.

1959 Trades Union Split healed with formation of Irish Congress of Trade Unions.

1964 McAteer's Nationalist Party becomes official opposition at Stormont.

1948 Fianna Fáil defeated in General Election and Coalition government forms. • Irish Republic enacted (inaugurated Apr. 1949) after Costello's repeal of External Relations Act.

1955 Republic admitted to United Nations Organization.

1961 Republic's unsuccessful application to join European Economic Community (repeated 1967). • Last execution is carried out in Northern Ireland at Crumlin Road Jail.

1971 Gunner Robert Curtis of the Royal Artillery is first British serviceman killed in Belfast in the years of warfare that follow. Internment introduced in Northern Ireland in August, almost completely for Catholics. Key IRA officers and men escape because lists are not up to date.

1976 11 Protestant workmen are taken from a minibus; 10 of them killed at Kingsmills in South Armagh. • 'Dirty protest' at the Maze prison. • British ambassador in Dublin killed.

1978 Provisionals' fire-bombs in Down restaurant kill 12.

Police vehicle ignited by petrol bomb, Londonderry 1969

1946 New Republican Party, Clann na Poblachta, founded, led by Séan Mac Bride.

1949 On Easter Monday Ireland formally leaves British Commonwealth: a Republic is declared. • British Parliament recognises the Republic. It guarantees the political position of Six County region if a majority continues to support it. • Minister for Health resigns after Catholic hierarchy's campaign against Mother and Child Scheme (similar scheme put through by de Valera, 1953).

1963 Liberal Unionist, Captain ← Terence O'Neill, succeeds Lord Brookeborough as PM of Northern Ireland.

1975 Northern Ireland Convention convened; NI internment suspended (abolished 1980).

1979 First ever Papal visit to Ireland, by Pope John Paul II (September) is a remarkable success.

1944 Split in Irish Labour Party (healed 1950); American attempt to have Axis legations in Dublin closed. • Children's Allowance Act passed. • C.I.E. established to control transport system.

1958 First programme for Economic Expansion in Republic (others in 1963-4, 1969).

1965 Seán Lemass, Taoiseach of the Republic, and Terence O'Neill Prime Minister of Northern Ireland meet at Stormont – first meeting ever between the two persons holding these offices.

1971 In September Democratic Unionist Party is founded by Rev. Ian Paisley and Desmond Boal.

1973 Republic and UK (including NI) enter EEC; proportional representation restored for NI local elections; Northern Ireland Assembly created, power-sharing executive agreed, and tripartite Sunningdale conference held.

1966 Anglo-Irish Free Trade agreement.

1974 Unionists leave Assembly in protest against plans for a 'Council of Ireland' (Jan.)

1976 Convention collapses; British ambassador in Dublin killed; Republic's Emergency Powers Bill referred to Supreme Court by President, who subsequently resigns after ministerial denunciation. • European Court of Human Rights finds UK guilty of torture of Republican prisoners.

1945-1959 Sean Thomas O'Kelly President

Houses of the Oireachas, Leinster House, Dublin ↓

1948-1951 John Aloysius Costello Taoiseach.

1951-1954 Éamon de Valera Taoiseach.

1954-1957 John Aloysius Costello Taoiseach.

1957-1959 Éamon de Valera Taoiseach.

1959 Eamonn de Valera resigns as Taoiseach and head of Fianna Fáil. and is elected President of Ireland. Seán Lemass is his successor.

1959-1973 Éamon de Valera President

Outstanding soldiers of Irish birth or descent include Lord Kitchener, Lawrence of Arabia and Field Marshal Montgomery.

1966-1973 Jack Lynch succeeds Lemass as Taoiseach.

1969 Terence O'Neill resigns as PM of Northern Ireland amid opposition to his plans for reform at Stormont.

1970 IRA split into official IRA and Provisional IRA. Provisional Sinn Féin formed after split, reflecting similar split in IRA; Social Democratic and Labour Party form from moderate nationalist groups.

1955 Short Bros pioneer first vertical take-off craft, the SC1.

1960 *Canberra* launched from the Harland & Wolff shipyard.

1972 'Direct Rule' imposed.

1973-1974 Erskine H. Childers President.

1973-1977 Liam Cosgrave Taoiseach.

1974-1976 Cearbhall Ó Dálaigh President.

1976-1990 Patrick J. Hillery President.

1977-1979 Jack Lynch Taoiseach.

1979-1982 Charles Haughey Taoiseach.

Jack Lynch at the signing of the EEC treaty of accession, 1973

↑ *The world's first vertical take-off aircraft*

1949 Aircraft constructors Short Bros (formerly Short & Harland) begin building Passenger flying boats.

→ *De Valera talking to President Kennedy, shortly before Kennedy's assassination, on his visit to Ireland. Kennedy was of Irish descent*

1966 Goodyear tyre company opens a factory in Craigavon.

1970 *Sea Quest*, the only oil rig built by Harland & Wolff launched.

1976 Economic Recession, originating in international oil crisis, begins to bite in Republic.

1946 Large-scale clearing of peat-bogs begun. Milled peat, briquettes, moss peat produced as well as traditional sod peat. One seventh of Ireland is under peat-bogs.

1956 Ronnie Delaney wins 1,500 metres race in Olympic Games at Melbourne, Australia.

1953 John Dalton, Archbishop of Armagh, created Cardinal.

1963 President John F. Kennedy visits Ireland.

1958 The Irish golfers, Harry Bradshaw and Christy O'Connor, win Canada Cup.

1965 William Conway, Archbishop of Armagh, created Cardinal.

1969 Bernadette Devlin, aged 21, elected in a by-election in Mid-Ulster to the British Parliament, is youngest woman MP elected until then.

1970 Taoiseach Jack Lynch dismisses Charles Haughey, → Neil Blaney from Cabinet, later charged with (and acquitted of) conspiracy to import arms ('Arms Crisis').

1979 Tomás O'Fiaich, Archbishop of Armagh, created Cardinal.

1979 Lord Louis Mountbatten killed by a bomb on his boat in August. • Airey Neave, a former escapee from Colditz, demands tougher action against the IRA. He is killed by a car bomb.

1953 Edmund Hilary and Sherpa Tensing reach the summit of Everest.

1946 League of Nations formally ended.

1957 Sputnik 1, first orbiting satellite launched.

1957-75 Vietnam War.

1950-53 Korean War.

1961 Yuri Gagarin is first man in space. • Berlin Wall erected.

1958 Invention of microchip.

1963 President Kennedy assassinated.

1969 Neil Armstrong and Buzz Aldrin become the first men on the moon.

1973 October War: Arab states attack Israel.

1977 Pompidou Centre opened.

Culture & heritage / Lifestyle

1980 Founding of Aosdána. • Brian Friel's *Translations* performed by Field Day Company, Derry.

1980 Derrynaflan hoard of silver and bronze antiquities found in Co. Tipperary.

1983 Shergar (racehorse; 1981 Derby winner) stolen from the Aga Khan's stud at Ballymany, Co. Kildare.

1980 The Boomtown Rats UK number one with *I Don't Like Mondays*.

1982 Maeve Binchy's novel *Light a Penny Candle*. • Frank McGuinness's first play, *Factory Girls* at the Peacock, Dublin. • Graham Reid's play *The Hidden Curriculum*.

1990 Jim Sheridan's film *The Field* is shown. • Painting by Caravaggio discovered in Dublin.

1989 The University of Limerick inaugurated. • Jack B. Yeats painting *The Harvest Moon* sells for £280,000. • Roddy Doyle's first novel *The Commitments* published.

Early 1990s Ireland has record-breaking run of successes in Eurovision Song Contest.

1993 Boyzone is formed. • Roddy Doyle awarded Booker Prize for his novel *Paddy Clarke Ha Ha Ha*. • *Riverdance* starring Michael Flatley is launched as intermission item in the Eurovision Song Contest; will soon achieve spectacular success as a stage show in London.

1995 Seamus Heaney awarded Nobel prize for literature.

1992 Samuel Beckett's first novel, *Dream of Fair to Middling Women*. • Eugene McCabe's novel *Death and Nightingales*. • Patrick McCabe's novel *The Butcher Boy*. • Boxer Michael Carruth wins first boxing gold medal for Ireland at the Olympic Games in Barcelona.

1990s Dublin attracts pop stars a[s] U2's hotel bears witness. Success[ful] entertainers pay vast sums for th[e] houses along coast south of the ci[ty].

Battle and conflict

1982 Multiple killings of soldiers at Knightsbridge (July) and Ballykelly, Co. Londonderry (Dec.).

1985 Principal year of 'moving statues', the reported movement of open-air statues of the Virgin Mary.

1986 Referendum confirms Republic's constitutional ban on divorce.

1990 Republic of Ireland reach quarter-finals of soccer world cup in Italy, under manager Jack Charlton.

1992 3 referendums on abortion issues.

1995 People of the Republic vote narrowly to allow divorce.

1996 Michelle Smith, Irish swimmer, wins three gold medals at Olympic Games, the first Irish person to win a swimming medal but is later discredited after drugs investigations.

1998 National Irish Bank accused of aiding resident Irish customers to lodge money in off-shore accounts to avoid Irish income tax.

1981 Republican prisoners go on hunger strike in H blocks of Long Kesh prison near Belfast, demanding to be treated like prisoners of war. 10 die before British government agree to this demand.

1983 In September 19 IRA men escape from Long Kesh prison. • 5 die in the IRA bombing of the Grand Hotel, Brighton, during Conservative Party annual conference.

Sinn Féin headquarters, Falls Road, Belfast

1986 IRA declares as 'legitimate targets' anyone working for security forces including contractors and British Telecom.

1994 After years of behind the scenes talks, initially between SDLP leader John Hume and Gerry Adams, leader of Sinn Féin, the IRA announces cessation of military activity, followed by a Loyalist ceasefire. IRA ceasefire midnight 31 Aug. • British army patrols cease in Derry & roads to frontier are opened.

1998 Condemnation in all quarters of the Omagh bombing by the 'Real IRA', a dissident IRA group. • Three sons of a Catholic mother burn to death in an arson attack on their house at night at Ballymoney, • Co. Antrim. General condemnation of sectarian violenc[e] • Orange Order parade from Drumcree blocked by barricades mounted by soldiers and policemen. • Th[e] bombing of Omagh by the Real IRA. People of all religions and mostly women and children are among the 28 that die then or later. • Huge bomb explodes [in] Omagh 15th August by a break-away republican grou[p].

↑1987 11 killed and 63 injured before Enniskillen service for Remembrance Sunday.

1992 UDR and Royal Irish Rangers merge to form Royal Irish Regiment. • In September a huge IRA bomb destroys Belfast forensic laboratory and damages hundreds of houses.

1996 Delays in progressing the Peace Process lead to break-down of IRA ceasefire (Feb 9) and Canary Wharf bombing.

Bertie Ahern, George Mitchell and Tony Blair (left) during peace agreement negotiations with (above) Sinn Féin's Martin McGuinness and Gerry Adams

28 killed and 200 injured in Omagh bomb explosion

Politics, law and religion

Easter Rising mural, Belfast

1916 EASTER 1982
"From the graves of patriot men and women spring LIVING NATIONS"

Apprentice Boys' March in Londonderry

1992 Bishop Casey of Galway flees when his fatherhood of a son is exposed. This proved to be but the first in a series of sex scandals which rocks the Catholic church and erodes its authority. • Treaty on European Union is subject of a referendum; results in 69.1% Yes, 33.9% No.

1988 Fianna Fáil under Haughey forms first ever coalition partnership with the break-away group, Progressive Democrats, led by Desmond O'Malley; continues to tackle successfully the country's economic problems.

1987 Fianna Fáil minority government introduces stringent financial restraints to solve the country's spiralling debt crisis. Spearheaded by Minister for Finance, Ray McSharry, they are supported in the national interest by the 'Tallaght Strategy' pursued by opposition leader, Alan Dukes of Fine Gael.

1996 Referendum removing ban of divorce narrowly carried in Republic.

1997 Rainbow Coalition of John Bruton defeated in general election. Succeeded by Fianna Fáil-Progressive Democrat coalition led by Bertie Ahern. • Return of Fianna Fáil to government and labour victory in the UK general election leads to restoration of IRA cessation and the commencement of all-party talks on North.

1993 Mary Harney succeeds O'Malley as leader of Progressive Democrats; first woman to lead a party in Dáil Éireann.

1998 Good Friday agreement signed in Belfast provides for a power-sharing administration in Belfast. • 94% vote in favour of the Good Friday agreement in a referendum. • The Dáil meet in emergency session to pass stronger legislation against groups such as the 'Continuity IRA' and 'Real IRA'. • Dr Mowlam, Secretary of State, visits Loyalist prisoners to convince them to support peace movement. • The Dublin government agree to abolish constitutional claim in Northern Ireland In return a council will deal with matters common to both parts of Ireland. • Agreement on future of Northern Ireland is reached on Good Friday. US former Senator George Mitchell guides all parties through intensive talks • Opposition to agreement from Ian Paisley, Bob McCartney and their parties; also from republican Bernadette Sands and her group. • 71% vote in favour of Good Friday agreement in a referendum. • Election for Assembly members under the Good Friday agreemen[t] takes place. A majority of elected candidates favour agreement. • The Parades Commission ban The Orange Order's march from Drumcree on the Garvaghy Road, Portadown, a Nationalist area. • The Northern Assembly convene at Stormont and elect David Trimble, of the Ulster Unionists, as First Minister and Séamas Mallon of the Social Democratic and Labour Party as his Deputy. This is first time that power is shared thus and that all parties sit together with Sinn Féin. • Tony Blair, UK Prime Minister, addresses the Dáil and Seanad.

Rule

1983 All-Ireland Forum held in Dublin Castle, boycotted by Unionists; referendum approves constitutional ban on abortion in Republic.

1985 Anglo-Irish Agreement signed by Dr. Garret Fitzgerald (Taoiseach) and Margaret Thatcher (Prime Minister) at Hillsborough, Co. Down. A north-south administrative body is to be established in Belfast, generating bitter Protestant protest.

1982-1987 Garrett Fitzgerald Taoiseach.

1987-1992 Charles Haughey Taoiseach.

1992-1994 Albert Reynolds Taoiseach.

1994-1997 John Bruton Taoiseach.

↑1997- Bertie Ahern, Taoiseach.
President's residence, Phoenix Park, Dublin→
↓1997- Mary McAleese, President

Agriculture and industry

1982 Goodyear company factory in Craigavon closed down with 770 job losses. • Since 1979, 110 businesses close because of Northern Ireland situation.

1986 Connacht Regional airport, promoted by Monsignor James Horan, opens at Knock, Co. Mayo in May.

1990-1997 Mary Robinson President, first woman elected to highest elected office in the land.

1990 and 1992 Nelson Mandela visits Ireland and addresses Dáil and Seanad.

People and personalities

1984 John Treacy wins silver medal in the marathon at the Olympic Games, Los Angeles.

1987 Stephen Roche of Dublin wins Tour de France.

1991 Cahal Daly, Archbishop of Armagh, created Cardinal.

1986 Monsignor James Horan dies in August at Lourdes.

1988 Seán McBride, former Chief of Staff of IRA, distinguished lawyer and founder of Clann na Poblachta party, dies. He had been granted both the Nobel and the Lenin Peace Prizes.

1992 Mary Robinson is the first President to visit Belfast.

1987 Richard Branson and Per Linstrand land in Limavady after 1st Atlantic crossing in a hot-air balloon.

1984 US President Ronald Reagan and his wife, Nancy, make 4-day official visit to Ireland.

Chri[s] Patte[n]

1998 ↑United States President Clinton given a warm welcome on his visit to Dublin, Limerick and Adare because of his support for peace in Northern Ireland • Tony Blair addresses the Dáil, first British Prime Minster to do so. • Chris Patten, last governor of Hong Kong, appointed to review operation and structure of Royal Ulster Constabulary. • President Clinton visits Omagh and Belfast. • David Trimble and John Hume informed that they have been awarded the Nobel Peace Prize.

World events

1980 ↑Margaret Thatcher visits Dublin.

1989 Tiananmen Square massacre.

1986 Chernobyl disaster.

1990 East and West Germany reunited. • Launch of Hubble Space telescope.

1994 Channel Tunnel opens to rail traffic.

1995 World Trade Organization established.

1997 A sheep is cloned. • Hong Kong returned to China. • Diana, Princess of Wales killed in car crash.

2000 Memorial to Oscar Wilde near Reading jail unvailed 100 years after his death.

Plaque in Paris where Oscar Wilde died 13 October 1900

1999 Civil Rights lawyer, Rosemary Nelson, murdered by a sophisticated car bomb in Lurgan. • Dr. Mowlam, Secretary, declares that IRA cease-fire is intact despite shooting. • IRA states it has appointed an interlocutor to discuss arms decommissioning with General John de Chastelaine. • All prisoners from Maze Prison at Long Kesh go home on Christmas leave. The prison has no inmates for the first time.

1999 Republic of Ireland joins the European currency. • Tribunal chaired by Judge Fergus Flood to investigate payments by businessmen to politicians begins hearings in Dublin Castle. • A Supreme Court judge and a High Court judge seem to have compromised themselves in the release of a man from jail after an arranged trial. Both resign. • Minister for Foreign Affairs, David Andrews, and Peter Mandelson, Northern Secretary, sign agreement on North-South administrative bodies. Articles 2 and 3 of the Constitution, with their claims to the northern counties, are repealed and Government of Ireland Act 1920 is amended. • Meeting in London of British-Irish Council. Irish and English government ministers, ministers from Northern Ireland, Scotland, Wales, the Isle of Man and the Channel Islands meet in this first meeting of its kind – a culmination of the peace efforts since the 1998 Good Friday Agreement. • David Trimble, First Minister for the assembly, boycotts Assembly when ministers are to be nominated. His deputy, S. Mallon, resigns but Trimble does not.

Report by Chris Patten on the RUC published. It advises change of name, uniform and a fixed percentage of Catholic members. • Already the review of the Good Friday

agreement by George Mitchell is in progress, but it is boycotted by Rev. Ian Paisley and his party and Bob McCartney. • At the demand of the Unionists Peter Mandelson is appointed to succeed Dr. Marjorie Mowlam as Northern Secretary. • Agreement reached between the Ulster Unionist Party and Sinn Féin. David Trimble makes statement recognising republican aspirations if pursued in a peaceful way. Gerry Adams reciprocates and IRA support verbally the peace movement for the first time. George Mitchell declares his review complete and returns to US. • Agreement between United Unionist Party and Sinn Féin results from talking directly to one another for the first time – instead of 'through the chair'. • David Trimble wins vote from Unionist Council to take part in new power-sharing executive. • Assembly meet in Belfast to receive nominations for ministries. Ulster Unionists 3 ministries, SDLP 3, Sinn Féin 2, Democratic Unionists 2. • Devolved government passes at midnight 1 Dec. to Belfast Assembly; 1920 Government of Ireland Act is repealed. • Inter-governmental bodies from both Irish governments meet in Armagh with some ministers of Belfast Assembly. This is first step in close and structured co-operation between the two parts of Ireland since 1920.

1999 Dana Rosemary Scallon (former singer) elected European Parliament in Connacht-Ulster constituency.

1999-2000 EU: Since 1973, membership of the European Union has contributed greatly to the transformation of Ireland. Now the country's economics, its road network, the restoration of Dublin and the stable punt all show the benefits. Ireland has emerged as a modern European country, with a distinctive identity.

1999 Former Taoiseach, Charles J. Haughey, appears before the Circuit Court. His £1.3 million debt of 1979, is cleared by Ben Dunne, supermarket owner, with some written off by Allied Irish Bank. • Ex-Senator George Mitchell is asked to review the state of the Good Friday agreement in the autumn. • Death of Jack Lynch, former Taoiseach. Two days later he is buried after elaborate State funeral in Cork.

A healthy nation . . .
In 1990 UNICEF reports that Ireland has the lowest mortality rate in the world for women giving birth, and the joint-lowest mortality rate for children under the age of five. • In 1994 Eamonn Coghlan becomes the first person in the world over 40 years of age to run a mile in under 4 minutes. • Dublin fish-and-chip shop owner, Ivan Beshoff, survivor of *Potemkin* mutiny in 1905 – does not die until 1987 aged 104.

2000
January
Government concerned that number of asylum-seekers surpassed 8000 in 1999, double the previous year.

February
Northern power-sharing Executive and Assembly suspended to avoid Unionist walk-out over IRA refusal to disarm.

April
The Flood Tribunal discovers widespread allegations of past abuses by public servants and politicians in the planning process in Co. Dublin.

May
Northern Executive restored when Unionists agree to re-enter government with Sinn Féin, following IRA decision to open arms-dumps to inspection by international observers.

July
Former Taoiseach, Charles Haughey, appears before the Moriarty Tribunal to answer charges that his lavish lifestyle was made possible by donations made in return for political favours.

October
Northern First Minister, David Trimble, bans Sinn Féin ministers from attending meetings of North-South Ministerial Council because of lack of movement on IRA 'decommissioning'.

November
British parliament enacts many of the provisions of the Patten Commission on the reform of the RUC, and changing its name to the Police Service of Northern Ireland.

2000
September
Sonia O'Sullivan wins silver medal in women's 10,000 metres at Sydney Olympics.

Our peacemakers David Trimble (left) and John Hume (right) are awarded the Nobel Peace Prize

1999 War in Kosovo.

1999 Floods in India.

1999 Global warming becomes an issue.

1999-2000 Millennium celebrations around the world.

2000 Olympic Games, Sydney.

2000 Widespread flooding in Europe.

Peace negotiations

Peace Statue, Derry City, Londonderry

The move towards peace

The path to reach a peaceful solution to the conflict in Northern Ireland and the last three decades' spate of troubles has been both protracted and fraught with difficulties.

Following intense negotiations, on 10 April 1998, an agreement on the social, political and economic future of Northern Ireland was signed. In the immediate aftermath there was a rush of hope that this historic agreement would deliver peace, security and prosperity. If fully endorsed by the will of the people from all sides of the conflict, the dream was possible.

Despite all this optimism, the peace process, unfortunately remained incomplete. There were further outbreaks of violence. Inevitably, such a long-drawn-out conflict will, just like an earthquake, continue to experience after-shocks which can take a heavy toll even as the population are recovering from the main thrust of tremors.

In July 1998, three Catholic children from Ballymoney, Co Antrim died when their home was fire bombed. Then, three months after the agreement was ratified in referendums on both sides of the border, a bomb in Omagh, Co Tyrone, killed twenty-nine people and seriously injured hundreds more.

But even in the face of such resistance, the negotiations continue.

The process is complex. Great courage, diplomacy and determination to succeed will be needed to meet the difficulties, to achieve, and maintain, a truly workable situation – one in which peace can thrive.

Discoveries and inventors

The 'discovery' of America is attributed to St Brendan, a 6th-century Irish monk.

Robert Boyle (1627-91), son of the Earl of Cork, author of *Boyle's Law*, is regarded as the founding father of modern chemistry.

John Tyndall (1820-93) of Carlow in 1859 discovered the 'Tyndall effect' explaining why the sky is blue.

John R. Gregg, from Monaghan, (1876-1948) invented shorthand.

The world's first submarine *The Fenian Ram* was invented by John Philip Holland (1841-1914).

The world's first tank, used at the battle of the Somme in 1916, was co-designed by the Dubliner, Walter Gordon Wilson (1874-1957).

John Desmond Bernal – from Tipperary designed the landing craft and Mulberry Harbours used in the Allied invasion of Normandy in 1944.

Ernest Walton, educated at Trinity College, Dublin, winner of a Nobel Prize for Physics, designed the world's first nuclear particle generator. He is credited with first splitting the atom in 1931.

Culture, sport and entertainment

The inaugural performance of Handel's *Messiah* took place in Dublin in 1742.

The Joshua Tree by the Irish group, U2, became the fastest-selling album in British pop music history in 1987.

Dublin is second only to Paris as the city to have produced most winners of the Nobel Prize for Literature (W.B. Yeats, George Bernard Shaw, Samuel Beckett and Seamus Heaney).

Ireland has the highest rate of cinema attendance in Europe.

Irishman, Peter O'Toole, is the actor who has received the most Academy Award nominations (7 for best actor) without actually winning an award.

In 1987, Stephen Roche became the only cyclist in history to win all three Grand Slam titles (Tour de France, Tours' Italia, and the World Championship) in one season.

Arkle, the greatest steeplechaser of all time, was foaled in Kildare in 1957.

The world's first ladies' tennis championship was played in Dublin in 1879.

Facts and figures

Almost one third of the Republic's population live in Dublin.

Standing at 205 feet, (62.5 metres) the Wellington Monument set in Phoenix Park, Dublin, is the tallest obelisk in Europe.

As strict attitudes to family life are changed by the more global outlook, one late member of the Parliament claimed that there had been no sex in Ireland before television!

The British Museum in London was founded by Sir Hans Sloane of County Down, after whom Sloane Square in London is also named.

Rear-Admiral Charles David Lucas, the first man ever to be awarded the Victoria Cross was of Irish blood.

The President of Israel from 1983-1993 was Irish. Chaim Herzog was born in Belfast and educated in Dublin.

A provision in the Irish tax system allows income that is derived from artistic endeavour to be tax free. This is one reason why so many artists choose to live in Ireland.

Dublin, like many of Ireland's first towns, was founded by the Vikings.

Historical perspective: background to the 'Troubles'

1169-1691: Early conflict
These begin with the Normans' first incursion into Ireland. • Treaty of Limerick is signed in 1691.

1695-1843 : Penal Laws
Penal Laws restricting Catholic liberty are introduced in 1695. The fight for emancipation begins.

1798: Rebellion
Atrocities on both sides.

1845-1914: The Great Hunger and its aftermath
Famine devastates the population. • The Fenian uprising is crushed. •

Struggle for Home Rule begins.

1916-26: Great conflict
The Easter Rising. • Conflict tears the country apart. • Sinn Fein obtain a political mandate. • Partition is introduced.

1927-49: From free state to Republic
Fianna Fail enter the Dail. • IRA declared illegal New constitution is drafted. • The Republic of Ireland is established.

1951-66: Peace movement
IRA campaign in Northern Ireland called off. • Co-operation between North and South develops. • Civil Rights campaign begins.

The 'Troubles'

1968-91: Fierce conflict
Civil Rights marches. • The Troubles escalate. • Although peace talks begin, there are mixed emotions among victims of the strife.

1985: Anglo-Irish Agreement
Establishes role of the Irish government in the affairs of Northern Ireland.

1991-97: Ceasefires
As killings continue, ceasefires come and go Great struggle to find a solution.

The progress of the peace negotiations is outlined under the flap on the left

---

Fact finder

Person or subject	Event	Place	Date
Abbey Theatre	Opens on the 27 December		190-
Abbey Theatre	Riots at *The Playboy of the Western World*		190-
Abbot Adomnán of Iona	Author of *Life of St Columba*		AD 69-
Abbots	appointed for some abbeys		163-
Abstract art	Metal-work		300-250 B(-
Act of Explanation	Cromwellian grantees obliged to surrender land		166-
Act of Parliament	Catholic clergy banished		169-
Act of Parliament	To stop soldiers robbing peasants and often killing workers		144-
Act of Parliament:	One self registered catholic priest allowed for each parish		170-
Act of Settlement:	New regime accepts Cromwellian land settlement		166-
Act of Supremacy	Acceptance that monarch is supreme governor of the church on earth obligatory for public office-holders		156-
Act of Uniformity	Compulsory use of the *Book of Common Prayer*		156-
Act of Union	Passed by Irish Parliament		180-
Ahern, Bertie	Taoiseach		199-
Aidan	Columba's disciple goes to Northumberland to found monastery, Lindisfarne (Holy Island)		AD 63-
Aircraft	Short Bros build passenger flying boats		194-
Aircraft	First lands Shannon Airport		193-
All-for-Ireland League	O'Brien founds this		191-
All-Ireland Forum	Held in Dublin Castle		198-
All-Ireland Hurling	First final played in Birr	Co. Offaly	188-
American Civil War	Troops sent from Ireland to America		177-
American troops arrive		Belfast	194-
Amnesity campaign	Begins for Fenian prisoners		186-
An Claidheamh Soluis	Publication begins		189-
Ancient laws			AD 46-
Ancient sites	Lough Boora,	Co. Offaly	6000 B(-
Andrews, David, Minister	With Peter Mandelson, Northern Ireland secretary for Foreign Affairs, signs agreement on North-South administrative bodies		199-
Andrews, John	Resigns as prime minister of Northern Ireland		194-
Anglo-Irish Agreement	Signed by Dr. Garret Fitzgerald & Margaret Thatcher	Hillsborough,	198-
Anglo-Irish Free Trade	Agreement		196-
Anglo-Irish peace conference		London	192-
Anglo-Irish Treaty	Ratified by the Dáil	In Dublin	192-
Anglo-Irish	Joint military consultations		194-
Anglo-Norman coins	Minted by Prince John,		118-
Anglo-Norman Ireland	Parish-system developed		
Anglo-Normans	Build Motte-and-baileys		1170-120-
Annals of the Four Masters	Chronology of Irish history		160-
Anti-Parnellite Irish National Federation	Formed		189-
Anti-Whiteboy Act	Passed		177-
Aosdána	Founded		198-
Apparitions	Gable-end of chapel	Knock, Co. Mayo	1879
Apprentice Boys Club	Founded by Colonel Mitchelbourne	Derry	171-
Aquila, Don Juan del	Captures town	Kinsale	160-
Archbishop Cullen	Issues St Patrick's Day pastoral condemning Fenians	Dublin	186-
Archbishop Dowdall	Opposes new forms of Protestant worship	Armagh	155-
Archbishop Marrh's	Library built		170-
Archbishop O'Lonergan	Resigns		122-
Archbishop of Dublin	Browné, a former friar, burns *bachall osa* (Jesus' staff),		153-
Archbishop Rinuccini	Comes from the Papacy to provide direction to Rising		1644--
Architecture	Stone-built houses		1500
Armagh	Under Uí Néill control	Armagh	750-85-
Ashe, Thomas	captures police barracks	County Meath,	191-
Ashe, Thomas	Dies in Mountjoy		191-
Assassination	of joint high-kings of Tara, Colmán & Áed Sláine		AD 60-
Assembly		Belfast	199-
Assembly members election	Under Good Friday agreement		199-
Asylum seekers	Numbers double from previous year		200-
Axis legations	American attempt to close these in Dublin		194-
Balfour Declaration	Proclaims Commonwealth co-partnership		192-
Ballot Act	Secret voting in parliamentary elections		187-
Bank of Ireland tokens	Issued		1760-189-
Barry, Kevin	Executed in Mountjoy jail		192-
Barrys & Roches	Murder Lord Philip Hodnet and 140 retainers	Munster	132-
Basil Brooke, Sir	Succeeds as prime minister of Northern Ireland		194-
Battle of Athenry	Bloodiest battle in Ireland since Anglo-Norman invasion		131-
Battle of Aughrim	Irish Jacobites defeated	Co. Galway	169-
Battle of Callan	John Fitz Thomas of Desmond & his heir defeated & killed by Finghin MacCarthy		126-
Battle of Dow	Defeat & death of Brian O'Neill		126-
Battle of Dysert O'Dea	Richard de Clare defeated & killed by O'Brien		131-
Battle of Towton Field	Earl of Ormond taken prisoner & beheaded		146-
Beckett, Samuel	*Waiting for Godot*		195-
Behan, Brendan	*The Quare Fellow*		195-
Belfast Academical Institute	Opened	Co. Kildare	181-
Belfast Assembly	Devolved government passed to		199-
Belfast explosions	First in series		196-
Belfast Shipyard	Engineers' strike		191-
Bermingham, John de	Created earl of Louth		131-
Bermingham, Sir John	Ambushed & slain	Ardee	132-
Bermingham, Sir Piers de	Invites O'Conor Falys to feast	Co. Kildare	130-
Bermingham, Sir William	Hanged		133-
Bianconi, Charles	Founds first passenger transport service in Ireland	Clonmel	181-
Bigod, Roger earl of Norfolk and Lord of Carlow	Co. Carlow constituted following death of	Co. Carlow	130-
Birmingham pub bombing	Six are released after 3rd appeal against verdicts		198-
Birrell Act	Compulsory powers of land purchase		190-

Ussher, James	Achbishop of Armagh		1625
Valera de	Peace Conference		1919
Valera de	Leaves Sinn Féin & founds Fianna Fáil		1926
Valera de	Replaces Cosgrave as presidentof Executive Council		1932
Valera de	Visits German Representative		1945
Valera, de & Chamberlain	Agree to end tariff dispute & returns 'Treaty ports' to Éire		1938
Valera, Éamon de	Becomes President of Sinn Féin & Irish Volunteers		1917
Valera, Éamon de	Dies		1975
Valera, Éamon de	President		1959-1973
Valera, Éamon de	Resigns as Taoiseach & head of Fianna Fáil. Elected President of Ireland.		1959
Valera, Éamon de	Taoiseach		1937-1948
Valera, Éamon de	Taoiseach		1951-1954
Valera, Éamon de	Taoiseach		1957-1959
Vere, Robert de, Earl of Oxford	Flees abroad		1387
Viceroyalty	Of Townshend	Townshend	1762-72
Viking	Raids - Iona, Rathlin, Inishmurray, Inishbofin		AD 795
Viking fleets	Around Munster coasts	Munster	AD 914
Viking	Attack monasteries		AD 800
Viking	Close of 2nd period of raids		AD 950
Viking	Fleet overwinters	Lough Neagh	AD 840-1
Viking	Raids penetrate deep inland		AD 836
Viking	1st settlements		AD 837
Viking-Irish alliance	1st reported		AD 842
Vikings	Led by Sitric Gale, return to Dublin	Dublin	AD 917
Vikings	32 Viking ships attacked but churches spared, Lough Foyle, and Armagh		AD 921
Vikings	Capture Forannán, abbot of Armagh		AD 845
Vikings	Defeat Osraige (Ossorm)		AD 825
Vikings	Defeated		AD 902
Vikings	Found port & city of Limerick	Limerick	AD 922
Vikings	Raid Lindisfarne	Lindisfarne	AD 793
Vikings	Raid Skellig Michael & capture the hermit Étgal		AD 824
Vikings	Seize Waterford	Waterford	AD 914
Vikings	Series of victories over Vikings		AD 848
Vikings	Struggle between Dublin Vikings & kinsmen in York		AD 867
Violence	Follows removal of tricolour	Belfast	1964
Vocational Education Act	Establishes technical colleges		1930
Volta Cinema	1st cinema in Dublin	Dublin	1909
Walls of Galway	Built by the de Burgos		1270-78
War	Major outbreak of war by the Irish of Leinster		1274
Warbeck, Perkin	Hanged at Tyburn		1499
Warbeck, Perkin	Arrives in Cork		1491
Ware, Sir James	Major works published	Dublin	1664-5
Warfare between Connacht	Theme of the *Cattle raid of and Ulster Cooley* story		300 BC
Wars of the Roses	Earls of Kildare & Desmond side with House of York & the Earl of Ormond with Lancastrians		1453
Waterford city	In custody of Robert le Poer		1177
Waterford electors	Reject Beresford family's nominee		1826
Wentworth, Thomas	Executed 12th May		1641
Wentworth, Thomas	Lord Deputy		1633
Wentworth, Thomas	Recalled & tried		1640
Wesley, John	1st visit to Ireland		1747
Westport House	Designed by Richard Cassels with alterations by James Wyatt		1731
Whiskey	1st historical reference		1405
Whiteboy Act	1st Act		1763
Whiteboy Act	2nd Act		1766
Whiteboys, The	Secret society founded	Co. Tipperary	1762
Wide Streets Commission	Appointed to oversee development of Dublin		1758
Wilde, Oscar	Found guilty of homosexual acts; imprisoned		1895
Wilde, Oscar	*The Importance of Being Earnest* performed for 1st time		1895
Wilde, Oscar	Memorial	Reading	2000
William & Mary	Reign		1689-94
William III	Arrives near Carrickfergus; defeats James' forces at the Boyne		1690
William III	Reigns		1694-1702
William of Orange	Victory is final act in reconquest of Ireland		1691
Wilton, Arthur de, Lord Grey	Appointed governor		1580
Wogan, Sir John	Appointed justiciar		1295
Women	Allowed to register as physicians		1876
Women	Qualify as poor law electors		1896
Woodroffe's School of Anatomy		Cork	1812
Workman Clarke shipyard	Closes due to lack of orders		1935
World War II	Ireland remains neutral		1939-1945
World War II	10,000 serve in British Armed Forces & war industries		1939-1945
Writing of Críth Gablach	Law tract on status		AD 700
Wyatt, James	Designs town of Westport		c. 1780
Wyndham's Land	Purchase Act		1903
Yeats, Jack B.	Exhibits 5 pictures in the Armory Show, New York.	New York	1913
Yeats, W. B.	Dies		1939
Yeats, W. B.	Nobel Prize for Literature		1923
Yeats, W. B.	*The Celtic Twilight*	London	1893
Yellow plague	Sweeps through Ireland		AD 664
York, Duke of	2nd visit to Ireland		1459-60
Zeuss, Johann Casper	*Grammatica Celtica*	Germany	1853

Alliance Party A moderate, non-sectarian Northern Ireland party.

Árd Fheis Annual convention, usually of a political party.

Bawn A castle enclosure or castlefold.

Bodhrán (pronounced bore-run) A hand-held, shallow, goatskin drum.

B-Specials Auxiliary Police force of the Stormont government; disbanded in 1971.

Bunreacht na hÉireann The Constitution of Ireland.

Cashel A kind of rath (see overleaf), distinguished by a circular outer stone wall instead of earthen ramparts.

Clochán A beehive-shaped, weatherproof hut built of tightly fitted stone without mortar. Clocháns date from the early Christian period.

'The Crack' Good conversation, a good time, often accompanying drinking. 'What's the crack?' means 'What's the gossip?' or 'What's going on?'

Crannóg An artificial island in the middle of a lake, dating from the Bronze Age.

Currach/Curragh Small fishing vessel used off the west coast; traditionally made of leather stretched over a light wood frame, modern currachs are of tar-coated canvas.

The Dáil Lower house of the Irish parliament.

Dáil Éireann Seat of Irish parliament.

Dolmen (or 'portal tomb') A chamber formed by standing stones that support a massive capstone. The capstone often slopes to form the entrance of the chamber. Dates from the Copper Age (2000-1750 BC).

Drumlin Small, oval, hummocky hill formed from the detritus of a retreating glacier.

DUP The Democratic Unionist Party. A traditionalist, anti-Republican right-wing party founded by Ian Paisley and Desmond Boal in 1971.

Éire Irish name for Ireland, but officially indicates the 26 counties.

Fenian A term, for a Catholic that implies that he or she is a Republican.

Fianna Fáil The largest and most successful of Ireland's two main political parties since Independence. Essentially a conservative party, it has its origins in the Republican faction of Sinn Féin, and fought against pro-Treaty forces in the civil war.

Fine Gael Ireland's second largest political party, Fine Gael sprang from the pro-Treaty faction of Sinn Féin which formed the first Free State government in 1921.

GAA Gaelic Athletic Association.

Gallery Grave A simple burial chamber of squared stones, generally found under a long mound.

Garda Police – Full name is Garda Síochána.

H-Blocks Colloquial name for buildings in the Maze Prison where most paramilitary prisoners are held.

INLA Irish National Liberation Army. Small republican paramilitary organisation.

IRA Irish Republican Army. The upholders of the Irish Fenian tradition, ultimately dedicated to the establishment of a united 32-county republic.

IRB Irish Republican Brotherhood.

IRSP Irish Republican Socialist Party. The most revolutionary, if small, party in Northern Ireland and the political wing of the INLA.

LVF Loyalist Volunteer Force. Active loyalist paramilitary group.

Loyalist A person loyal to the British Crown, usually a Northern Irish Protestant.

Martello Tower Circular coastal tower once used for defence.

Motte A circular mound, flat on top, which the Normans used as a fortification.

Nationalists Those who wish to see a united Ireland.

The North Term referring to Northern Ireland used by many people.

Ogham (rhyming with poem) The earliest form of writing used by the Irish (fourth to seventh centuries), and found on the edge of standing stones.

Oireachtas Name to cover both houses of the Irish Parliament (ie The Dáil and the Seanad) and the President.

Orange Order A Loyalist Protestant organization, found throughout Northern Ireland, which promotes the Union with Britain. The name comes from William of Orange ('King Billy'), the Protestant king who defeated the Catholic James II at the Battle of the Boyne (1960) and at the Battle of Aughrim (1691).

Passage Grave A megalithic tomb from the Neolithic period. A simple corridor of large, square, vertical stones leads to a burial chamber, and the whole tomb is covered with earth.

Poteen/Poitín (pronounced potcheen) Highly alcoholic (and often toxic) and illegal spirit, usually distilled from potatoes.

PUP Progressive Unionist Party. Seen as the political wing of the UVF.

Rath or Ringfort A farmstead dating from the first millennium AD. A circular timber enclosure banked by earth and surrounded by a ditch, within which roofed dwellings were built and, in times of danger, cattle were herded. Today raths are visible as circular earthworks.

Republicans Supporters of the ideals incorporated in the 1916 Proclamation of the Republic.

Round Tower Narrow, tall (65-110 ft) and circular tower, tapering to a conical roof. Built from the ninth century onwards, they are unique to Ireland. They are found on the sites of early monasteries, and served to call the monks to prayer.

RUC Royal Ulster Constabulary. Northern Ireland's regular, but armed, police force.

SDLP Social Democratic and Labour Party. The largest Nationalist party, centrist left, founded in 1970.

Sinn Féin ('Ourselves Alone') Nationalist party sometimes described as the the political wing of the IRA.

Souterrain Underground passage that served as a store or hiding place in times of danger.

Stormont The seat of government in Northern Ireland.

Taoiseach Irish prime minster.

TD Teachta Dála. Member of the Irish parliament.

Tricolour The green, white and orange flag of the Republic.

The Twenty-Six Counties The Republic of Ireland (Éire).

Tuath The basic Territorial Unit of Early Irish Society, consisting of a population group with between 700-3,000 soldiers and including land it occupied.

UDA Ulster Defence Association. A Protestant paramilitary organization, the largest in Northern Ireland.

UDF Ulster Defence Force. Illegal paramilitary Protestant organization.

UDP Ulster Democratic Party. Political wing of the LVF, led by Gary McMichael.

UDR Ulster Defence Regiment. A regular regiment of the British army recruited in Northern Ireland.

UFF Ulster Freedom Fighters. Another illegal Protestant paramilitary faction.

UKU United Kingdom Unionists. Virtually a one-person Unionist Party, sharing similar views to the DUP and led by Robert McCartney, MP for North Down.

Unionists Those (predominantly Protestant) who wish to keep Northern Ireland in union with the rest of the United Kingdom.

UUP Ulster Unionist Party. Founded in 1905 by Edward Carson, the UUP was in power in Northern Ireland from 1921 until the dissolution of Stormont in 1972.

UVF Ulster Volunteer Force. Another illegal Protestant paramilitary organization, originally formed in 1912 to oppose any British plans to impose a united Ireland on Northern Irish Protestants; banned in 1966.

The Effects of Geography

The first emigrants entered the country on foot as there was originally a land bridge between Scotland and Ireland. This land bridge was broken as the ice retreated in the post-glacial period. From that point onwards, travellers had to reach Ireland by sea.

It had become an island off the north-west coast of the European mainland and

Neolithic Court Tomb at Sligo

has ever since been subject to gales from the Atlantic. In particular, in the west coasts of Ireland, the rough seas made landfall very difficult and, in ancient times, almost impossible for a small craft. For this reason, the main points of entry to the country were established in the east.

A 'time lag'

Ireland's isolation as an island cut off from the rest of Europe caused a time lag in the transmission of ideas and the developments in human activity that were taking place elsewhere. Travel to Ireland was time-consuming, especially when it depended on sailing ships. Meanwhile, communications remained difficult inland too as its industry and road system were somewhat primitive.

Poulnabrone dolmen (right)

However, the invention of the telegraph and telephone, and then the radio, shortened this effect significantly and the 'time vacuum' effect was gradually eroded. Since air travel has become common and the internet widely used, the time gap between Ireland and the rest of the world is no longer of great significance.

Landfall

In early times there were serious difficulties about where to make landfall in Ireland. A frail craft could not contend with the fierce currents at many places where seafarers wished to land. The easiest landing points were all on the east coast.

In the Irish Sea the tidal currents enter from the north and from the south. The southern tidal current enters at 4.63 km an hour (2.5 knots) and increases to about 7.408 km (4 knots) at Wicklow Head. It slackens markedly when it reaches Lambay Island outside Dublin Bay and becomes sluggish. The northern current comes into the North Channel at 5.556 km (3 knots) and this increases to 11.112 km (6 knots) but slackens as it passes Dundrum Bay. Any sea craft entering from the south, for example, found it simplest to make landfall between Dublin and the coast of County Louth.

On this stretch of coastline were the estuaries of the Rivers Liffey at Dublin and the River Boyne at Dundalk. Thus Dublin harbour and port was very accessible to even the frailest craft in early times.

The Boyne valley became the centre of a very important agricultural community in the New Stone Age, and their builders constructed the tombs at Newgrange.

On the west coast there was a Neolithic settlement in Sligo and the remains of a large burial area of about sixty tombs is found in Carrowmore.

Waterford harbour is just outside the tidal stream of the Irish Sea and a seafarer coming towards it could navigate safely before coming in sight of the harbour entrance. Then, in the distance, two hills on either side of the mostly northerly part of the estuary acted as landmarks which had to be steered between. These are Tory Hill and Slieve Kielts. This brought the boat exactly into the harbour entrance. The land served by the harbour has many portal dolmens that may date back to 4000 BC.

Dublin was and is the capital city. Waterford City remained the second city of the country until the 19th century.

The west coast

The winds and heavy rain which sweep over the island of Ireland are strongest on the west coast. This inhibits the growth of trees, which are seldom found in West Clare, Connamara, West County Mayo and much of Donegal. The difficult terrain restricts the population in many of these areas. Unpopulated areas are found in West County Kerry, West Counties Galway

and Mayo and in much of Donegal.

The houses of people who live in these areas are situated in valleys sheltered from the wind and weather. There are also scattered areas in the Counties of Galway, Mayo and Roscommon, which remain relatively unpopulated.

Forest and woodlands

The island of Ireland was heavily forested in ancient times due to the temperate climate and the constant rainfall. Only in the 17th century was a determined effort made to clear the land of the last of them. The thick forests that still remained in the 16th century hid rebels and outlaws as well as people and their domestic animals during war. These were the 'fastnesses'. There was a fastness in the Glen of Aherlow stretching westwards into Counties Tipperary and Limerick. There was also a fastness west of the River Bann and northwards from Lough Neagh in Ulster.

The equable climate of some valley parts of County Kerry around Killarney, Glengarriff and Kenmare allows natural woods of oak, hazel and rowan to grow today – with arbutus on their fringes around Killarney in sheltered valleys. The arbutus may grow to a height of some 9 metres (29 feet). Trees will grow behind shelter in West Clare only at sea level, but

in these Kerry woods they reach heights of 180 to 250 metres (590-820 feet).

Natural woods are also found in Glendalough in County Wicklow, a deep valley where there is adequate shelter. In the Wicklow Mountains trees are confined to valleys everywhere and the widespread dome-topped mountains and hills are bare. Only the Big and Little Sugarloaf are pointed peaks because of the presence of quartzite.

Geographic boundaries

There were thirty-three dioceses in the whole country when the church reforms of the 11th and 12th centuries were complete. Thirty-one of these were based on the old tuath kingdoms or a combination of two or more of them to form larger ones. All, except the diocese of Leighlin, either has a maritime boundary or touches on an estuary or else the River Shannon.

They were all based on rural areas in the old native Irish fashion. Each of these was confined within natural geographic boundaries, which aided the defence of the tuaths.

There were two dioceses which were based on cities, Waterford and Dublin; these were the Viking settlements that had never followed the native system.

Counties

The counties were formed over a period from the 13th century to the 17th century. County Tipperary, for example, has within it a part of the Diocese of Killaloe in the north, the Diocese of Cashel on the central plain of Tipperary and lastly part of the Diocese of Lismore south of the Galtee Mountains and Slievenamon.

Waterways

The rivers were the main highways in a forested country and they remained of great commercial value until the 20th century. The River Shannon, which traverses the Central Plain, has never been fully navigable by substantial river craft. Some distance north-eastwards from the tidal water limits there are waterfalls at Doonas which prevent full use of the river. However, from this point upwards the river is eminently navigable.

The Rivers Suir, Nore and Barrow created a very useful network of navigable rivers in the south of Ireland. They formed means of communications with the world outside Ireland through the estuary and port of Waterford. The important inland town of Clonmel, an Anglo-Norman town, is built on the Suir and its trade in medieval times with Waterford and beyond made it a busy highway. It also formed part of the general route from Waterford to Limerick.

On the River Nore the city of Kilkenny is situated. It was originally a religious settlement at an important ford on the Nore.

Carlow on the Barrow was originally an Anglo-Norman military point that was set astride the main route from Dublin to Waterford through a break in the mountains and hills. The traveller reached the Liffey valley from the Barrow and could then go on into Dublin.

The building of canals in the late 18th and early 19th centuries was an extension of the various river systems for inland transport. Roads could not carry the amounts of merchandise that the rivers (and later the canals) could. The Central Plain was a perfect area for canals and both the Grand Canal and Royal Canal were pushed westwards to the River Shannon. To join Dublin and the Shannon with the southern river system, a branch of the Grand Canal was built into the Barrow valley. Merchandise could now be carried by water from Dublin to Waterford and Clonmel. There were no canals built west of the Shannon; none were built in Munster because of the unsuitable terrain.

Practically all Irish towns and cities are situated on estuaries or on rivers. The biggest cities, Dublin, Waterford, Cork, Limerick, Galway, Derry, Belfast and Drogheda are all ports.

The only exception is the town of Cashel in County Tipperary, officially declared a city in the 17th century. It was an ancient Irish settlement, which became the chief ecclesiastical centre of Southern Ireland and later of Munster.

With the development of the internal combustion engine, roads are now the main highways and rivers have lost their importance as thoroughfares.

Horses

The geological structures of much of Ireland made some areas eminently suited to the breeding of horses. The limestone in the soil is excellent for bone and body-building and Irish stock is famed for its sturdiness and hardiness. It is no accident that the country's great racecourses, surrounded by stud farms, are in Counties Dublin, Kildare, Carlow, Tipperary, Limerick and East County Galway.

Industry

Ireland did not experience an industrial revolution like the one in Great Britain – largely because of the lack of suitable coal

and iron ore. However, in the middle and late 19th century, heavy industry was developed in Belfast and throughout much of North-War Ulster. There coal could be imported more cheaply from Scotland and Northern England than was possible in the rest of Ireland.

Shipbuilding was conducted in Belfast. Throughout the area, steam-driven machinery made the linen mills also very profitable, where the finest linen cloth was manufactured.

The farmers of this area grew flax, a crop which needed much care and labour to cultivate and save. The damp climate was also suited to the successful spinning of the linen thread. The result was that from being a small town in 1941 with only 75,000 people, Belfast had become a major city by 1911 with a population of 387,000.

The Titanic and her sister ship, the Olympic in Belfast lough, both built in the Harland and Wolff shipyard, Belfast

Climate and agriculture

The heavy rainfall demanded an architectural response. The first stone churches built in Ireland, dating from about 800 AD onwards, have steeply pitched roofs, which were obviously designed to throw off the rain. It seems that the roof pitch was moderated later when experience proved such a steep angle to be unnecessary.

The climate of the island also dictated what foods could be produced. Plenty of rainfall meant cows produced plenty of milk. This resource was also used for making butter. Cheese was made but since butter could be preserved for a reasonable length of time in the normal cool temperatures of the country, there was little real need for it.

The sowing, harvesting and milling of some wheat for bread were always part of Irish agriculture. The frequent rain made it difficult to produce dry grain so by the 20th century this was mainly imported. The sowing of oats and its use as porridge for humans and fodder for horses has always been part of Irish land use.

The landscape of mountains, and lakes has also contributed to the romance of Ireland, to its legends and mythology and the poetry of its people.

Cows have always been an essential part of the Irish economy and in earliest days were used as currency

Towns and cities

Armagh

The city's name derives from the Irish, *Ard Mhacha*. A city, a seat, and a district: formerly in County Armagh, Northern Ireland, the modern Armagh city developed around the ancient hill fort of *Ard Mhacha*, an important place in the 4th cen-

View of Armagh at the turn of the 19th century

tury. It was here in the 5th century that Saint Patrick established his principal church in Ireland on this hill-fort site, which grew to become a medieval ecclesiastical capital. By the end of the 7th century, its primacy was generally admitted everywhere and its head took precedence over the clergy of Ireland.

Protestant English forces captured Armagh in the 16th century and then went on to establish a Royal school (1627), a library, and an observatory (1765). The Protestant clergy and gentry were a prosperous set in the 18th century and were responsible for the erection of the city's many Georgian monuments and buildings.

Today Armagh is the seat of both the Anglican Church of Ireland and Roman Catholic archbishoprics.

Those areas of County Armagh near the Irish Republic's border were hotbeds of sectarian and political violence during the late 20th century.

Located south of Lough Neagh, Armagh district covers an area of 261 square miles (676 square km). Its rugged southern terrain slopes down to more fertile lowlands in the north – the main fruit-growing region in Ireland, with market centres for apples and strawberries. The once important linen mills in the district have closed or diversified into the production of synthetic fibres. The city itself has become a market centre for the district and manufactures textiles, chemicals, optical items, and processed foods.

Belfast

The city's name derives from the Gaelic *Béal Feirste* (Mouth of the Sandbank or Crossing of the River). Capital of Northern Ireland, this town on the River Lagan became a city by royal charter in 1888. After the passing of the Government of Ireland Act in 1920, it became the seat of the government of Northern Ireland. Some fifty years on, its former county borough became the district of Belfast after the local government re-organisation of 1973. Its boundaries were then expanded to 44 square miles (115 square kilometres).

During both the Stone and Bronze ages, the site was occupied and the remains of Iron Age forts are still to be found on the slopes near the city centre.

The Norman conqueror of Ulster, John de Courci, was probably responsible for the castle built there after 1177 which survived until the beginning of the 17th century. It was in 1611 that Belfast's modern history began when Baron Arthur Chichester built a new castle there. He greatly encouraged the growth of the town, which received a charter of incorporation in 1613. Belfast survived the 1641 Irish insurrection and, by 1685, had a population of about 2,000. Brick, rope, net, and sailcloth making were the main occupations at that time.

City Hall, Belfast (centre)

Despite the castle's destruction in the late 1730s, Belfast began to acquire economic status, becoming an important port and the market centre of the Ulster linen industry: this was developed by French Huguenot refugees at the end of the 17th century. Mechanization of the spinning and weaving of linen made Belfast one of the greatest linen centres in the world.

This busy port with small shipbuilding interests, became firmly established when William Ritchie founded a shipyard in 1791 and a graving (dry) dock in 1796. In due course, its chief shipbuilding firm, Harland and Wolff went on to build the ill-fated *"Titanic"* and to become a huge concern with a shipbuilding yard covering about 300 acres and facilities for building vessels up to 1,000 feet (300 metres) in length. In the 1970s the firm was acquired by the Northern Ireland department of commerce, subsequently returning to private ownership, producing steel plates for bridges as well as supertankers. Belfast has continued to develop as a port, despite air raid damage in 1941.

Ulster became the scene of a largely Roman Catholic civil rights campaign in 1968, and from 1969 street riots and increasing violence took place in Belfast. After British troops were called in to police Catholic-Protestant disorders, the riots were marked by an increased use of firearms and bombs by both Catholic and Protestant extremists and by the killing of civilians, police, and soldiers. Unremitting violence continued into the 1980s.

Notwithstanding these scenes of unrest, Belfast has grown to become the retail, educational, commercial, entertainment, and service centre for Northern Ireland. Ships, aircraft, agricultural produce, livestock, and linen textiles are exported while other industries include tobacco and food processing.

Educational institutions in Belfast include Queen's University at Belfast. There are many other renowned seats of learning and nearby Stormont houses the seat of government.

Cork

The city's Irish name is *Corcaigh*, meaning a marsh. The second largest city in the Irish republic after Dublin, Cork was originally a religious settlement, founded by Saint Finbar in about AD 622.

Cork stands at the head of Cork Harbour on the River Lee. An island in the River Lee housed the centre of the old city. Its original site was probably near the present-day Cathedral of Saint Finbar, whose 7th-century monastery was visited by many students and votaries. Norsemen raided and burned Cork in 821, 846, and 1012 but eventually settled there to found a trading centre on the banks of the Lee. The walled town was granted its first charter in 1172. It was later held by the English.

Ever politically aware, Cork supported Perkin Warbeck, the pretender to the English throne, when he visited Ireland in 1491-92. Then in 1649, the city revolted in favour of Oliver Cromwell. In 1690 it was taken by John Churchill, Earl of Marlborough, for William of Orange. By the 1920s Cork had become a centre of

Irish nationalist resistance to British military repression. So much so that the ambush of a military convoy led to the British burning down parts of the city in retaliation. Further devastation followed the Anglo-Irish treaty in 1921. Irish Republican forces, who were unwilling to accept the treaty, held the city for a time.

The site of the 7th-century monastery became the site of another structure built in 1735, the Roman Catholic St. Mary's Cathedral built in 1808 and then the Protestant Cathedral of Saint Fin Barr, completed in 1880. Queen's College, opened in the city in 1849, became a college of the National University of Ireland in 1908.

Today this seaport is the county town of County Cork. Cork Harbour is one of the finest natural harbours in Europe, and one of the world's first yachting clubs was built there in 1720. The port of Cobh is on Great Island at the head of the outer harbour.

Cork's butter market has been famous since the early 17th century while today it has a wide variety of food-processing and manufacturing industries.

Dublin

In Irish, *Dubh Linn* means 'Black Pool' but the city is also called *Baile átha Cliath* (Town of the Ford of the Hurdle). Viking raids in the area began in about AD 830. The invaders first overwintered there in AD 841-2 – this is marked by a 9th-century cemetery with some well-furnished graves for women that have been uncovered to the west of the city at Kilmainham. Their most serious defeat was at the Battle of Clantarf near Dublin in 1014. In this battle the renowned King Brian Boru was killed.

Dublin was seized again in 1170 by the Norman knight Richard de Clare known as Strongbow whose armies proceeded to take much of Ireland.

Dublin is set in east-central Ireland at the head of Dublin Bay on the Irish Sea and is the largest port in the republic. The city stands on a hill-ringed plain and embraces the lovely River Liffey, which flows eastward into Dublin Bay. The city itself stretches little more than 4 miles (6.5 km) in any direction from central Dublin Castle but it has wide suburbs that extend towards the ring of hills and the sea for some 16 miles (26 km) or so.

Halfpenny Bridge links the North and south sides of the city. Built in 1816, this arched cast-iron footbridge is one of the earliest of its type. The halfpenny was the toll which was charged until 1919.

The capital of County Dublin and of Ireland, Dublin is the country's chief port. It is a vital centre of financial and commercial power, and has been long renowned as a seat of culture.

At one time famous for its textiles, especially wool, cotton, silk, and poplin, today the Guinness Brewery, producer of beer and stout, is the nation's largest private employer and Dublin's main industrial exporter. Other industries include food processing, making glass and cigarettes, and shipbuilding, while government and trade are major activities. The surrounding region is devoted mainly to agriculture.

The city's architectural heritage derives primarily from Norse, Norman, and Georgian sources, and these three influences combine in historic Dublin Castle, Christ Church and St. Patrick's. Few buildings date from before the 17th century. Both Protestant cathedrals were rebuilt by the Normans in the 12th century and

restored in the 19th century. Several of Dublin's most impressive government buildings were originally built as homes for leading citizens, including Leinster House (1745-48), now the seat of the Irish parliament, and the lord mayor's residence – built by Joshua Dawson in 1705 and the site of the ratification of the Irish declaration of independence from Great Britain in 1919. Other fine buildings include the Neo-classical Custom House (1781-91) and

Halfpenny Bridge, Dublin (pronounced Ha'penny) officially called the Liffey Bridge

the Four Courts (1786-1802), both damaged during the rebellions and civil war of 1921-22, and rebuilt since.

St. Stephen's Green, now a neatly manicured park, used to be an open common where locals cut their firewood and the mayor left his livestock to graze. It was also where public executions took place. The University of Dublin, or Trinity College, houses the famous medieval *Book of Kells* while The National Library and National Museum both have fine collections and interesting exhibits.

Quayside in Cork (left)

Galway

Galway's Irish name is *Gaillimh*. Set on the northern shore of Galway Bay, this seaport and county town originated with the building of its walls by Anglo-Norman settlers in about 1270. The Norman Lord of Connacht gave the city to fourteen of his supporters and their families to keep and defend against local Irish tribes – which they did successfully for many years.

A Franciscan friary was founded in 1296. Galway grew into a commercial centre, trading a good deal with Spain.

Richard II gave Galway its charter of incorporation in the 14th century and this was extended in 1545 to give the port jurisdiction over the Aran Islands. Export of all goods except linens and woollens was permitted. A shipping service still connects Galway with the Aran Islands.

In the early 17th century, James I issued a charter establishing the town and land within a 2-mile (3-km) radius as a county. During the English Civil War the town was captured by Parliamentary forces and was seized again during the campaigns of William III.

The town is the seat of a Roman Catholic diocese. St. Nicholas' Church dates from 1320 while University College, founded in 1849 as Queen's College, received a new charter in 1908 as a college of the National University of Ireland. Claddagh, the Irish part of the town in earlier times, is now a suburb.

Aerial view of Galway showing the port and the River Corrib

The Diamond in Derry City, Londonderry (centre)

An example of the famous Waterford crystal (right)

A major feature of the city is the River Corrib which is famous for its colony of mute swans and its salmon school which can be seen from April to July, heading upstream to Lough Corrib.

Galway's chief exports are wool, agricultural produce, marble, china, and metals. Its industries include flour milling, iron-working, hat-making, furniture, refrigeration units, electric motors, computers, medical and sports equipment.

Londonderry

Known in past times and to the locals today as Derry, its name comes from the Irish word *doire*, meaning 'oak grove'. Derry is set about 4 miles upstream from where the Foyle widens into the broad Atlantic inlet

of Lough Foyle. In an area first inhabited by fishermen and hunters, then Celts and Vikings, the old city area of Londonderry was centred on a hill on the west bank of the River Foyle. Saint Columba had established a monastery in Derry in the middle of the 6th century but the early settlement was repeatedly attacked by Norse invaders, who apparently burned it down some seven times before 1200.

Later, during the Tudor wars against the Irish, the town became a strategic battle point. The English seized Derry in 1600 and destroyed the Irish churches and the monastery. By 1613, James I of England had granted Derry to the citizens of London who laid out the new city, built its stout walls, gave the town its official name of Londonderry, and introduced Protestant settlers from both England and Scotland. The well-preserved city walls, about 18 feet thick and one mile around, were completed in 1618 and the city is still partially contained by these.

The city was besieged several times during the wars and rebellions of the 17th century and by James II's forces in 1688-89 but all these attacks failed St. Columba's Cathedral, originally built in 1633, contains many relics of the 1688-89 siege.

By the 1850s, linen shirt making became important and clothing manufacture remains a significant industry today.

Londonderry served as a naval base during the two World Wars. Following the civil rights campaign seeking equal rights for Roman Catholics, street violence occurred in Londonderry in 1969, with recurring disturbances right into the 1980s.

The old city, together with adjacent urban and rural areas, administratively merged in 1969 and became one of Northern Ireland's 26 districts during local government reorganisation in 1973. Its rolling lowlands and valleys rise to the wooded slopes of the Sperrin Mountains in the south-east.

Salmon are commercially fished in the tidal portions of the River Foyle, while sheep, barley, and poultry are raised by farmers in the district. Local factories process foods, manufacture chemicals and make other light industrial products, as well as linen and shirts.

Waterford

In Irish, the city is called *Port Láirge*. The major town of south-eastern Ireland, Waterford is a city, an important port, and a county borough. Set on the south bank of the River Suir, it lies 4 miles (6 km) above this river's junction with the Barrow at the head of Waterford Harbour – a sheltered, winding bay.

Waterford became the base for the second period of Viking raids which began in 914 AD, when a great sea fleet arrived in Waterford harbour. By 1096, Waterford had become a cathedral city. Strongboy, the Earl of Pembroke, seized Waterford in 1170; Henry II landed there in 1171. His son, King John, gave Waterford its charter in 1205 and defined the shire. By the later Middle Ages the city was virtually an independent commune.

Waterford's Roman Catholic cathedral was completed in 1796, and its Anglican Church of Ireland cathedral was built in 1773-79 on the site of an earlier church founded in about 1050. Norsemen enclosed some 15 acres (6 hectares) of the city with walls and fortifications that were rebuilt by the Normans. There was also a Dominican friary.

The city sent two members to Parliament from 1374 to 1885. However, in 1603 Waterford was involved in fierce opposition to the government and the Anglican church but the approach of the forces of Baron Mountjoy, lord deputy of Ireland, led to its submission. In 1649 the city resisted Oliver Cromwell but the next year surrendered to his son-in-law Henry Ireton. In 1898 it became a county borough.

Waterford is now an important export centre for fruit and meat. It is also a centre for extensive salmon and sea fisheries. The main industries are food processing, brewing, paper-making, and glass-making. Waterford crystal is world famous.

Wexford

In Irish, Wexford is known as *Loch Garman*, while the name Wexford derives from the Norse settlement of Waesfjord. Seaport and county seat on the River Slaney, Wexford Harbour, formed by the Slaney estuary, is large, but cannot accommodate vessels drawing more than 12 feet (4 metres) because of a bar. It is now served by an artificial harbour which is connected with Wexford by rail – which opened in

1906 at Rosslare.

Ptolemy mentioned a tribe called the Menapia in the area and certainly Belgic Gauls settled here. Wexford was an early colony of the English, having been taken by Robert FitzStephen in 1169. The town received a charter in 1317, which was extended in 1411 by Henry IV and in 1558 by Elizabeth I. Later charters were granted in 1608 and 1686 by James I and James II.

Sacked by the forces of Oliver Cromwell in 1649, Wexford was captured and garrisoned for William III in 1690. Wexford was most actively involved in the 1798 rising when the unrest and rebellion – due to land hunger, the fall in grain prices and an increase in taxes – led to the declaration of martial law in the April of that

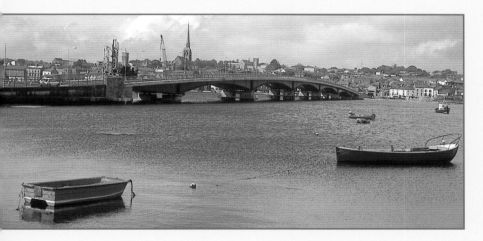

year. Other claims to fame are that the Arctic explorer who discovered the Northwest Passage, Sir Robert McClure, was born here in 1807.

Under the Municipal Corporations Act of 1840, the city lost its charter but was granted another in 1846 by Queen Victoria.

Today parts of the old walls remain and one of the five towers of the town. Alongside the ruins of the ancient abbey of St. Sepulchre, a de-consecrated Protestant church is supposed to occupy the spot where the treaty was signed between the Irish and the English invaders in 1169.

Wexford's principal exports are livestock and agricultural produce while the town's industries are based on agriculture and light engineering. It is a base for salmon and sea-fishing, and is popular as a centre for tourists.

Irish place names

Practically all Irish place names are derived from Gaelic, English or Old Norse.

English names, while in the minority, are still a vital element. There are many beginning with 'Newton' and 'Newcastle' as well as hybrids such as: **Danesfort** – from *Dún Fearta* (fort/enclosure of the grave/trench), a misunderstanding of the original place name.

Only a few few names have Old Norse origins. These include: **Waterford** – *Vedra Fiord*, the (good) weather fiord *Leixlip, Lax hlaup*, salmon leap. **Wexford** from *Weissfiord*, western fiord.

Hybrid names, where the Gaelic name is linked with the Old Norse word for place (*ster*) include the names of three provinces:
Ulster from Uladh + *ster*,
Leinster from *Laighean* + *ster* and
Munster from *Mumham* + *ster*.

Gaelic names

Names with Gaelic derivations are often drawn from geographical features and the names of people that lived there.

'**ard**' *ard* (high or height), eg Ardpatrick, Patrick's height.

'**bally**' *baile* (homestead, eg Ballyneale, Neill's homestead.

'**bawn**' *bán* (cow-field or courtyard of castle), eg Bawnmore, the great cowfield.

'**beg**' *beag* small 'kill', eg Ballybeg, the little homestead.

'**ballagh**' *bealach* (road), eg Ballaghadereen, the homestead of the little oak-wood.

'**barna**' *bearna* (gap), eg Barnaderg, red gap.

'**boher**' *bóthar* (road), Boherlahan, wide road.

'**booley**' or '**boola**' *buaile* (milking place), eg Boolavogue, Mogue's milking place.

'**carra**' *ceathrú* (quarter, a land measure), Carraroe, the red quarter.

'**carrick**' *carraig* (rock), Carrick-on-Suir, the rock on the River Suir.

'**cloon** or **clon**' *cluain* (a pasturage), eg Clonard, the high and noble one's pasturage.

'**cashel**' *caiseal* (stone ringfort), Cashel city.

'**cool**' *cúl* (nook), eg Coolderry, nook of

the oakwood.

'**curragh**' *currach* (marsh or racecourse), eg the Curragh of Kildare.

'**derrig**' *dearg* (red), Gathaderrig, red gate.

'**derry**' *doire* (oakwood), eg Derry city.

'**drehid/droghed**' *droichead*, eg Droghed, the bridge of the ford.

'**dun**' *dún* (fort or enclosure), eg Dunmore, the great enclosure/fort.

'**gort**' *gort* (tilled field), Gortavilly, the tilled field of the sacred tree.

'**inch**' *inis* (river-holm), eg the Inches.

'**inish**' *inis* (island), Inishbofin, the island of the white cow.

'**kill**' *cill* (church), but in rare cases wood, coill, eg Kildare, church of the oak-tree.

'**knock**' *cnoc* (hill), eg Knockroe, red hill.

'**liss**' *lios* (ringfort), eg Lisboy, yellow ringfort.

'**lough**' *loch* (lake), eg Lough Cullen, the lake of the holly trees.

'**ma**' *mágh* (plain), eg Moynalta, the plain of the bird-flocks.

'**maghery**' *machaire* (a plain), eg Magherybeg, small plain.

'**maum**' *mám* (a raised mountain pass), Maumturk, the mountain gap of the boars.

'**moan/mona**' *móin* (pasture-moor), eg Ballinamona, homestead of the pasture-moor.

'**money**' *muine* (thicket), eg Ballymoney, the homestead of the thicket.

'**more**' *mór* (big or great), eg Curraghmore, the great racecourse.

'**rath**' or '**rah**' *ráth* (ringfort), eg Rathmore, the great ringfort.

'**ring**' *rinn* (a point), eg Ringaskiddy, Skiddy's sea-point.

'**ross**' *ros* (a wood or point of land), eg Roscrea, Crea's wood.

'**roe**' *rua* (red), eg Knockroe, the red hill.

'**shan**' *sean* (old), eg Shanbally, old homestead.

'**slieve**' *sliabh* (mountain), eg Slieve Felim.

'**seskin**' *seiscin* (marsh), eg Ballinteskin, the homestead of the marsh.

'**turlough**' *turlach* (winter lake, dry in summer), Turloughmore, the great dried lake.

'**tulla/tully**' (semi-conical hillock), Tullamore, the great semi-conical hill.

'**tra**' *trá* (strand/beach), eg Tralee, strand of the River Lee.

'**villa**' *bile* (sacred tree), eg Knockavilla, the hill of the sacred tree.

View of the seaport of Wexford seen from the harbour

Religion and Irish culture

From time immemorial, religion has been a major pivot of the Irish way of life and culture.

Early Irish belief: sun worship

In the Boyne valley the tomb entrances face the rising sun of mid-winter's day. The cairns are circular, like the sun's dial. They are built on the land near the River Boyne – derived from *Bóinn + find*, which means white cow (probably a goddess) – and the river flows towards the east and the rising sun. In the Newgrange tomb, spirals carved on the stone may be sun emblems.

In Irish country tradition, good luck is associated with the right-hand side, and moving (or working) clockwise. This is probably a survival of sun worship – as was the lighting of bonfires on hills on St. John's Eve (23rd June), almost the summer solstice. These aspects of sun worship survived in many places into the 20th century.

Celtic worship

Little is known of the religion practised by the Celts in Ireland. Their chief divinity was a mother goddess, Anu, described as mother of the gods of Ireland. The feasts of the good god, Lug was held in August, which in Gaelic, means the feast of Lug.

Early Christianity

When Christianity came to Ireland in the fifth century, it brought literacy (hitherto confined to a minority), church regulations and a Roman Canon Law completely foreign to the Gaelic customs. A diocese was founded in each tuath. Most accepted in the country, the church was monastic, without parochial or diocesan divisions, or central government. Bishops' powers were limited to spiritual functions. Real authority rested in the hands of the abbots, who dominated the Irish church.

Monasteries soon became centres of literacy, learning and art. Latin, doctrinal and moral theology and the Bible were studied, and the monks reached high standards of craftsmanship, working with leather and precious metals – and illuminating manuscripts, especially the Scriptures. The most celebrated monastic schools were at Clonard, Co. Meath, Bangor and Moville, Co. Down, and Clonfert, Co. Galway.

Celtic design and the Early Church

Missals and copies of the gospels were provided for the monks. At first they were not ornamented but in time Celtic design reached its highest peak of excellence, culminating in such masterpieces as the *Book of Durrow* and the *Book of Kells*. For the first time the trumpet pattern is seen in its perfection. Celtic design contains the interlacing lines, which look like elaborate weaving, stylised heads of animals, spirals, the key pattern and every intricate ornament from the scribe's imagination.

Metal work also reached a high point. Gold, bronze, silver and gems were used in the fashioning of venerated bells, shrines, reliquaries and croziers. The High Crosses of this era, which still stand at each monastic site, appear to have some of their features modelled on the metal crosses. They have, for example, a circular band of stone, which suggests the band stabilising the two main parts of a metal or wooden cross. There is also an imitation of the binding wire holding the metal surfaces on the corners of the stone.

In the late 8th or early 9th century the first written versions of notable ancient Irish heroic stories were put on paper, including the epic tale *The Cattle Raid of Ulster*. Ireland was the first European country to have a vernacular literature.

The Brehon Law

The Brehon Law was written out in the 5th century. Its provisions for divorce still remained until the last areas were conquered and new laws enforced in the early 17th century.

Monasteries

The influence of Irish monasteries upon Britain and the continent from the late 6th century onward is attributable not only to their reputation as teaching centres but to the fact that companies of monks detached themselves to wander in search of places to practise their ascetic rule. It was this 'wandering for the love of Christ' rather than conventional missionary zeal that took Irish monks to Britain and deep into Europe, probably to Iceland; possibly, even, to the coast of North America. St. Columba and St. Columban are probably the most influential of these missionaries.

St. Columba and St. Columban

Columba, who was of royal blood, studied under the two Finnians at Moville and Clonard and later established monasteries in a number of places including Durrow, Co. Offaly. In about 563, he left Ireland with twelve companions and settled on the island of Iona, off the western coast of Scotland. The monastery he established there was to become the base for the conversion of a large part of Scotland and, eventually, of northern England.

Columban went, about 590, by way of Britain to Gaul. He settled in Annegray in the Vosges mountains and built a permanent monastery at Luxeuil. A man of strong personality, he quarrelled with the French bishops, withdrew to Switzerland and subsequently to Italy, where he died at his monastery of Bobbio. Other Irish monks who made their mark on the continent were Gall in Switzerland, Fergal in Austria, Disibod in Germany and Fursey in France.

Irish church and monastic movement

This missionary activity was most intensive during the 7th century but continued for the next two or three centuries when Johannes Scotus Erigena, theologian and philosopher, and Dicuil, a geographer who described journeys by Irishmen to Egypt and Iceland, were especially notable.

The Irish church was proud of its independence of Rome and clung firmly to its own usages in preference to those adopted by the rest of Christendom. Its method of calculating the date of Easter was maintained in face of protests from advocates of the Roman calendar until 704. This caused rifts in the Irish-managed church in Northern England and Scotland. In 664 the Roman Easter was accepted there and efforts were made to enforce it in Ireland in what was now a Celtic rather

Oratory of Galarus, a drystone beehive structure built for a monk or hermit, for prayer or contemplation

than a Roman church. Eventually it was accepted. However, even after this, the Irish church did not submit to any real jurisdiction from Rome until the 12th century.

The Irish monastic movement also had an ascetic wing, *céli Dé*, the partners of God or the Culdees. Founded in the 8th century, it involved extreme forms of austerity, self-inflicted hardship and fasting.

Viking influence

The Norse invasions, beginning at the close of the 8th century, precipitated a decay of culture and learning in Ireland. The era of artistic advance ended in the 9th century when Viking raids became frequent and monasteries a main target. Some of the loot they seized has been found in Denmark and Norway. Vikings settled in walled towns at Dublin, Waterford, Limerick and elsewhere on the coastline. The Vikings worshipped the Norse gods.

Many of the old monasteries had fallen into secular hands, and about the middle of the 12th century St. Malachy, friend of St. Bernard, introduced a new monastic system based on the Cistercians. The weakness of an unco-ordinated ecclesiastical organisation became evident, and the influence of Rome, through Canterbury, began to be felt for the first time.

In the 11th century the former Vikings became Christians but they did not participate in the Irish church organisation. The kings of Dublin and Waterford petitioned the Archbishop of Canterbury to appoint bishops to their cities. English bishops, chief among them Gilbert of Limerick, seized the most important sees.

Celtic church, reform and abbeys

There was much criticism of the Celtic church in England and mainland Europe. Priestly celibacy was not observed, bishops had little power and there were too many of them – some not even ordained priests. Reform was urged but there were no fundamental changes until about 1110-1111, when Gilbert held a synod at Rathbreasail. This divided Ireland into two provinces, Armagh and Cashel. The number of bishops was reduced to twenty-three. Among these were the bishops of Limerick and Waterford. The Dublin bishop did not become a member of the Irish hierarchy until the synod of Kells in 1152. Then the dioceses were reorganised into four Provinces – Armagh, Dublin, Cashel and Tuam, with an archbishop over each diocese. The synod had divided Ireland into 25 sees subject to Armagh's primacy.

The final step in the process of reform was taken at the synod of Cashel (1171-72), when obedience to Rome was accepted. Regulations were made for baptism and marriage, tithes and papal tribute. The native liturgies were abandoned and the usage of the English church was adopted.

The first Cistercian abbey was at Mellifont, north of Drogheda where the church was consecrated in 1157. In 1228 there were thirty-six abbeys throughout the country. They cultivated the reform of the church and the old monasteries either conformed or became casualties of the new orthodoxy.

In two of the old monasteries manuscripts were written which were compendia of Gaelic literature and tradition: *The Book of the Dun Cow* at Clonmacnoise (pre-1106) and the *Book of Leinster* at Terryglass, Co. Tipperary (about 1160). They were the last contribution of the old church to Irish letters.

In general, the medieval history of the church in Ireland would follow that of the country as a whole, only at intervals being made conscious of English overlordship, while the tribal kings continued to wield authority. In the church, Englishmen were appointed to the more important positions. The native orders were gradually replaced from abroad, but most of the secular clergy were Irish and retained some of the old Celtic spirit. Had this remnant of independence been considered and fostered at the Reformation the Church of Ireland might have become the church of the majority. In the event, the native Irish were antagonised and came to look on the attempt at reformation as a political expedient and a weapon of conquest.

Architectural styles

In 1134 Cormac's Chapel was consecrated on the Rock of Cashel. It was built in the Irish Romanesque style, with its European influence. Churches were built in this style in Glendalough, Roscrea and many other places. The church in Clonfert is a fine example, with semi-circular arches and lavish ornamentation.

In the early 13th century an architectural style transitional between Irish Romanesque and pure Gothic appeared in the abbey churches at Boyle and Jerpoint. The triple lancet east windows at Jerpoint bear the ornamentation, characteristic of Irish Romanesque, retained in what is Early English Gothic.

From about the middle of the 15th century there was a general refurbishment of churches and monastic buildings in Ireland. Thus in a church with the Anglo-Norman barrel pillars and transitional east window, a stone cloister could be provided in the Irish late Gothic style and even some of the pillars might be replaced.

English dominance

With the Anglo-Norman invasion, King Henry II declared his object to be the con-version of the people of Ireland to full church reform. He produced a Papal Bull, which was granted to him by the English pope, Adrian, to go to Ireland to stamp out evil practices and bring people into conformity with the church. In the parts of Ireland which the invaders conquered, parishes were organised, the new lords founded abbeys on their lands and supplied money for parish churches. Strict celibacy was enforced on the clergy.

In the 13th century the island was divided between the English-ruled portion and Ulster west of Lough Neagh – where the old native people were still the masters and there were no Cistercian abbeys or houses of Augustinian Canons.

The English government appointed Englishmen to Irish dioceses. Men of pure Gaelic race had no rights under English law. In 1317 Donal O'Neill of Tyrone addressed *A Remonstrance of the Irish Princes* to Pope John XXII. He pointed out that Pope Adrian had empowered Henry II to restore Christian life in Ireland but the English had deprived the Gaelic people of all rights under the laws.

Religious houses

The mendicant orders of Franciscans, Dominicans and Augustinian Friars founded houses in most of the early towns. Thirty-three Franciscan, twenty-four Dominican and eleven Augustinian houses were built between 1220 and 1336. Not one of these was in Gaelic Ulster. In later years religious devotees of native blood were forbidden to live with those who were not. However, between 1400 and 1508 forty-three of the new Franciscan Third Order of Penance houses had been built in Ireland: twenty-two of these were in the province of Armagh and in Gaelic-dominated areas.

The virulence of the dissension between friars on matters of race was so intense, that Franciscan friars were divided into two separate groups in Ireland. On the contrary the Augustinians remained part of the English province of the order.

Reformation and Tudor subjugation

The Reformation period began with the passage in 1537 of the Irish Supremacy act, which asserted the English king's supremacy in the Irish as well as the English church. But it was a very superficial Reformation: the dissolution of the monasteries was only partial, and scant knowledge of English meant that liturgical changes were few. No attempt was made to win the mass of the Irish people to Reformation principles, nor were the differences of religious outlook of succeeding English sovereigns brought home to the Irish. There was no effort to preach the doctrines in the towns and cities

– with the exception of Dublin.

However, monasteries and abbeys were dissolved. Their lands were bought willingly by men who never accepted the doctrines of the Reformation. At Mary I's accession five bishops either abandoned or were deprived of their sees; but the Anglo-Irish who remained faithful to the Reformation were not subjected to persecution, as would have been their fate on the other side of the Irish sea.

The Tudor subjugation of Ireland proceeded in the reign of Queen Elizabeth I: two bishops were deprived for open resistance to the new order of things and stern measures were taken to suppress treasonable plotting against the constitution, but the uniform policy of the government in ecclesiastical matters was one of toleration. The nobles had no support except from the Spaniards. Out of this an Irish nationalism grew, aided from abroad. The Franciscans, especially, were zealous promoters of Catholicism, particularly in Ulster.

Irish Protestantism

After Queen Elizabeth's death in 1603 the officials of King James made a determined effort to promote Protestantism. They rigorously enforced the Supremacy act, but on political rather than religious grounds. Enforcing laws imposed heavy fines on absentees from Divine Service.

Charles I sold concessions to Irish Roman Catholics, taking little interest in the progress of Irish Protestantism. The earl of Strafford, however, inaugurated a period of rigorous high Anglicanism – this to be followed, under Cromwell, by strictness in the opposite direction, but still toward the strengthening of English rule. James Ussher, appointed archbishop of Armagh in 1625, successfully defended the independent character of the Irish church against the reforms of William Laud, archbishop of Canterbury. On the accession of Charles II, the church was strengthened by John Bramhall (a most learned, zealous prelate) being moved from Derry to the primatial see of Armagh and by the consecration of twelve other bishops.

Religious struggles

The Plantation of Ulster after 1608 introduced a Protestant stock, which continued to hold sway until the present day. Elsewhere the vast majority of landowners were Catholics who remained loyal to the monarchy. When they were defeated in a rebellion in 1642, most of these landowners forfeited their lands.

In 1658, largely through the work of William Bedell, bishop of Kilmore, the Bible was printed for the first time in the Irish language – just a century too late.

The Williamite War from 1689 to 1691 was the last religious war in Ireland. After this conflict the triumph of Protestantism was assured. The Irish Parliament then passed laws depriving Catholics and Dissenters of all civil rights and of any public or municipal office. These laws were designed to make Catholics poor and ignorant and thus protect the ruling minority. The one lucrative business for a Catholic was to be a merchant.

In spite of many strictures the Catholics diocesan system continued to operate and priests were trained at colleges in France, Spain, Italy and Belgium. They became leaders of their people.

Changing regimes and enclosure

A stricter penal code introduced by the English government (1702-15) made the church unpopular. The English government, for political reasons, tended to choose Englishmen for Irish bishoprics, and the consequent involvement of higher clergy in state affairs weakened the church. In 1703, at the request of the clergy, the Irish convocation met after a 37-year interval and tabled many necessary reforms. William King, bishop of Derry and subsequently archbishop of Dublin, reorganised the work of the church, and his influence was felt right through the 18th century. This was also the period of Jonathan Swift and George Berkeley.

The later 18th century saw the Irish parliament asserting its independence and, at the same time, an atmosphere of reform within the church was stimulated by new pride in its missionary heritage and by a rising evangelical movement. Schools and charitable institutions were founded. Roman Catholics and Presbyterians alike received more tolerant treatment, but the privileged position of the Church of Ireland minority remained a grievance.

The Church of Ireland began to take its place as an independent national church, but, once again, political considerations hindered development.

Some of the new landlord family members became popular with their tenants, who admired their rollicking ways. Many landlords organised hurling teams and fox hunting in the winter. More often than not the priests could carry out their duties but with the greatest discretion.

Presbyterians, who were the hardest working Irish people, especially in Ulster, suffered from the laws, as did the Catholics. During the 18th century they began to emigrate to North America where they had more freedom than at home.

In the 1760s land was enclosed to form farms and Catholic priests tended to be the sons of well-off farmers. A secret society, the Whiteboys, was formed among poor Catholics to oppose enclosures and defend their patches of land against eviction. There was also a protest against paying tithes to the established Church of which they were not members. However, there was gradual relaxation of the laws against Catholics and Dissenters as the century went on. In 1798 the last serious disability was a Catholic's exclusion from parliament because he was required to take an anti-Catholic oath.

1798 Rebellion

In 1798 a serious uprising took place inspired by the French Revolution. The Society of United Irishmen was founded in Belfast: Presbyterians willingly joined. They appreciated the democratic spirit and the call for freedom. Both Protestant and Catholics bishops disapproved of this society as they did of the French Revolution.

In Wexford some Protestant gentlemen and three priests led the rebels. They were defeated in a few weeks. In the neighbourhood of Dublin and in Meath and Kildare the uprising was a fiasco. In Antrim and Down the Presbyterians were defeated in a few days. The so-called 'new lights', a liberal group of Presbyterians, provided the leadership for the uprising. After this failure the Presbyterians never again joined in any revolutionary effort. The Catholics stood by their Catholic nationalism. After this time both Ulster and the rest of Ireland developed in separate political and religious ways.

Resurgence of the Catholic Church

In 1829 Daniel O'Connell was elected for the second time to parliament and the British Government substituted the members' oath to a more acceptable one. Henceforth Catholics sat in parliament. The election organisation was based on the Catholic parishes and generally led by priests. Thus began the close influence of the Catholic Church on politics in Ireland.

In Ulster the Presbyterian 'new lights', represented by Rev. Henry Montgomery, whose brothers had fought in the uprising, was foremost in founding an excellent school, the Academical Institute, Belfast. The local Catholic bishop, Dr Crolly, subscribed to the building of the school.

Rev. Henry Montgomery and Rev. Henry Cooke both lived from 1788 to 1865. Montgomery was a liberal, non-subscribing Presbyterian who favoured Catholic Emancipation. Cooke, who urged the political union of Presbyterians with the Established Church, succeeded in forming a Protestant unity against the resurgence of Catholicism after 1829. Montgomery's liberalism became a weak force in Ulster. The rift between Ulster Protestants and the rest of Ireland deepened.

Tithes

The 1830s saw a passive resistance against payment of tithes – as much resented by

Presbyterians as by Catholics. Some violence and loss of life accompanied the campaign in Counties Kilkenny, Cork and Tipperary. There were so few Established Church members that in 1833 ten bishoprics were abolished. The matter was resolved by adding reduced tithe payments to rents.

Catholic influence

Rev. John Cullen became Archbishop of Armagh in 1849 and, in 1852, Archbishop of Dublin. He was the first Irishman to become a Cardinal in 1866. In 1850 he held the first Synod of the Church in Ireland since 1152. The church was guided henceforth in a path of strict conformation to Rome. Discipline among the clergy was enforced and the authority of the bishops strengthened. Now more (and larger) churches were required to accommodate the bigger congregations that came to Mass on Sunday. Irish Catholics became the most regular churchgoers in the world.

Dr Cullen destroyed the Tenant League, founded in 1850 to curb the unjust excesses of some landlords. He ordered priests to leave it because they were working with Protestant clergymen in its ranks. He also encouraged the forming of an Irish Brigade to fight in the Papal army against Italian nationalists in 1859. At Cullen's death in 1878 the Catholic Church's bishops and priests had established a formidable spiritual and political influence.

The Orange Order

The Orange Order for the defence and promotion of Protestantism was founded in 1795. It spread rapidly throughout Ireland and British colonies among Irish-born soldiers and officers. It held marches to assert its presence and display its power. So irksome did its activities become that all public marches were banned in 1835. In 1868 a march was held in spite of the ban and the leader jailed but parliament repealed the 1835 law soon afterwards. After this, Orange Lodges thrived only in Ulster .

Education

In the 19th century congregations of teaching and nursing brothers and sisters were founded in Ireland. They did remarkable work and shaped the minds of the ancestors of those who would found the Southern Irish State, as well as introducing a civil discipline. These religious orders stressed discipline among their members.

The great debate of the 19th century was over education. In the 1830s the government created a nondenominational National Board of Education to give an elementary education to all. Rejected at first by the Presbyterians and then by most of the Established Church bishops, the major-

ity of Catholic bishops accepted it and gradually it was established but schools of one religion became the norm. In 1850 a Catholic University was founded in Dublin: the medical school thrived. Trinity College was not acceptable to most Catholics. It was in opposition to the Queen's Colleges of Dublin, Cork, Galway and Belfast, founded just before the bishops forbade Catholics to attend them. In practice Catholics remained without university education until 1904 when the National University of Ireland (with colleges in Dublin, Cork and Galway) was founded and made acceptable to Catholics.

Church of Ireland disestablishment

The Act of Union of 1800 aimed to remedy the disaffection that had culminated in the 1798 rebellion. Now the parliaments of England and Ireland were united; the church became part of the United Church of England and Ireland. But the dissatisfaction felt by the majority of Irishmen about the privileged position of the Established Church, grew – along with resentment of the church tithes exacted largely from Roman Catholic tenant farmers. In the 1830s agitation against this privilege became known as the tithe war.

The census of 1861 showed that less than one-eighth of the population belonged to the Established Church; four-fifths were Roman Catholics. Supposedly the church for all the Irish people, when the majority did not become members, it was necessary eventually to disestablish it. The passing of the Act of Disestablishment was only a question of time. Introduced by William Gladstone, it was passed in 1869. The Established Church of Ireland was disestablished in 1870 and became known as the Church of Ireland in 1871.

The church was suddenly thrown on its own resources and had to reorganise its ecclesiastical system and provide for its future clergy. Back in 1865, with disestablishment imminent, the foundation stone had been laid in Cork for an elaborate cathedral. Many cathedrals and churches were restored during the twenty years following the passing of the act.

The first act of the convention of the bishops, clergy and laity summoned in 1870 was to declare the adherence of the Church of Ireland to the ancient standards and its determination to uphold the doctrine and discipline of the Catholic and Apostolic Church, while reaffirming its witness, as Protestant and Reformed, against the innovations of Rome.

Under the constitution then agreed, the supreme governing body of the church is the general synod. This synod consists of the bishops and 208 clerical and 416 lay representatives of the several dioceses – whose local affairs are managed by diocesan synods.

The twentieth century

After 1922 the two new Irish States became subject to religious pressures. In the northeast of Ireland a permanent Unionist and Protestant majority of about two to one over Catholics made it impossible for a Catholic to secure employment or often any advancement in many walks of life. By the end of the century the gap between the numbers narrowed considerably.

In the Southern Irish State, Catholics were about 90% of the population, which over the years rose to 95%. The Catholic ethos became the policy of the State. In 1925 divorce was forbidden and in 1929 the Censorship of Publication Act was passed. This banned much English language modern literature, including the works of distinguished Catholics. The Act was directed almost exclusively against expression of sexual matters. It remained until 1967 when it was modified, and has been implemented very little since then.

Foreign missions

The greatest Catholic movement in Ireland from the 1920s to the 1960s was the growth of foreign missions. Nuns and priests were sent to India, British African colonies, Korea and China. Special religious orders were founded to carry out this work and the foreign missionary movement seemed to be the chief expression of the dynamism of the new Ireland. The missionaries were drawn from both parts of Ireland.

Changing traditions

From the 1960s onwards new trends were followed in church building which broke with tradition. Moreover, European and American cultural influences began to flood the country through television and the growing popularity of foreign holidays and travel.

A visit by Pope John Paul II was arranged in late autumn 1979 and he was welcomed with great warmth. However, in the years that followed, church attendance dropped and fewer people entered the religious life. By 1990 many convents and monasteries had closed, religious schools were handed over to lay teachers and a scarcity of priests made it difficult to manage some parishes. Many nuns and priests returned to secular life.

In spite of vigorous campaigns by certain Catholic groups and clergy a referendum to permit divorce was successful.

The issue of abortion was still not fully resolved in the 1990s but by then, the world was changing fast. The young people of Ireland were not emigrating in such large numbers as they had done hitherto. A more open society was emerging as religion and the Irish culture embraced the new millennium.

The Ardagh Chalice is a fine example of early Irish Christian art

Languages of Ireland

Prior to the arrival of the Celtic settlers in Ireland (sometime after 300 BC) the original inhabitants must have conversed in their own languages and it is unlikely that these simply vanished immediately. However, we can only guess at their existence.

Celtic settlers and Old Norse

In historic times, the language of the Vikings, Old Norse, was the first significant imported language. It was spoken in Dublin, Waterford and Limerick but by 1300 seems to have become extinct.

Norman, Middle English and German influences

With the arrival of the Norman invaders, by 1169 Norman-French and English were being spoken. While the French influence affected the pronunciation of Gaelic in the south of Ireland the language never became fully established.

By contrast, the contemporary Middle English did not disappear until the 19th century in parts of County Wexford – where it was known as Yola.

During the 18th century German peasants from the Rhineland settled in parts of Munster but their culture was soon absorbed into the Gaelic-speaking population and their particular form of German became extinct.

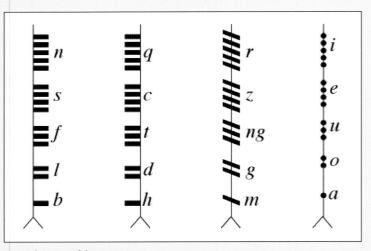

An explanation of the meanings of the Ogham inscriptions

Gaelic

Gaelic remained the principal language of Ireland over some sixteen centuries. It is the one Celtic language that has survived in Europe – as Gaelic, Welsh, Breton and Scots Gaelic (Manx died out in the last century). The word Gaelic derives from an early form *Goedelleg* which comes from Welsh *Gwyddel*, literally 'wild man of the woods'. Gaelic is a Celtic language.

The first written forms were commemorative personal names found on stone pillars and written in Ogham. This was a series of strokes and dots cut on, across or at a central line in fives. The vowels a, o, u, e, i, were indicated by one to five dots for each, respectively, on the central line. One to five strokes to the right represented b, l, v, s, n, respectively. One to five strokes to the left represented h, d, t, c, q, respectively. One to five strokes across the line indicated m, g, ng, z, r.

Ancient laws and manuscripts in Swiss, German, Italian and French libraries exhibit Gaelic forms as words borrowed from Latin and Welsh in this period.

Quite sophisticated grammar and syntax changed rapidly in the oldest forms of the language. Nouns had singular, plural and dual numbers and there was a full complement of tenses, just as in Latin.

This old form of Gaelic mutated into to a simpler language in about 800 AD. This was used in Ireland for the next four hundred years. Many interesting stories and documents were written in it until Viking raids and settlements hastened modern development with words that had been borrowed from Old Norse.

Early Modern or Classical Gaelic

Early Modern or Classical Gaelic appeared after 1200 and the Anglo-Norman conquest. Some of the complex grammar was replaced by simpler forms. It is interesting that the words for 'yes' and 'no' disappeared. It was not safe for anyone subject to tyranny to use either of these words and so make a firm commitment. Even in today's Gaelic, questions still receive a reply in sentence form – not a simple affirmation or denial.

Many of the first settlers married local Irish women and their children spoke Gaelic. As the Elizabethan poet, Edmund Spencer, stated: *'since the language is Irish, the heart must need be Irish'.*

In Ulster, where the conquest had largely failed, Gaelic was spoken in the old way. In the South of Ireland, generally, Gaelic was spoken with a nasal Norman-French tone. In Connacht the speech pattern lay between the two. Words borrowed from Norman-French include *garson*, meaning boy. Efforts made by the authorities to force the descendants of the settlers to stop speaking Gaelic failed. By 1400 the Irish language was spoken by all people outside the main cities (Dublin, Waterford, Limerick, Cork and Galway) which alone kept contact with Europe and were loyal supporters of the Crown.

Anglicisation

With Tudor domination, the Anglicisation of Ireland began. Gaelic was still being spoken by large numbers of the ruling classes but the new settlers were usually English speaking.

During the Cromwellian Plantation, many of the wealthier Gaelic-speaking people lost their lands and the status of the language diminished – so much so that by 1700 it had become the speech of the poor and underprivileged.

The Protestants generally spoke English and gradually it became the language of Catholic businessmen and priests too. There was no longer a standard literary Gaelic but three main dialects, Northern, Western and Southern, and many local dialects.

By the mid-1800s, Gaelic was widely spoken west of a line from Derry to Cork, and in certain places to the east of that line in Counties Waterford, Kilkenny, Meath, Louth and the Glens of Antrim where Gaelic was predominantly used and understood.

About 23% of the population spoke Irish. However, by 1893, huge numbers of these people emigrated to the UK and the USA, English was taught in the National School, the clergy and businesses encouraged its use and the Anglicisation of Ireland was virtually complete.

Saving the language

The Gaelic League, devoted to the revival of the language, grew from Dr Douglas Hyde's powerful speech on the subject in 1893. This enthusiasm was undermined by politics and, in 1923, by the teaching of Gaelic in schools being made compulsory – this had the contrary effect of turning many people against the language.

After World War II a complete modernisation of both Gaelic spelling and grammar was gradually introduced into the education system. Gaelic script was replaced by the Roman script which simplified the printing of works in the language. This Gaelic script was an old form of an early Roman one that had been adopted by the scribes in the first manuscripts. Elementary schools now tried to use more sympathetic methods of teaching the language.

However, despite the salvation of written Gaelic, the decline of spoken Irish seems to have been inevitable. It is now confined to the few remaining Gaelic-speaking areas. Today only a few hundred thousand people in Ireland can converse comfortably in the Irish language.

The Old Irish Laws

Ancient laws emerged from the need to control some aspects of daily life in pre-historic times. These were transmitted from one generation to another by what might be regarded as folk memory.

The Brehon Laws

Known as the Brehon Laws, these earliest laws first existed in written form at about the same time as Christianity arrived. They could not be repealed, nor could new laws be added.

However, the laws could be 'glossed' and, with the passage of time, this led to some strange interpretations: for example, a prostitute was described in one source as a woman who had more than six partners in a single night.

The class structure

Society was divided into strict classes. It was possible to move upwards from one class to the next but often it took several generations for a family to become fully accepted within the new structure.

The chief classes were king, noble and common person and, inevitably the laws were slanted to favour the more elite groups. For example, a free client was granted stock for which he paid a yearly tribute and which he would then own after seven years.

By contrast, a 'base' client paid tribute each year, gave free labour to his lord and was obliged to share with him any legal compensation that he received for injury.

In spite of the use of words for High King and other rulers that appear in Gaelic stories and annals, the highest rank the laws actually recognised was *rí*, 'king', which denoted the king of a small kingdom (called the *tuath*). This was the standard area of legal jurisdiction.

If someone needed to travel outside his *tuath*, he or she was required to go to a ford or other crossing point where someone of his own class had to provide his legal guarantee in the next *tuath*. Only poets and clergyman were exempt from this obligation.

The system of justice

The old Irish laws did not involve judges, jails, courts of law or police. There was no capital punishment. If a complaint was recognised, the male relatives of each of the parties involved would meet to resolve the problem. These could be fathers, grandfathers, cousins to two degrees, sons or grandsons.

After hearing what the complainant and/or the defendant had to say, a legal expert was summoned to give his opinion. This expert was called a *briethem*, (brehon) – hence the term, Brehon Laws. The brehons of both parties then met and decided what should be done.

Each man or woman had an 'honour-price' and the penalties were based upon the degree to which this honour had been violated. Eventually the matter would be settled by the payment of cows, gold or other valuables.

Murder

There was a separate penalty for homicide called the *raic*, sometimes translated as 'blood-money'. The lord or nobleman of a base client received one third of this. Generally, the penalty charged was seven *cumals* (female slaves – worth one-heifer each) for every free person.

Divorce

According to the Brehon Laws, divorce was readily available. This was never subject to church law and remained free of church jurisdiction in the Gaelic-ruled places until these areas were finally all subdued by 1603.

When a divorced woman left her husband, she took with her all the property that she had owned when she was married and half of what she and her husband had earned together.

If a former husband brought a new wife or lover into the house within three days of his divorce, his former wife – if she was still in situ – was initially permitted to draw blood from the new woman. For a further short period, the wife was still legally permitted to assault the incomer – but this time without drawing blood. Then, the first 'old' wife was required to leave.

Child care

All children were legitimate in the eyes of the law except those unfortunates that had been born to a prostitute. The father and his kin had to be clearly identified in order to guarantee the legal protection of each young individual.

There were further laws covering fostering. After the birth, a son or daughter might be given out to be fostered. The foster parents were generally paid, receiving more for the care of a girl than they did for a boy child. This fostering lasted for seventeen years. A male foster-child had to be taught to ride a horse and then be provided with his own horse after the age of seven. He was also taught chess playing – and swimming if there was a suitable stretch of water available. A girl was instructed in sewing and embroidery.

Children played an important part in the yearly *transhumance* or *booleying*. The modern Irish *buachaill*, a boy, meant simply 'cow-herd', while *cailín*, a girl meant 'little herd'. The youngsters herded cows on the summer pastures.

Animals

Cows were the most important domestic animals in ancient Ireland. They provided food, drink, butter and cream. They were also used as currency. At nightfall cows were enclosed in a secure place where a herdsman with a dog watched over them. The laws described a herdsman's dog as being distinct from a yard dog. Anyone who killed a 'cow-dog' had to pay five cows and supply a replacement one. Cows were sometimes trained to follow a leading cow that wore a bell.

The laws listed five types of 'houses'; these showed the importance of the animals that were kept and read as follows – a dwelling house, a cowhouse, a sheep field, a calf field, and a pigsty. Pigs were tethered securely by iron collars at night.

Changing times

Right up to the end of the 16th century, the Anglo-Irish lords generally had brehons to handle any legal issues with their Gaelic neighbours. The Earls of Ormond, for example, employed the McClanychys of County Clare. Inevitably, as the British held greater sway, so English law was introduced and soon replaced the old laws right across the whole country. By 1603, it was said that the Brehon Law was defective because it 'compounded the felony'.

The Brehon Laws had proved eminently suitable for a rural situation with subsistence farming and thus had been a workable system for centuries. But by the seventeenth century, with the development of an urban society, the old laws were regarded as totally unsustainable.

Old Irish sayings

Neither break a law nor make one.
No matter who comes off well, the peace-maker is sure to come off ill.
A good retreat is better than a poor defence.
Justice melts in the mouths of the faint-hearted.

Music in Ireland

The Irish are a musical people. It is a vital element of their culture whether the first ever performance of Handel's *Messiah* or a fiddler entertaining in a public house.

The Harp

The harp was the musical instrument of the rich and noble in ancient Ireland. Harpists had to grow their nails long to pluck the steel strings. The sound-box, upper shoulder and connecting wooden column appear to be much the same as in the modern harp. However, this column seems to be missing in an old carving of a harp on a High Cross and there is speculation that it may well have been omitted in some of the instruments.

An elegant Celtic harp in Birr Castle, County Offaly, home to the Earls of Rosse

Harp music in Ireland consists generally of dance music and haunting Irish traditional airs. It remained popular for centuries, and, for example, Turlough O'Carolan (1670-1738), the composeer of *Carolan's Concerto,* was always a welcome guest at the houses of the settlers and their descendants.

By 1792 traditional harp players were few and far between. In an attempt to preserve their music, a great harp festival was held in the Linenhall Library in Belfast. Blind Art O'Neill (1727-1816) and Denis Hempson who had played before Bonny Prince Charlie were among the ten harpers that played. Edward Bunting recorded the harpers' music. He published a first volume of this music in 1796, followed by two other volumes in 1809 and 1840, eventually rescuing some 300 airs for future enjoyment.

Thus, although the last of the great Irish composers for the harp had died at the beginning of the 19th century, the traditional music for the harp was preserved for posterity.

Pipes and dance

Pipes were also very popular traditional Irish instruments. There are various kinds; one is just like the Scottish bag-pipes with a limited musical range, while another, the uilleann or Irish pipes, is rather more sophisticated.

Irish dance music has undergone various influences. The hornpipe music is often from Scottish origins while the reel music derives from England. Jig music is generally an original Irish composition while the ancient Gaelic songs can be Ionian, Mixolydian, Dorian and Aeolian. In fact, more than half of the genuine Irish airs are in the Ionian mode.

During the twentieth century, there has been a revival of the old style of Irish music and dancing. In 1951 *Comhaltas Ceoltas ireann* (the Association of the Musicians of Ireland) was founded. The intention was to cultivate Irish music of all kinds, including the harp and the uilleann pipes. In the event, one of the instruments that became popular was the tin whistle. The bodhrun, a one-skinned hand-drum made of tanned goat-skin, has also emerged as a popular instrument.

Out of *Comhaltas Ceoltas ireann* grew the *Flea Cheoil*, which means the 'Feast of Music'. This festival of Irish music and competitions is held every August in an Irish town.

Meanwhile the phenomena of Michael O'Flaherty's *Riverdance* and *Lord of the Dance* have created an incredible theatrical experience world-wide and made Irish dancing remarkably popular.

Seventeenth century development

At the dawn of the seventeenth century, when two Englishmen, John Farmer and Thomas Bateson, were appointed as organists in Christchurch, Dublin, Irish music was to reach new heights. They composed many madrigals and Farmer wrote the anthem, *Holy God Almighty*. In 1612, he was the first to be made a Bachelor of Music by Trinity College.

This was the beginning of Dublin leadership in the development of music in Ireland. Musical recitals were held in both the cathedrals of Dublin. In 1694 the centenary of Trinity College was celebrated with a performance of Henry Purcell's *Commemoration Ode*.

The Eighteenth century

Handel visited Dublin in 1741 to 1742 to conduct almost twenty concerts, including two recitals of his *Messiah*. These musical events took place in the New Music Hall, designed by Richard Cassels and opened in 1741.

Meanwhile, Geminiani settled in Dublin. Here he taught the violin, wrote the first treatise on the violin in Ireland and Great Britain, and held his 'Concerts and Great Music Room' in Spring Gardens in 1739. In 1742 this was taken by the first clarinet-player in Great Britain and Ireland.

During this century, operatic performances were given by Pietro Castrucci and Tomasso Giordani, who dedicated their lives to cultivating opera in Dublin.

Lord Mornington was the first Professor of Music in Trinity College Dublin in 1764. He founded a Musical Academy for gentlemen while his work as a composer inspired some of the first Irish composers – including John Field who settled eventually in St. Petersburg. In his wake he left many fine pieces for piano, music which had a clear influence on the work of Chopin.

Michael Kelly from Dublin was a renowned tenor who emigrated to Europe – there to become a friend of Mozart and to sing in the very first performance of *The Marriage of Figaro* (1786).

The Nineteenth century

Thomas Moor wrote the very popular *Irish Melodies*, the first of which appeared in 1808 and became a source of entertainment for the concert hall, salon and drawing room. Adding verse to modernised versions of old Irish airs and introducing historic Irish characters, these songs proved popular everywhere. Sir John Stevenson of Dublin composed the accompaniments.

In the wake of the Act of Union of 1800, patrons of music and art deserted Dublin for London. Like their patrons, many composers chose to live out their lives abroad. Music was given little support until 1856 when the Royal Academy of Music was founded. Then, when Michele Esposito was appointed its director in 1882, his teaching and composition greatly influenced the course of music in Ireland.

The Twentieth century

In the 20th century the new and independent State in the South of Ireland has once again encouraged music and composition. Brian Boydell, John F. Larchet and Seoirse Bodley have all worked in Ireland.

Sir Hamilton Harty composed *With the Wild Geese* and *An Irish Symphony*, while Sean O'Riada set out to compose a native Irish music based on the ancient music of Ireland. He also composed the theme-music for two films, and a Gaelic Mass. His early death was a serious artistic deprivation for Irish music.

Ballad-singers

Over the years, Irish musical recitals have taken many forms. Ballads may be sung in the open street or in a public house, hymns sung in church and formal renditions of songs performed in a concert-hall or salon.

In the 14th century the Bishop of Ossory, Ledrede, forbade his clergy to sing love-poems on holy-days. A stanza of one such poem, an early example of an Irish ballad in Modern English, goes:

Alas, how shall I sing?
Lost is my fun;
How shall I with that old man
Live and lose my lover,
Sweetest of all things.

This was innocent wording compared to what was sung on the streets. In 1829 a letter from Clonmel described:

'the croaking of two ballad-singers chanting verse . . . which exceeded in immorality anything of the kind I ever heard'

and:

'the idle and strolling vagabonds' gave 'displays in ribaldry and scurrility as are heard in the town every evening'.

Up to the 17th century there was what was called *crosantacht* in the Irish language which was a bawdy mixture of verse and prose – sung and recited at weddings. Here is how a poet began his advice to a newly married groom:

Fortunate is your wedding,
good luck to your work!
Till you put a son in the womb
don't go off to sleep!
Sweep her off to the bedroom
with no by-your-leave. . .

Most ballads began with one of two types of openings:

'Come all ye tender Christians . . .'
or
'One fine morning as I roved . . .'

They were frequently described as 'Come-all-yees'!

Having sung their songs at markets and fairs, the street-singers then sold paper sheets with the words of the ballad. Their lyrics commemorated games and significant events such as murders, hangings, or great deeds of bravery. The performers earned money and managed to evade the laws against begging.

The foundation of the *Nation* newspaper led to the appearance of literary ballads in the 1840s. Held in greater esteem than street ballads, these patriotic songs celebrated the deeds, lives and deaths of patriots. After being published in the newspaper, they then appeared in *Spirit of the Nation* which reached its 58th edition in 1828. The writers included Thomas Davis,

Charles Gavan Duffy and D. F. McCarthy.

In time, street-ballads lost respectability. However, during the 1960s, it became recognised once again as a popular form of form entertainment in Ireland. This was mainly because of the enthusiasm of several young modern Irish performers. In particular, the Clancy brothers and Tommy Makem promoted Irish ballad music in New York when they appeared on the Ed Sullivan Show. Dressed in woollen jackets and wearing cloth caps, they went on to sing Irish ballads at concerts, becoming famous right around the world. The Irish ballad became the latest 'craze' in both Ireland and the USA. Soon the Dubliners, led by Ronnie Drew, were performing a more earthy kind of ballad-singing and introducing the Dublin element.

Opera and concerts

Since Castrucci and Giordani dedicated their lives to cultivating opera in Dublin in the eighteenth century and Michael Kelly sang in the first performance of *The Marriage of Figaro*, opera has had its Irish performers and supporters but it was not until 1941 that the Dublin Grand Opera Society was founded. Since then it has performed many operatic works while opera companies from many other nations have been invited to perform in Dublin.

Meanwhile, the Royal Irish Academy has contributed enormously to music in Ireland while the annual *Feis Ceoil* competitions have continued to discover and encourage Irish musical talent since its inception in 1897. The tenor, John Count McCormack, first came to public notice at a *Feis Ceoil* and so did Hamilton Harty and Margaret Burke Sheridan. In later years Bernadette Greevy won a *Fies Ceoil* award.

Dublin had no concert hall for many years. However, when the new university

campus was built in Belfield in the Dublin suburbs, a concert hall was erected in the old college at Earlsfort Terrace.

Dr Tom Walsh founded the Wexford Opera Festival in 1951. Each year since then the festival has been held in the Theatre Royal in Wexford town during the last week of October.

There are also annual 'opera weeks' in Cork. The Cork Grand Opera Society was founded in 1952 while the Limerick Grand Opera Society, founded in 1957, hosts annual seasons of opera. Meanwhile, founded during 1945, the Waterford Grand Opera Society, provides regular seasons of opera in the city, with the full co-operation of the Waterford Orchestral Players.

Contemporary music

Ireland has had enormous success in popular music in recent decades with a run of wins at the Eurovision Song Contest, Bob Geldof and the Boomtown Rats, Thin Lizzy, U2, Daniel O'Donnell, Boyzone and the Corrs – to name but a few – while *Riverdance* has had a huge international impact, bringing Irish music and dance to the attention, and applause, of millions.

Ireland has emerged as a strong supporter of cultural activities of many kinds, capitalising on its rich heritage, encouraging fresh talent and setting new standards. Music is no exception to this.

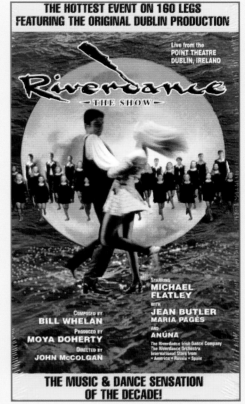

Irish music and dance, performed by professional or amateur entertainers can be enjoyed in the theatre – and in pubs

Art

The first artistic expression of Irish people is found in the Neolithic tomb at Newgrange, County Meath. It consists generally of intricate patterns of spirals and lozenges. There is no record of the artists except what can be surmised from the spiral patterns.

Bronze Age

Gold ornaments have been found from about 2000 BC to about 700 BC. In some hoards, collars, necklaces and bracelets again exhibit curves and spirals.

Celtic Art

This arrived in Ireland after c.700 BC. Examples have been found over the years in which the La Téne influence is apparent. Discoveries have been made of beautiful vessels of gold and fine jewellery.

Above right
The golden boat from the
first century AD has minute
masts, oars and seats for
rowers. It was probably an
offering to the sea-god,
Mananan

period. Irish Celtic design reached its greatest glory ever.

In the twelfth century there was a revival in the metal work which is represented by the Cross of Cong. In the twelfth century also, Irish Romanesque architecture was introduced. Cormac's Chapel on the Rock of Cashel was one of the first examples of this.

The High Crosses on monastic sites are also distinctive of this period, when much of the artistic endeavour of the era was religious in origin.

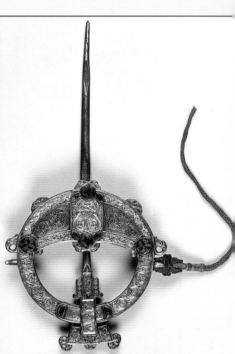

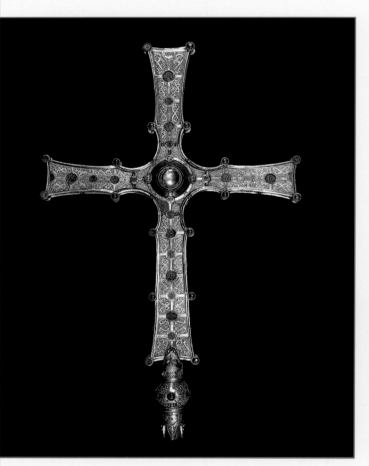

Above
Dating from about AD 1120,
the Cross of Cong is a
masterpiece of medieval Irish
art and supposedly held a
fragment of the True Cross

Christian Celtic Art

From about the 6th on to the 8th century a form of design was developed in Ireland, which reached a very high standard of artistic excellence. Illuminated manuscripts such as the *Book of Kells* and the *Book of Durrow* were written at this time when this design reached it's highest form. Artefacts in gold such as the Tara Brooch and the Ardagh chalice were made in this

Medieval Art

From about 1200 to 1250 the great abbeys of Ireland were erected. They are all basically built in the Gothic style, although the rounded arches in early ones reflect the transition from Romanesque to Gothic. In churches, stone carvings are set in pillars.

Some wooden statues survive from this era. It appears that there were two types. One was the purely Irish statue from the west of Ireland such as that of Saint Molaisse showing an ascetic face. There were also some Madonnas carved in this style. The other style of statuary, such as *Our Lady of Dublin in Whitefriars,* was practised in Dublin and Waterford cities.

Once more the church was the chief, if not sometimes the only, patron of the arts in this period.

In the late 15th century there was some building done but much of the work was the refurbishment of earlier buildings, not always satisfying to the eye.

The 17th to 18th Century

In the year 1670 the Cutlers' Stainers' and Engravers' Guild was founded in Dublin. This marked the modest beginning of an Irish school of painting.

The 18th century was distinguished by the development of the Georgian house in Ireland in the peaceful conditions of the country. In the second half of the century the City Hall, the Four Courts, the front block of Trinity College and the Custom House were built in Dublin. Already the House of Parliament was built. Elaborate stucco-work ceilings distinguished the buildings in town and countryside. It was an age of elegance for those who lived in these fine buildings.

Meanwhile, the demand for portrait painting grew. . . .

Hugh Howard
Hugh Howard of Dublin (1675-1737) studied painting in the Netherlands and provided portraits of Fellows of Trinity College and others.

James Latham
The first major portrait painter to live and work exclusively in Ireland was James Latham (1786-1747) – who had spent some time in Belgium.

Nathaniel Hone and Horace Hone
Nathaniel Hone senior (1718-1784) was an eminent portrait painter. An enamelist, he lived and worked in Dublin and created many fine miniatures. He left behind him ten self-portraits, eight in oils and two miniatures. His son, Horace Hone (1756-1825), who outshone his father, worked in London before returning to Dublin in 1782. Here he found many clients during the last years of the Irish parliament and while Dublin was still a capital city.

The 19th Century

Irish painters began to interest themselves in the Irish landscape. The painters, James Arthur O'Connor, George Petrie and Francis Danby were among those who followed this tendency.

In 1823 Irish painters were given a focal point when the Royal Hibernian Academy was founded. Its first president was William Ashford, an English landscape painter who settled in Dublin.

James Arthur O'Connor
O'Connor was one of the greatest of the Irish landscape painters of this time, although he was not so regarded during his lifetime. He painted some notable pictures of the West of the Ireland and its variable skies and countryside.

George Petrie
Petrie, on the other hand, produced watercolours of the Irish landscape, which have a haunting quality and light. As an archaeologist he had a special feeling for the spirit of the Irish countryside as he saw it through its past.

Left
The Four Courts, Dublin, epitomises Ireland's elegant 18th-century architecture

Far left
The beautiful Tara Brooch from the 8th century is made from silver gilt and gold foil, decorated with gold filigree, in interlacing spiral patterns, as well as amber and glass studs

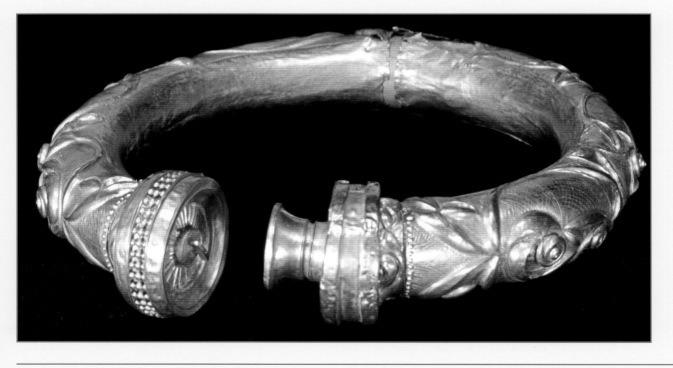

Left
Bracelet from the Broighter hoard that dates from the Bronze Age

Painting depicting the marriage of Strongbow to Princess Aoife by Daniel Maclise (1805-70)

Daniel Maclise

Daniel Maclise (1805-70) was a great artist who worked mostly in England. He began as a portrait painter and later went to live in London. His huge picture, *The Marriage between Princess Aoife and Strongbow*, a symbol of unity between Ireland and England, was painted for Westminster.

William Mulready

William Mulready (1786-1863) from County Clare painted landscapes and portrayed Irish people in their everyday lives. He also painted nudes.

John Hogan and John Henry Foley

The two great sculptors in Ireland in this time were John Hogan (1796-58) and John Henry Foley (1818-74).

Hogan's work such as his *Minerva* owed much to classical models. His travels in Italy, where he studied sculptors of the classical period, influenced his style. He became one of the greatest Irish neo-classical sculptors. In the North Chapel of St. Mary's in Cork city are twenty-seven statues of saints and apostles and a bas relief of the Last Supper. He had no successor as sculptor of religious statues in Ireland and, as the century went on, Italian plaster statuary of little merit filled Catholic churches.

Most of Foley's work is in England but in Dublin the magnificent monument to Daniel O'Connell in O'Connell Street and the statue of Oliver Goldsmith in College Green are his work.

Into the 20th Century

Nathaniel Hone the Younger

The greatest Irish landscape painter of the late 19th century was Nathaniel Hone the Younger (1831-1917). After some years abroad he returned to Ireland in 1875, where he painted scenes of land and sea. Above all, he portrayed the skies, with ever-changing blending of light and colour. Hundreds of his paintings are stored in the National Gallery but his work was exhibited very seldom in his lifetime.

John Butler Yeats the Elder

John Butler Yeats the Elder (1839-1922) was a portrait painter and a Pre-Raphaelite. His son, the poet W. B. Yeats, wrote of his reaching for perfection by painting 'a square inch at a time' with constant revision and erasion.

Roderic O'Connor

Roderic O'Connor (1861-1940) lived at Port-Aven and spent his life mostly in France. He knew Gauguin and admired the work of van Gogh.

George William Russell (Æ)

George William Russell (1867-1935), known as Æ – whose mystical world included a belief in the existence of fairies – expressed this in most of his paintings which give them a quality not readily understood or appreciated in many quarters. This man was otherwise a very practical social reformer.

Jack B. Yeats

Jack B. Yeats (1871-1957), son of John Butler Yeats, who attended art school in London, evoked on canvas the people of Ireland and their lives. Fairs and public assemblies supplied him with material, while the tinker, the circus clown and the Arranmore fisherman were among the characters who came to life in his watercolours. He evoked the life and soul of Ireland in his figures whose essence stored a single moment for posterity. Jack B. Yeats was the first Irishman who was invited to provide a one-man exhibition at both the Tate and the National Galleries in London.

Paul Henry

Paul Henry (1876-1958) celebrated in his paintings the west of Ireland, its ever-changing colours and ravishingly beautiful landscape. Above all, he captured in form and colour the light that emphasises hill, bog and sea or softens it in a wispy haze.

Seán Keating

Seán Keating, born in 1889, was a portrait painter who often chose the country people of Ireland for his subjects. His paintings are meticulously drawn. They have a sense of repose in contrast with those of Jack B. Yeats where the life of his subjects seems to bubble over.

Sir William Orpen and Sir John Lavery

The two great portrait artists, Sir William Orpen (1878-1931) and Sir John Lavery (1856-1941) were born in Dublin and Belfast respectively. They both worked outside Ireland. Lavery designed the new Irish currency notes after 1924 and he placed one of his portraits of his wife on them. Later it was used as a watermark on the Irish paper money.

Stained glass

The development of the art of stained glass in Ireland owes much to Michael Healy (1873-1941), Harry Clarke (1889-1931) and Evie Hone (1894-1955). They were members of the co-operative society of artists, *An Túr Gloine* (The Tower of Glass) which was founded by Sarah Purser in 1902.

Clarke and Healy developed a technique using hydrofluoric acid in the preparation of stained glass. Clarke's work includes the Honan Chapel in University College Cork and Newport parish church, County Mayo. Evie Hone used a much simpler technique on her glass than the other two. Her work appears in such diverse places as Eton College Chapel, the Jesuit College Chapel in Tullabeg and the C.I.E. office in O'Connell Street, Dublin 1.

Michael Healy, Sarah Pursar, Hubert McGoldrick and Evie Hone made the stained glass for the windows of Loughrea Catholic cathedral in County Galway.

Sculptors

Among the sculptors in this time there were Albert Power (1883-1945) and Oliver Sheppard (1864-1941). Sheppard sculpted the fine statue of the epic hero Cuchulainn in the General Post Office in Dublin and Inisfáil in the Municipal Gallery. Power provided the tympanum in Mullingar Cathedral and also a head of W. B. Yeats, which expresses the brooding poetic genius of the poet. Power is said to have been inspired by Rodin.

Andrew O'Connor

Andrew O'Connor (1876-1943) was an impressionist artist who worked mostly outside Ireland. The collection of his work in the Municipal Gallery is probably the largest of Irish artists in Ireland.

Later 20th Century

Louis le Broquy

Louis le Broquy (1916-) has the odd distinction of being a major artist whose work the Royal Hibernian Academy rejected. Although he is not a portrait painter, his interest is paradoxically in the human form. This representational form of the human person gives way to an attempt to reach the essence of the person. There is a sense of individual isolation in his figures.

Tory Island School

A very interesting phenomenon of Irish art is the so-called Tory Island School. This began when Derek Hill (1916-), an Englishman, came to Ireland and drew his subjects from the sea and the landscape of the isolated Tory Island off the coast of Donegal. One of those who were inspired to paint a series of primitive works was James Dixon (1887-1970). These were based on the bleak island, which faces the fury of the North Atlantic storms.

Dan O'Neill

From Belfast came Dan O'Neill (1920-1974), who produced landscapes of the Irish countryside painted with clarity and striking colour treatment.

Michael Farrell

One interesting Irish painter is Michael Farrell (1940-2000), who settled in France. He was very conscious of being an Irishman who was reared in an independent Ireland. He studied in Martin's College of Art in London but represented Ireland at the Paris Bienniale in 1967 and regarded Yeats and Celticism as his models. He moved to live in France in 1971. One of his artistic comments on Ireland may be experienced in *Madonna Irlanda*, which the Huge Lane Gallery bought in 1978 but kept hidden until 1988. It shows a naked woman on a bed crowned by a saint's halo. He has exhibited his works in the Hugh Lane Municipal Gallery, the Ulster Museum and the Centre Pompidou in Paris.

Sculpture of the epic hero, Cuchulainn, by Oliver Sheppard, stands in the General Post Office in Dublin

Séamus Murphy

One of the most distinguished sculptors in the 20th century was Séamus Murphy (1907-1975) a native of Mallow, County Cork, who came to sculpture from the stone carver's yard. His work was chiefly on religious themes. His *Black Madonna* and a figure of Michael Collins are displayed in the Sculpture Park in Cork city. He also collaborated with Lawrence Campbell on themes arising from the national revolution from 1916 to 1922.

Art Galleries:

The National Gallery of Art

Merrion Square, Dublin 2

Formally opened in 1864, from the beginning it exhibited a collection of European painting from about 1250 – Italian Renaissance paintings, Early Flemish and German Masters, as well as examples of all European painting since then. Irish painters all represented here. There are, for example, pictures by the Hones, Maclise, Roderic O'Connor and so on.

The Municipal Gallery of Modern Art

Parnell Square, Dublin 1, or Hugh Lane Gallery

Situated in the former Charlemont House, it has works by Orpen, Lavery, the two Yeats, and painters of the second half of the 20th century, such as le Broquy, Scott and Nora McGuinness. There are also pictures by the French Impressionists, some on loan from the Lane collection, as well early 19th-century French paintings.

The Ulster Museum Belfast

Botanic Gardens, Belfast BT9 5AB

This has an important collection of Irish paintings after 1945. There is a small Old Masters section with works by Italians and painters from the Low Countries.

Lavit's Gallery

Cork Arts Society, 5 Fr. Matthew Street, Cork

Here are exhibited a large collection of mainly 20th-century and modern works. Ceramics and batiks are exhibited in addition to paintings and sculpture. It was founded in 1963.

Crawford Municipal Art Gallery

Emmet Place, Cork

The exhibits include Irish and English paintings of the 18th and 19th centuries and a large, representative collection of 10th-century Irish paintings and sculpture. It was founded in 1830.

Irish Folklore and the 'Little People'

Irish people, especially country folk, have long maintained a belief in the existence of other strange little people who live close to human beings. The stories remain fairly consistent. Although not human themselves, these mysterious beings try to influence the lives of their human neighbours, and are sometimes quite malevolent creatures.

Belief in these supernatural 'other people' persisted right into the 20th century.

Hills, ringforts and the shee

In earliest times the little people were said to inhabit a fairy residence called a *'shee' (sidh)* which was always set on a mountain, a hill or a high place. A diminutive form of *shee* is *'sheeaun'* and this term appears in place names such as Shane, Sheeny and Sheena. The fairy people who lived in the *shee* were generally described as mischievous and seemed to want to annoy people rather than to help them.

Fairy folk dressed differently, so the stories say. An ancient story describes how the two young daughters of a king went to wash themselves at a well in the morning, as was their daily routine. When they saw Saint Patrick and another foreign missionary they thought that these strangers were from the *shee*.

The ringforts of Ireland are the remains of circular fences, which enclosed dwellings. They are very numerous and were the sites of well-off country people from medieval times and in some cases two millenniums ago. They have been uninhabited for at least four centuries. These ringforts were said to be dwelling places for fairies. So the stories go, anyone who risked interfering with a ringfort or ploughing it up, was likely to die soon afterwards. At best, some other misfortune would beset him or his family, his animals or his property. Several remarkable coincidences do seem to support some of these strange superstitions.

Even in the second half of the 20th century when such traditions were no longer accepted, few ringforts have been disturbed. In some parts of Ireland the ringforts are known as fairy forts. People feared to go near them in the dark and in many places it is claimed that lights could be seen inside – not supplied by human beings.

Female rulers often held high rank in the fairy world. For example Aoibhell, Clíona and Aine lived on a hill and Knockaney in County Limerick is named after Aine (*Cnoc Aine*).

Trickery and malice

Among the many beliefs about little people was that they could lead a person astray in a field at night. Stories tell how men can find themselves wandering about in fields, unable to discover where and how they had entered this place. It would be impos-

sible to find a way out until dawn. The fairies or the little people must have done this to them, it was claimed.

There was also the notion that the little folk that came out after midnight were the kind to be feared most of all. Believing that the 'dawn fairy' was the most malign, fishermen on the lower reaches of the River Suir would sometimes go ashore or land on an island until the moment of dawn was past, rather than risk a meeting with 'the light of day fairy'.

Even in hurling fields were not immune for here it was said that the fairies came out to play at night. No one should risk being there after dark for it was very dangerous to catch sight of the fairies at play.

One fable tells how a man with a hunchback watched the little people dancing and heard them chanting monotonously: 'Monday, Tuesday, Monday, Tuesday'. He then called out: 'Monday, Tuesday, Monday, Tuesday, Monday, Tuesday and Wednesday'. They were so pleased to have a suitable finishing piece that they removed his hunchback. When another hunchback added 'Thursday, Friday and Saturday', they added this hunchback to the wretched man's own one.

Leprechauns, banshees and other fairy folk

One of the best-known little people was the leprechaun. This individual was always seen alone. He was tiny and believed to be able to sit on a mushroom in a field. The name of this very mischievous sprite originated in a word meaning dwarf or pygmy.

This little fellow was believed to have a crock of gold. If anyone spotted him in a field on a moonlit night, it was in his or her interest to grab the wily leprechaun and refuse to let him go. This was a difficult task but worth pursuing for, it was said, the lep-

rechaun would be so desperate to escape that he would eventually give the crock of gold to his captor. However, the leprechaun was a master of deception and could usually divert his captor's attention in order to escape.

The banshee was yet another kind of fairy. She was the female fairy who lamented or keened the dead of the Gaelic people. She also announced a death beforehand by making a loud wailing at night.

One of the most popular tales was that of the three Children of Lir. When his wife died, he married again and his wife hated the children. She changed them into swans and they lived in the sea off the north-east of Ireland. Nobody could turn them back to humans again until Saint Patrick came to Ireland.

The fairies were tiny in all cases except one. In the *shee* of Slievenamon, County Tipperary, instead of being little people, the fairies assumed the form of adult women. Slievenamon means 'Mountain of the Women'. (Sheegowna was the fairy dwelling of the young deer.) These larger-scale fairies came down from the mountain at night to enter unlocked houses where the housewife was slovenly and the housework had not been undertaken to the fairies' satisfaction. These fairies then proceeded to do the work properly. The only way to frighten them away was to run out and shout: 'Slievenamon and the hill under it are on fire!'. Then the fairies fled back home to check if this was true as the hill under Slievenamon was their *shee*.

'Going with the fairies'

'Going with the fairies' was another well-known superstition. It was believed that the fairies could put a spell on someone. When this happened, the victim would become totally absorbed with the 'other world' – to the extent of completely withdrawing from human society. This sometimes occurred, for example when a fairy lover became attached to a human and ruled his or her life.

In a very old story, which is recorded in an early manuscript, Conla, a young man, is described as being enticed away by a fairy woman. His father, a king, implored a druid to save his son but the poet told him that this was beyond his powers. The fairy lady, who was invisible to all but to him, left him an apple and when he ate it, he disappeared., In a story from the 19th century a man was asked about a woman who disappeared, 'She is gone out the hill on a white horse', he replied.

While the saying: 'He (or she) is gone with the fairies' is often used colloquially to mean that the person concerned is acting strangely or is simply odd or distracted, there are tales of people actually crossing over into the other people's world. One story tells how Finn MacCool's son,

Far right
In moonlight and at moments of transition – such as nightfall and the dawn – fairies were most likely to be seen. The dawn fairies were especially feared.

Centre right
Banshees wailed to announce a death

Below
If you were lucky enough to capture a wily leprechaun, you might gain his crock of gold

Usheen, went to the Land of Youth with Niamh the Golden-haired. This is a typical literary example of how someone is supposed to have actually left his homeland to go with a fairy.

Changelings

Stories of changelings are numerous. In these rather sad tales, the little people's interference in human lives involves the swapping over of a human baby for a fairy one. If a baby boy or young son sickened and died, it was thought that fairies had taken the human child to their home and substituted a changeling. This changeling then died. In some places, the belief was upheld that a child could be stunted by the evil influence of the little people. It was common for mothers to threaten miscreant children with the warning 'Do it now or the fairies will get you!'.

There is one case where a changeling was supposedly substituted for a female adult. In the 1890s a woman was actually burned to death in a place just north of Slievenamon, County Tipperary, because of this belief. Purportedly, the real woman had been taken by fairies and so a group of men tried to burn the changeling away to force the fairies to restore the original human woman. They stripped her and placed her on an iron plate over the fire to drive the fairy out of her. After the poor woman's death, one of her murderers claimed, 'She's gone out the mountain with a fairy on a white horse!'.

W. B. Yeats' poem, *The Stolen Child*, is based on this theme. He concludes the final stanza with the words:

The world's more full of trouble
Than he can understand.

Yeats professed to believe in fairies as the mystical expression of Ireland. He was much derided about this until the death of the woman in 1895 took place.

Speculation

The origins of the belief in the little people or fairies remains uncertain. Some speculate that in every society there is the need to account for happenings that might otherwise seem impossible to accept. For example, the sudden illness of a healthy child can be explained by its having been exchanged for a sickly changeling. The man 'lost' in the field may simply have been disorientated by a surfeit of alcohol but he finds it easier to blame the fairies.

Meanwhile ancient Irish 'historians' and story-tellers told tales of the earliest invaders. They also mutated the Gaelic gods and goddesses to form one group – the Tuatha D, Danann (People of the God Danu). Long ago it was believed that the little people belonged to these people of the gods.

Some people have suggested that there may indeed have been aboriginal peoples of slight stature who once lived in the remote mountains but who were rarely seen. They may have come out under cover of darkness to play mischievous tricks on those whose ancestors had ousted them from their lands, and to dance in the fields in the moonlight. It was said that these genuinely small humans may have been a particularly fierce race and so regarded as a threat to the settlers and their descendants for generations – until their eventual disappearance.

With the passage of time – as one culture merges into another, and incidents from the past mutate into myth – real events often slide into the storytelling tradition of a nation. It is indeed credible that an aboriginal race who lived in the hills may have provided some basis for belief in the fairies from the *shee*.

The Influence of the Celts

Celtic man in a tunic and cloak

Celtic peasant woman

Celtic peasant in clothes worn when fighting

More than two thousand years ago, the European lands that lay to the north of the Mediterranean were dominated by the Celts, a collection of peoples with shared traditions of language, art, and culture.

The Roman opinion

Archaeologists and historians have long been fascinated by the Celtic settlement of Ireland. There are many interesting remains that contribute to the jigsaw puzzle of the past. Supposedly an insular people, we know of the Celts' existence in Ireland from Caesar's report of the migration of Belgic tribes to Britain. The inhabitants of both Ireland and Britain were regarded by the Romans as being similarly related to the Gauls but both the archaeology and language of Britain and Ireland show that, in fact, there were many differences between the Celtic tribes in these two islands – so their settlement obviously developed in distinct ways.

Greeks and Romans described the Celtic warrior classes as being remarkable for their height, muscularity and fair colouring but skeletal remains suggest considerable variations of stature in the general population.

Society, work, family: a way of life

The Celtic world was not a simple homogeneous whole. Instead, it was formed from a complex and varied group of societies. Social and religious customs differed widely between the various Celtic lands – which by 350BC stretched from the Atlantic to Turkey. Some Celtic tribes belonged to small, tightly-knit units; other groups were part of larger and less-structured entities.

Ireland was the far western outpost of Celtic power and so became the place where this ancient culture was to revel in

its final golden age. The Celts were highly skilled miners, smiths, builders and farmers. The economy was based on mixed farming with single farmsteads as the norm, except in times of unrest. Often cattle raising was more important than cereal cultivation – depending on the land. Meanwhile, Celtic merchants travelled and traded internationally.

The Celtic way of life developed into a threefold social system consisting of king, warrior aristocracy and freeman farmers. The family was patriarchal – a man with his wives, children and grandchildren. While land-ownership and social obligations were vested in the kin, the status of women varied according to the rank and prosperity of a particular community.

Druids, who supervised religious events and undertook magic duties, were recruited from the warrior class, but assumed a higher rank.

Celts were reputed to love warfare. Hill forts provided places of refuge, but disputes were often resolved by individual challenges and single combat rather than by general fighting. Magic, display and ritual were all-important: naked combat was supposed to invoke magical protection; chariots were used for display and retreat on the battlefield; and the Celts' enemies were decapitated for ritual purposes.

A belted tunic or shirt, worn with a cloak, was the usual style of clothing for men. Women wore a single long garment with a cloak. Coarse linen and wool were used, and bright colours very popular. Noted for their high spirits, the Celts were hospitable; they enjoyed feasting, drinking, quarrelling, music and telling stories.

Celtic religion and the Celtic church

Early Celtic religion expressed beliefs about omens, magic, and transformation: these beliefs were explored through the symbolism of the natural world.

Their places of worship were rarely housed in stone buildings. Instead, the Celts chose natural boundaries, such as trees or the edge of a lake. If temples were built, they were either open to the sky, or built of wood and thatch, such as Navan Fort in County Armagh, Ireland.

Belief in the afterlife was a vital element of Gaelic religion. The destination of the dead was the Otherworld, an unearthly, magical region – home to supernatural beings and monsters.

In the fifth century, St Patrick's mission established Christianity in Ireland. Over the next two centuries the Irish sent missionaries to Iona and Lindisfarne and

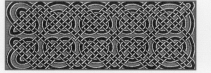

even further afield – to Switzerland and northern Italy.

As the Celtic church developed, it was Irish masters who taught the Scriptures to such saints as Aldhelm, Alcuin, Wilibrord and Chad. Welsh and Irish figures of the 9th century are well-known (such as Asser, Johannes Scotus Erigena and Sedulius Scottus) but many Irish influences contributed to the enrichment of Christian Europe. Collections of ecclesiastical laws and regulations were widely read and copied and had an enormous influence – as did Welsh and Irish penitentials, and great monastic leaders like David, Finnian and Columban. Their teaching lead to the development of private confession and the sacrament of penance.

Celtic Fairy Tales

Ireland was one of the first countries to collect her folk-tales. National and mythical heroes featured in a consistent body of oral tradition in tales and ballads that have perpetrated for about a thousand years. The Celtic folk-imagination is peopled with heroes from the past, with magic, charm and humour – invoking a vivid picture of life when the storyteller wove his spell.

Celtic art

There is a rich heritage of Celtic culture in the material that has been recovered by archaeologists. An amazing amount of early Celtic artefacts have survived, especially those items made in metal. Once the smiths in Britain and Ireland had mastered the technique of enamelling, they created superb intricate patterns, seen on ring brooches, shields, and scabbards.

Generally, the Celts drew their inspiration from nature with its infinite source of form and change. Delicate, curving, swirling lines suggest human, animal, and plant forms with great ingenuity. The exact meanings of some symbols can be difficult to decipher but since it is evident that the Celts loved metaphor and conundrum, perhaps the intricate asymmetrical and abstract patterns of their art are a puzzle that runs parallel to the symbolism of their medieval literature.

As the Celts moved west and north into new territories, they brought their language, art and religion with them and the surviving, magnificent metalwork and manuscripts of early medieval Ireland remain an inspiration today.

The books of the gospels were the not only the much needed tools of the Church and missionaries, but were the embodiment of Celtic art forms. Described by one

traveller as 'the work of angels', these manuscripts were written on fine calf skin, and epitomised Celtic vividness and intricacy.

The Eternal Knot, which traces an unbroken path without beginning or end, is a perfect example of Celtic book decoration. From its origins in the plait motifs of western Europe, intricate knotwork developed in Ireland – to culminate in the interlace patterning of 7th to 9th century manuscripts. Many months of painstaking labour produced ingenious eternal knot designs of exquisite craftsmanship, covering entire pages of gospels, psalters, and other religious works. To the pious scribe, the endless knot was a reflection of God and the Creation, in all its infinite diversity.

Celtic art is also famous for its fine stone carving. With the arrival of Christianity, came intricately sculpted stone crosses while inside churches, statues decorated walls. On White Island, in County Fermanagh, a Romanesque church exhibits saints and bishops with simple, calm faces just like those in the manuscript illustrations. It is possible that the statues were originally carved onto the wall of a ninth- or tenth-century monastery.

One predominant element in Celtic art was the use of triplication, or groups of three – either symbolically with threefold designs or as triple divinities, such as the triplicated mother goddesses and the three hooded spirits', the *genii cucullati*. Medieval literature in Ireland also used triplication, as a narrative device, while in myths, a hero is warned of imminent death by the appearance of three red-headed warriors riding before him.

Celtic Mythology

Real literacy began with the introduction of Christianity to fifth-century Ireland, and its subsequent spread to other Celtic lands. Meanwhile, in all Celtic countries, the folklorists recorded and translated huge volumes of oral tradition, most of which was drawn from ancient times.

Medieval Irish tales refer constantly to the nature of kingship and sovereignty, while adultery is another common theme and one that is portrayed surprisingly sensuously. Bloody vengeance was exacted in response to treachery, broken promises, or insult – real or imaginary. Monsters lurk at cross-roads, near dark pools, and in the remote hills. Boats of white bronze sail on glassy seas, and sweet damsels entertain heroes for centuries that can pass in a flash.

Visits to the afterlife, to the realm of 'Otherworld', became an important theme in Celtic literature. The realm's inhabitants were known as the *Tuatha Dé Danann* (People of the Goddess Danu), who lived in the *Tir na nÓg* (Land of Youth) or the *Tir na mBeo* (Land of Women). Death was not the only passport for entry into the Otherworld, so some stories tell of mortal women being kidnapped as brides for

Otherworld men, or of heroes who entered these strange lands, sometimes never to return. Ancient burial sites, known as 'fairy mounds' were reputed to be the entrance to these strange worlds and to Otherworld islands beyond great seas, islands haunted by strange beasts where springs gushed wine, and the trees were filled with fruit and exotic birds; others were peopled by beautiful Otherworld women.

Magical transformation was an important part of Celtic myths. The hero Oengus followed his lover into the Otherworld after assuming the form of a swan. Birds were frequently the result of human transformation in Celtic belief, while supernatural beings often assume animal form s.

Four great seasonal festivals marked important divisions in the Celtic year. Imbolg (Sheep's Milk), was the first to be celebrated – on 2 February. Then the summer began at Beltaine (Great Fire) on 1 May. On 1 August Lughnasa, the feast of the god Lugh, was celebrated as a traditional harvest festival; and winter began at Samhain (End of Summer) on 1 November.

The most famous Celtic celebration of all was Samhain (the Irish/Gaelic name for the festival). Many of the major events in Irish mythology took place at this time, when the boundaries of this world and the supernatural realm were believed to dissolve completely, and the fairy mounds were open to the Otherworld.

This literary tradition survived the many onslaughts that beset Ireland, from the Anglo-Normans through Cromwellian pogroms to the unrest of the eighteenth and nineteenth centuries.

Hillforts

Prehistoric Celtic hillforts exploited the natural terrain. These impressive structures were brilliant engineering achievements. Undoubtedly they were used for defensive purposes but also served as open-air temples, using both landscape and the building to enclose a sacred space. The walls may well have been believed to represent boundaries between this world and the next.

In Celtic tales, hillforts are frequently the setting for heroism and adventure. Just as castles were seen as the home of giants in European fairy tales, Irish forts often housed fearsome monsters. Defensive walls and pillars were sometimes flaming barriers or perhaps rings of stakes topped with human heads.

An exceptionally well-preserved stone ringfort can be found at Grianan Aileach in Co. Donegal. Some parts date back to the 5th century BC. In earliest times, the site was defended by four concentric ramparts and could well have been a centre for tribal power and trade. The

high fortifications and the physical demands of building such a structure would certainly have made an impressive display of political power.

The Irish language

For centuries, the spoken word was the main expression of Celtic culture. Writing was a relatively late innovation.

For the purposes of study, the history of the Irish language has been split into four periods: the Ogham inscriptions, probably AD 300-500; Old Irish (600-900); Middle Irish, (900-1200); and Modern Irish (200 to the present day). Modern dialects include Scottish Gaelic and Manx.

There are more than 300 Ogham inscriptions from the archaic period, but none is of more than a few words and the great majority are names of people and families. At this stage, writing developed along with Roman influences and inscriptions on monuments are the only remains of this period. A series of notches represented each letter.

Old Irish refers to the language which emerged from the archaic stage. It survived for some centuries but was simplified in the Middle Irish period to a point resembling the earliest recorded Welsh.

The Latin alphabet was introduced into Ireland in the 5th century and by the end of the 6th century was being used to write. Irish monks wrote in Latin but used Gaelic too, adapting the Roman lettering and developing it to express Irish speech. In fact they created the first vernacular literature in Europe.

Poets and bards traditionally set down their verse in Gaelic and this continued even when the old Gaelic order collapsed in the 18th century. Gaelic was still widely spoken in 1800 but as the century progressed, with the spread of formal education and the after-effects of the famine, English soon began to dominate. A Gaelic League was established in 1893 to try and redress the balance a little and to rescue the language from extinction.

Since then many fine Gaelic works have been published and, while English remains the first language, Gaelic continues to be revived and enjoyed as part of the Celtic heritage.

A Celtic chief in civil clothing

Celtic chieftainess

Celtic chief in war dress

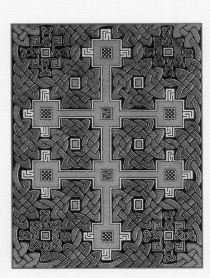

Maps over the centuries

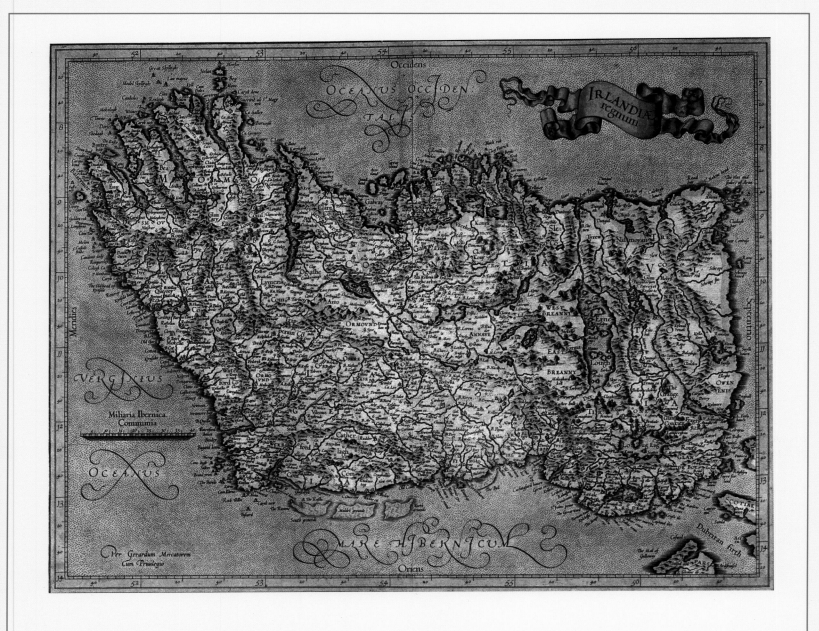

Maps abound of Ireland and the changing patterns they show over the centuries, as well as reflecting the contemporary styles of execution and knowledge of geography, are also a clear indication of the patterns in the way of life and political structure within the island.

The earliest known map of Ireland was the one drawn up in about AD 150 by Ptolemy, astronomer, geographer and mathematician – an outline representation of which is shown on the left.

The following few pages of the book include a selection of maps of Ireland from 1562 to 1850 – a time when the creation of the most magnificent, illustrated maps was at its zenith.

Mercator's map Irlandia Reginum 1562

Gerard Mercator 1512-94

For nearly sixty years, at the most exciting period in the story of modern map making, Gerard Mercator was the supreme cartographer. His name, second only to Ptolemy, is synonymous with the form of map projection still in use today. Although not its inventor, he was the first to apply it to navigational charts so that compass bearings could be plotted in straight lines, thus simplifying navigation at sea. He transformed land surveying and his researches challenged Ptolemy's conception of the size and outline of the Continents, drastically reducing the longitudinal length of Europe and Asia and altering the shape of the Old World as previously visualized.

He established himself as a cartographer and instrument and globe maker, drawing and engraving his first map (of Palestine) when he was twenty-five. He went on to produce a map of Flanders (1540) supervising the surveying and completing the drafting and engraving himself. His excellent work brought him the patronage of Charles V for whom he constructed a globe, but he became caught up in the persecution of Lutheran protestants

Irlande Accurata Descriptio
by Baptist Boazio, Antwerp, 1603

Baptista Boazio, 1585-1606

A naval cartographer from Italy, Boazio's information was gathered whilst sailing with Sir Francis Drake.

The map was published by Jan Baptist Vrients (1552-1612). He was the map engraver and publisher in Antwerp who, after the death of Ortelius in 1598, acquired the publication rights of the Theatrum. Between 1601 and 1612 he issued a number of editions which included some of his own maps and he was responsible for printing the maps for the English edition in 1606. He also published a number of important individual maps and a small atlas of the Netherlands.

and charged with heresy – fortunately without serious consequences. He moved in 1552 to Duisburg, where he continued the production of maps, globes and instruments culminating in large-scale maps of *Europe* (1554), the *British Isles* (1564) and the famous *World Map* on 18 sheets drawn to his new projection (1569). These early maps are exceedingly rare, some known by only one copy.

Later he devoted himself to his edition of the maps in Ptolemy's Geographia, reproduced in his own engraving as nearly as possible in their original form, and to the preparation of his 3-volume collection of maps to which, for the first time, the word 'Atlas' was applied.

The word was chosen, he explained, 'to honour the Titan, Atlas, King of Mauritania, a learned philosopher, mathematiciar, and astronomer'. The first two parts of the *Atlas* were published in 1585 and 1589 and the third, completing the edition, in 1595, a year after Mercator's death.

Mercator's sons and grandsons were all cartographers. Rumold was responsible for the complete edition in 1595. After a second complete edition in 1602, the map plates were bought in 1604 by Jodocus Hondius who, with his sons, Jodocus II and Henricus, published enlarged editions which dominated the map market for the following twenty to thirty years.

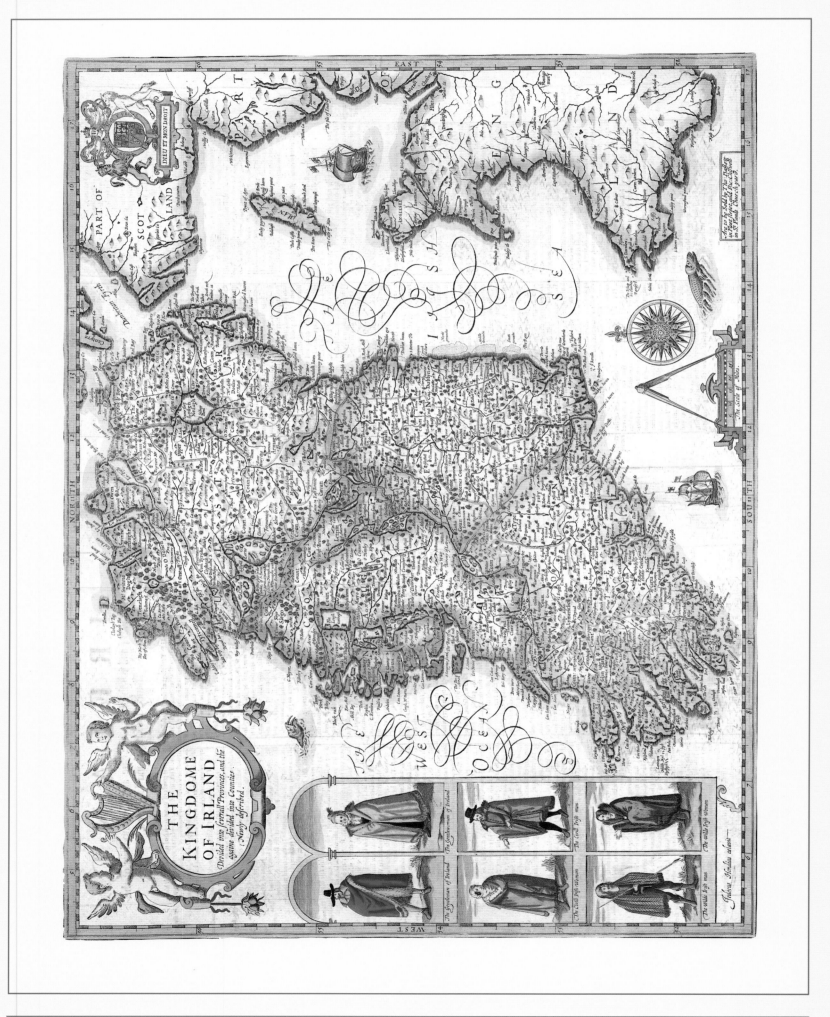

Left **Kingdome of Ireland**
Newly described
by John Speed, London, 1612-1676

*Are to be Sold by Tho: Bassett in Fleet Street
and Ric: Chiswell in St. Pauls Churchyard*

John Speed (1552-1629)

Speed was one of the most famous British mapmakers of the seventeenth century, and probably the most popular of all with map collectors around the world. He is noted for placing England into the mainstream of map publishing which had been dominated by the Dutch since the late sixteenth century. Speed began by issuing maps of Great Britain as early as 1611 in his famous *Theatre of the Empire of Great Britaine* that contained maps of the entire British Isles, their kingdoms, and their counties. Speed spent over fifteen years assembling the information for this atlas, which was first issued by John Sudbury and George Humble. It is one of the most influential atlases of the British Isles ever published. Not only are the maps historically fascinating, but Speed also improved the decorative features, which were all finely engraved by Jodocus Hondius. Speed's maps are some of the most appealing cartographic images ever produced. He included intricate calligraphy, coats-of-arms, town plans, small profiles of important buildings, vignettes of battles, compass roses, figures of local inhabitants, cherubs, and many other attractive features. Speed's British maps were immediately popular and remained so well into the eighteenth century.

Above **The Province Ulster**
by John Speed, London, 1610-1612

Performed by John Speede and are to be solde by John Sudbury and George Humble in Popeshead Alley at London. Cum Privilegio. An. 1610

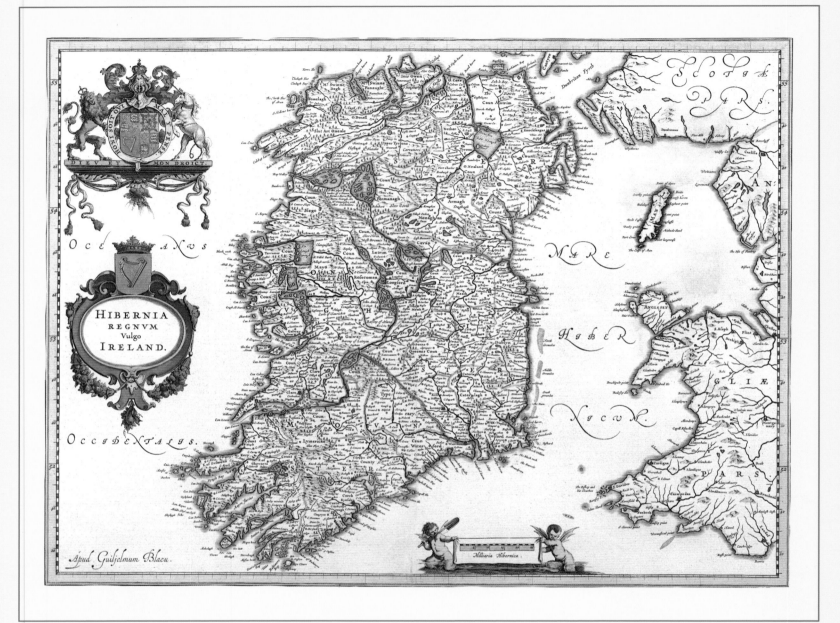

Hibernia Regnum vulgo Ireland
by Willem Blaeu, Amsterdam, 1636-c1645

Willem Janszoon Blaeu 1571-1638

Willem Blaeu founded a business in Amsterdam in 1599 as a globe and instrument maker. Soon the business expanded, publishing maps, topographical works and books of sea charts as well as constructing globes. His most notable early work was a map of Holland (1604), a fine *World Map* (1605-06) and *Het Licht der Zeevaerdt* (The Light of Navigation) – a marine atlas, which went through many editions in different languages.

Blaeu was planning a major atlas to include the most up-to-date maps of the entire known world. Progress on so vast a project was slow and not until he bought some thirty or forty plates of the *Mercator Atlas* from Jodocus Hondius II to add to his own collection was he able to publish a 60-map volume, *Atlantis Appendix* in 1630. It was five years before the first two volumes of his planned world atlas, *Atlas Novus or the Theatrum Orbis Terrarum* were issued. Blaeu was appointed Hydrographer to the East India Company but died in 1638. The business passed into the hands of his sons, Joan and Cornelis.

There is often confusion between the elder Blaeu and his rival Jan Jansson (Johannes Janssonius). Up to about 1619 Blaeu often signed his works Guilielmus Janssonius or Willems Jans Zoon but after that time he seems to have decided on Guilielmus or G. Blaeu.

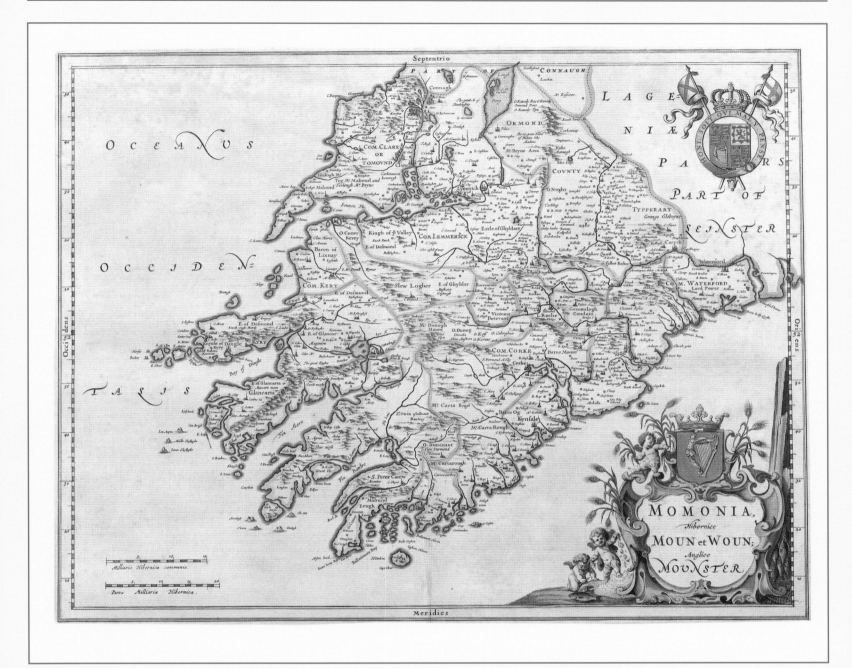

Momonia Moun et Woun; Mounster
by Joan Blaeu, Amsterdam, c1645

Joan Blaeu 1596-1673

The sons of Willem Blaeu continued their father's ambitious plans. After the death of Cornelis, Joan directed the work alone and the whole series of six volumes was eventually completed by about 1655. He immediately began the preparation of the even larger work, the *Atlas Major*, published in 1662 in 11 volumes (later editions in 9-12 volumes). It contained nearly 600 double-page maps and 3,000 pages of text. This was the most magnificent work of its kind ever produced with fine engraving and colouring, elaborate cartouches, pictorial and heraldic detail and splendid calligraphy.

In 1672 a disastrous fire destroyed Blaeu's printing house in the Gravenstraat and a year afterwards Joan Blaeu died.

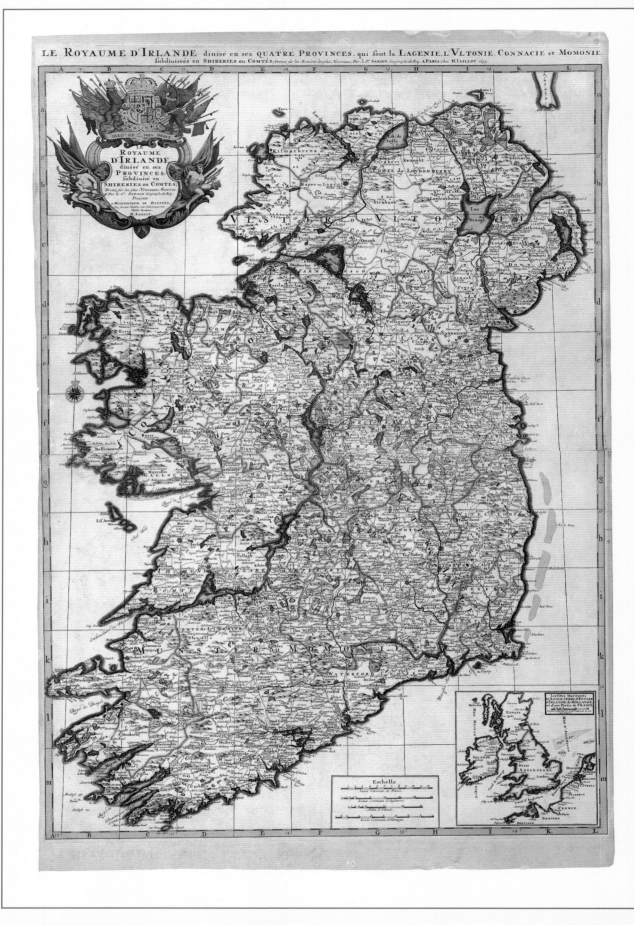

Le Royaume D'Irlande
by Alexis Hubert Jaillot, Paris, 1693

Alexis Hubert Jaillot, 1632-1712

The French mapmaker Hubert Jaillot. collaborated with the sons of Nicolas Sanson

(1600-1667). His maps were larger than normal and often highly decorative, with coloured cartouches, divine figures, wild animals and native people.

L'Irlanda Hibernia
by Giacomo Rossi, Rome, c1690

Giovanni Giacomo de Rossi, 1648-1691
A publisher from Rome

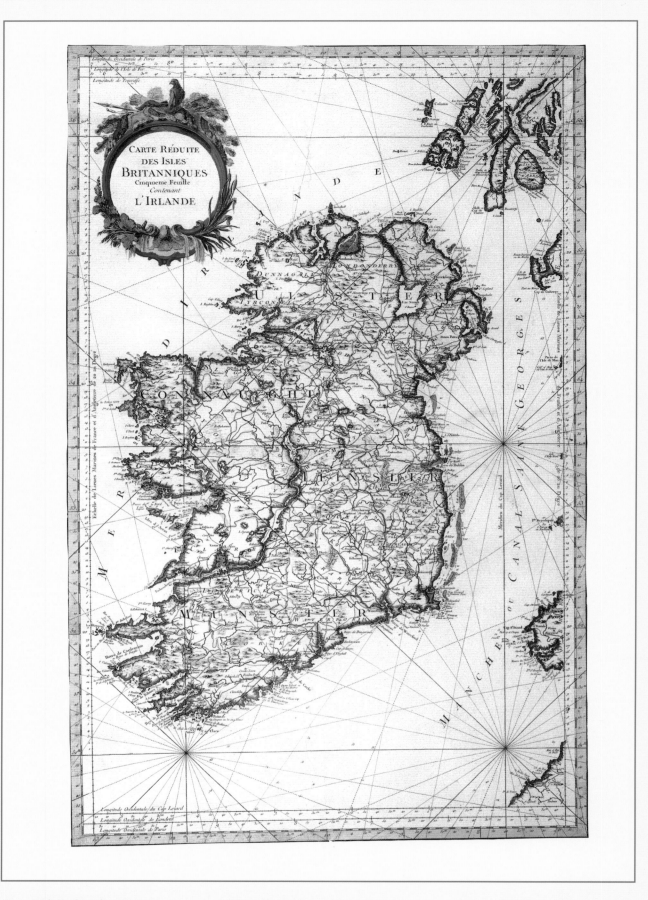

**Carte Réduite des Isles Britanniques
Cinquieme Feuille Contenant
L'Irlande**
by Jacques Nicolas Bellin, Paris, c1760

Jacques Nicolas Bellin (1703-1772)

Jaques Nicolas Bellin was the most important French hydrographer of the 18th century. He spent over fifty years at the French Hydrographic Service where he was appointed the first 'Ingenieur hydrographe de La Marine'. During his term of office he carried out major surveys, first of the coasts of France and later of all the known coasts of the world. This resulted in the production of a large number of sea charts of the highest quality which appeared in many editions. He was appointed 'Hydrographer to the King' and was a member of the Royal Society in London.

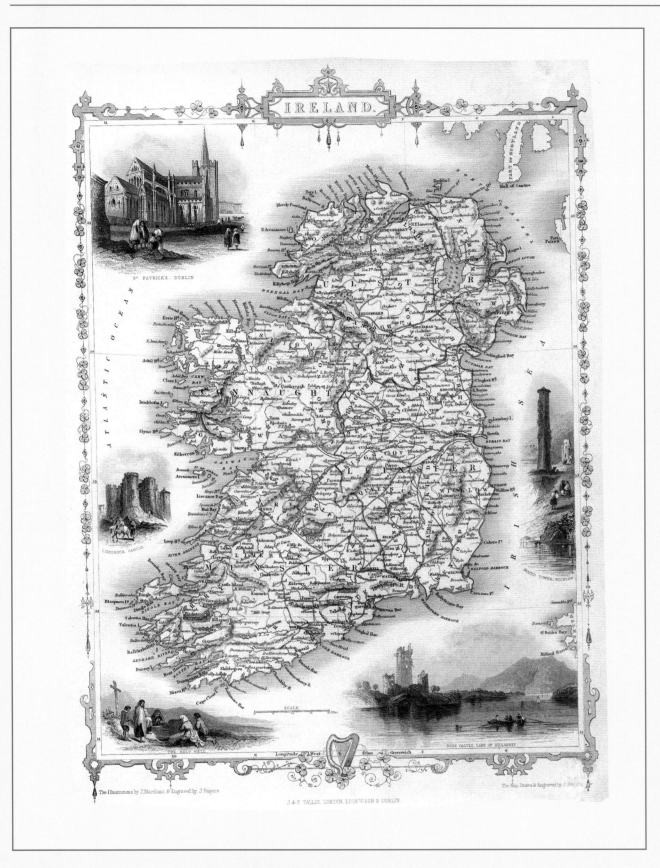

Ireland
by John Tallis, London, c 1850

John Tallis 1818-1876

All John Tallis maps are decorative with vignette views combining art, skilled engraving, hand painting and hand colouring in a distinctive early Victorian style. They are perhaps the most decorative maps of the world that were issued during the 19th century.

Gaelic games and sport

The Gaelic Athletic Association (GAA) was founded in 1884, as part of the Gaelic revival, to promote three Gaelic games: hurling, Gaelic football and handball.

Hurling

Hurling has probably been played in Ireland for at least two thousand years and is the national game of Ireland. It is played with a curved stick called a hurley. The original Irish game developed into shinty in Scotland and hockey in England. In 'bow' or 'loop' hurling, the goal was the shape of a circle's arc and one goal decided the winner. There was also the 'hole'

The fastest outdoor team sport in the world, hurling has been played in Ireland for at least 2000 years

game where a ball was driven into a hole in the ground or a hole in a fence or wall: this is believed to be the origin of golf. In another version, the ball was pucked back and forth over a fence, which may have been the beginnings of tennis.

During the 18th century the landed gentry in Ireland organised bow or loop hurling games between counties, baronies and their own teams. There was no goalman as such; the 'back', usually three hurlers, filled this role. Seven hurlers formed a kind of scrum. No referees were in evidence but in the 18th century the interested gentry rode about on horseback, trying to maintain order among both players and spectators.

In the North of Ireland hurleys were like hockey or shinty sticks. Elsewhere in Ireland a wide 'bossed' hurley was used. The ball in the south was the roansheen which was made of cow-hair when the animals were moulting in the spring. In the north the ball was a rounded piece of wood, called the 'crag'.

As the influence of the gentry diminished in the 19th century, the games often turned into rowdy affairs: hurling matches earned such a bad reputation that women were advised to avoid them. Nowadays, however, women have their own version of hurling, called camogie.

Today the game is played by teams of fifteen each. The goal consists of two uprights and a cross-bar. If the ball is driven between the goal-posts under the cross-bar, it is counted as a goal (a goal equals three points) but if it is driven over the bar and between the posts, it scores a single point. It is a very fast and skilful game. In modern hurling the ball may be handled.

Hurling is played all year and competitions such as the National League take place throughout the four seasons. Teams from the GAA parish clubs play one another in a knock-out competition that leads to the County Hurling Final. The greatest competition of the hurling year is the All-Ireland Final played by senior county teams on the first Sunday in September.

Gaelic football

Gaelic football is played by teams of fifteen players and their positions on the field are similar to those in hurling – as is the scoring count of goals and points. Handling of the ball and foreball are allowed but there is no scrum as in rugby. The great Kerry and Cavan teams of the past excelled in great feats of 'fielding' the football, jumping high in the air to catch it.

The All-Ireland Final competition in Gaelic Football, organised in a similar way to hurling, is played at Croke Park in Dublin where the GAA headquarters is sited. Gaelic football was introduced by the GAA to meet popular demand– largely because the GAA had banned their players and members from attending 'foreign games' such as rugby, soccer and cricket. This ban remained in force until April 1971.

Perhaps because the gentry never promoted football in Ireland, it was a disorderly game back in the 18th century. The matches were often called to a halt because they were causing breaches of public order. It was a regular event for players to be rounded up, imprisoned or transported.

Other very popular sports in Ireland today include rugby and horse racing.

Handball

In past times, handball was played against the gable-ends of houses. The ball used in Ireland is a hard ball, the 'alley-cracker'.

Sporting achievements
in recent decades

1982

Northern Ireland football team plays in World Cup Finals in Spain.
Ireland rugby team wins Triple Crown.
Joey Dunlop wins Formula One motorcycle world championship.
Alex Higgins wins World Professional Snooker Championship for 2nd time.

1984

John Treacy wins silver medal in the marathon, Los Angeles Olympics.

1985

Barry McGuigan wins WBA world featherweight boxing championship.
Ireland rugby team wins Triple Crown.
Dennis Taylor wins World Professional Snooker Championship.

1986

Joey Dunlop wins Formula One motorcycle world championship for 5th time.
Northern Ireland football team reaches 2nd rounds in World Cup Finals, Mexico.

1987

Stephen Roche wins Giro d'Italia, Tour de France and World Championship.

1988

Republic of Ireland football team plays in European Championship final .
Stephen Martin and James Kirkwood win gold medals with Great Britain hockey team, Olympic Games, Seoul.
Irish golfers win Dunhill Cup, St Andrew's.

1990

Republic of Ireland football team plays in World Cup Finals for 1st time, Italy.
Irish golfers win Dunhill Cup.

1991

Frank O'Mara wins world indoor 3000m championship for 2nd time, Seville.
Eddie Jordan enters his Jordan team in World Formula One Championship.
Seán Kelly wins Tour of Lombardy.

1992

Michael Carruth wins gold medal in welterweight boxing, Olympic Games, Barcelona.

1993

Mount Everest is climbed by Irish team, ascending its North Ridge.
Marcus O'Sullivan wins world indoor 1500m championship for 3rd time, Toronto.

1994

Republic of Ireland football team reaches last 16 in World Cup Finals, USA.

1999

Roy Keane and Dennis Irwin from Cork help Manchester United win FA Premiership, FA Cup and Champions' League.

The roansheen was used in Co. Armagh for handball while the wooden crag was used for hurling. It was 1924 before the GAA took control of handball.

Horse racing

Horse racing is a traditional national sport. The Irish passion for horses is famous and has been renowned for centuries. The Curragh, still Ireland's most famous course, was popular for stabling and racing as long ago as the 17th century.

Many famous race horses have come from Ireland – in recent years the Grand National specialist, Red Rum, the Derby Winner, Shergar (who was horsenapped and probably met a grisly end) and the famous steeple chaser, Arkle.

Rugby

It was English students at Trinity College, Dublin, who first introduced Rugby Union football to Ireland in the middle of the 19th century. Soon the game was being played at schools and colleges, while rugby clubs sprang up in many places. In 1874 the Irish Rugby Football Union was formed in the south and there were some clubs in the north. The first international rugby match was played in Dublin in 1875. In 1879 the IRFU included all clubs throughout Ireland and so it has remained, despite the partition of the island.

In 1883-84 England, Ireland, Scotland and Wales played the first Triple Crown series of matches. Then, when the International Board was established, Ireland became a member.

In England the game was even more boisterous than the old Irish football had been. The game was not allowed to be played on Sundays but in Ireland this also excluded any working class people from watching or playing the game. Nowadays rugby games are allowed to be played on Sundays in Ireland – with the exception of internationals.

Hockey

It was W.E. Paterson of the High School in Dublin who instigated the drawing up of the rules for hockey in 1892. In the following year the Irish Hockey Union was formed. The oldest hockey cup in the world, the Irish Senior Cup, was first competed for in 1894 while the first international hockey game was played in Ireland, against Wales, just one year later.

Hurling had already been played in the High School and other Protestant schools in Dublin so once the GAA had been founded in 1884, the change from 'hurley' to hockey was a natural development. All the hard striking and lashing at the ball, which characterised hurling, was controlled in hockey by the 'rule of sticks': this forbade the hockey stick to be raised higher than the shoulder and somewhat 'tamed' hockey.

In 1897 the first inter-provincial match was played between Munster and Leinster. By 1898-9 the Irish Hockey Union began forming branches throughout Ireland.

Association Football

Associated Football or soccer was first seen in Ireland in Belfast in 1878 when Queens Park and Caledonians, two Scottish teams, played at the Ulster Cricket Grounds. Two Dublin clubs, Bohemians and Shelbourne, were formed in 1890 and by 1901 Bohemians opened their grounds at Dalymount Park. This is now the principal soccer ground in the republic.

Initially it was the IFA, the Irish Football Association, who controlled the game in Ireland. In 1921 the FAI, Football Association of Ireland, was founded for what later became the Republic. Soccer was the only Irish field game to split this way in the wake of Ireland's partition.

In August 1923 the FAI joined FIFA, the international association of football associations, underlining this division. To begin with the FAI had some 100 teams but this escalated to over 1,000 by the end of the century.

During the late 1980s and early 1990s the influence of Jack Charlton, the former English international player, raised soccer standards in the Republic of Ireland to a higher level. It has achieved a new popularity and prestige – and great success in World Cup games.

Legendary Cheltenham Gold Cup winner, Arkle, parading at the Dublin show to receive honour

Irish Farming

Early farming and cattle

Evidence from both early literature and archaeology suggests that the agriculture of the ancient Gaelic peoples was mainly pastoral with some small-scale tilling. Because this was subsistence farming there was no need to market any surplus produce and so no stimulus for real urban development.

However, maintaining a herd of cattle was vital. Cows provided milk for drinking and for butter. Although butter could be preserved in the cool Irish climate – so that making cheese was not essential – the early farmers did produce a rough cheese called *mullchan*.

Arable farmland in County Donegal

The herds were moved out to the hills or summer pastures on May Day when the new growth of grass was available for grazing. The fresh grazing land was called a *buaile* – a cow field. The cows were tended by women, children and dairymen. The cows were brought home according to the laws on the eve of the first of November when the feast of *Samhain* marked the beginning of winter. Calves could not be over-wintered, so a bull and breeding cows were retained while the calves from the previous spring were slaughtered and eaten through the succeeding months.

Pigs and cocks

Ancient laws dictated that pigs must be held at night in their sties by collars. Pork was a much-prized meat, eaten at feasts and also salted to preserve it. Pigs were fattened on mast in the woodlands and forests and their slaughter began in the autumn. Only the sows and one sire were over-wintered for breeding in the spring.

On the eve that preceded 11th November (the 1st November according to the Julian calendar), the ceremonial slaughtering of a cock took place. Before the bird was boiled and eaten, its blood was sprinkled on the threshold and on the four corners of the house and hearth – a custom which survived until the 20th century in parts of Ireland.

Crops, bread and mills

Leeks, onions, garlic and a kind of cabbage was grown in herb gardens. Watercress, a seaweed known still as *dilisk* and a porridge made of nettles were also eaten. Crops of wheat, barley and rye were cultivated. Beer was made from barley.

The best bread was made from wheat grain. Ground in a quern, the grain could also be eaten as a porridge with milk. Irish mills had eight main components: a source of water to provide power, an upper millstone, a lower millstone, the shaft around which the stones spun, the shaftstone, the mill wheel or paddles, a pivot for the upper millstone, and a hopper for the grain. All the other parts were mounted on a central shaft. The price of a mill was a *cumal* – a female slave whose value was equivalent to three cows.

Fields and tilling

The earliest towns in Ireland were established by the Vikings who introduced the first tilled plots or fields, known as *stangs*. These small fields were oblong so that the plough horses did not have to be turned around too often.

Commercial farming arrived in Ireland with the Norman invasion. Now each manor or parish had three very large fields. One was tilled, the second one kept for pasture and the third left fallow. Rotating their use meant that each field underwent a three-year cycle.

Typical inventory

Inventory of a manor farm, leased by the Earl of Ormond at Donadea (Co. Kildare) in 1396:
  12 draught animals,
  50 acres of wheat
  48 acres of oats
  2 ploughs
In 1404, as well as the three field system, deeds describe meadows, a bridge, an orchard to be fenced in, 14 plough animals, 9 cows, and 7 score of sheep (140).

Rabbits

The descendants of the Anglo-Norman settlers introduced the rabbit and coneywarrens became a feature of the landscape under the manorial system. These proved a valuable asset and rabbit became a very useful addition to the Irish diet.

Monasteries

It was the monasteries, especially the Cistercians, that pioneered commercial farming. The Benedictines, who had spearheaded agricultural methods in Europe, introduced their new systems to Irish monks through their concept of work as a form of prayer. They had 'granges', large out-farms for supplies of grain, and huge herds of sheep. In the early summer, the sheared wool was sold, often to Italian merchants who visited Irish abbeys annually. The Italians were also money-lenders. In 1302, for example, the Abbot of Monasternenagh Abbey in County Limerick, owed a considerable sum to Ricardi of Lucca from the Arno valley.

While the monks worked the monastery lands, they also developed eel and salmon fisheries – and used tenant labour. On certain 'boon days and plough days' each year, labour was given in return for use of the land.

Meanwhile, in those parts of Ireland that remained unconquered, such as mid and western Ulster, the old Gaelic system of agriculture continued to be practised until after 1603.

Planters

Irish agriculture changed dramatically between 1554 and 1660 with the installation of English and Scots planters in certain areas. In Ulster, forests were cleared gradually and the land tilled for the first time ever. In Munster, the Earl of Cork introduced the cultivation of cherry and cider-apple trees. The potato was also introduced to Ireland by planters. Finally, the Cromwellian plantation in 1654 transferred the ownership of most Irish land to the planters. Irish labourers now worked for the new masters but no enclosing of fields took place.

The foundation for modern Irish farming

A new wave of Irish farming began after 1760 with more intensive farming. For the first time a portion of land was given to a tenant who then fenced it and divided it into fields. Butter markets sprang up in city, town and village and the export of cattle expanded. Turnips were grown to feed over-wintering cattle, a significant element of the agrarian revolution – in Ireland, as elsewhere. Growing of wheat increased, especially after 1784 when Corn Laws protected this crop against competition.

Cattle, meat, wheat, linen and butter were transported via rivers to domestic and export markets. Canals built from 1790 to 1830 linked the River Shannon with Dublin and the River Barrow. Towing paths on river banks accommodated boat hauliers who used horse power to pull yawls against the current.

Flax and fairs

In the 18th century flax was cultivated in Ireland, especially in Ulster. This provided the raw material for the linen which was exported and used at home for clothes, domestic articles and sail making.

Fairs in towns, villages and old manorial estates provided opportunities for selling cattle, sheep and pigs. Often cattle had to be driven on the hoof.

Poverty and 'land hunger'

Many landlords built fine Georgian houses but did not develop their tenants' farms or invest money in these. Tenants and labourers lived in mud-walled thatched cabins, generally unfit for human occupation. While they raised cattle and crops to pay heavy rents, these poor people depended on the potato for food. Farmers had to pay rent, an annual sum to the Grand Jury of the county for the care of roads and bridges – and annual tithes to the established Church of Ireland, even though few of them actually belonged to that church.

In the 1770s in Ulster, the farms were often so small that it was hard to eke out a living. In Connacht, especially, farmers lived in dire hovels while the land was largely poor and infertile. By the 19th century, land-seekers settled in areas that had been used for *booleying* in the past. This 'land hunger' led to violence; the high rents created hardship; evictions and feuds between families increased.

Flour mills were being built throughout Ireland in the main grain-growing areas by 1800. The growing of wheat paid the rent. Oats were used to feed the horses and as porridge or small cakes for human consumption. Barley served as animal fodder or was sold to breweries. The potato

was still the staple food for most people.

When the potato crop failed, the Great Famine led to starvation and greatly reduced the number of people working on the land. Small farms were bought by farmers to enlarge their holdings. Meanwhile, cheap imported American grain rendered wheat growing unprofitable so cattle became more important. Many ruined landlords had their land sold by the Encumbered Estates court and most of the new landlords that seized control were interested only in financial gain.

Agricultural machinery and the creameries

The first agricultural machinery arrived during the 1870s. The new hay-cutting machines were strongly opposed by the labourers but this resistance was soon submerged in the struggle of the farmers for a fairer land system and, in due course, their demanding to be sold their farms. From 1885 onwards, a series of Acts of Parliament enabled the farmers to buy the land with money advanced by the British government, these sums to be re-paid by yearly instalments (land annuities). The Labourers' Cottage Act of 1881 meant that farm labourers were properly housed at last – often in better homes than the poorer farmers.

At the turn of the 19th and 20th centuries, creameries were built to encourage milk production and butter-making. Proprietary creameries were followed by the co-operative creamery movement which stimulated the development of dairy farming and operated shops where seeds, farm implements, groceries and clothes were sold at a fair price. Finally free of landlord oppression, farmers became shareholders in the 'co-op' venture.

The twentieth century

New machinery was now being used on the land. Horse-pulled reaper-and-binder machines for corn appeared in the 1930s on many farms.

In 1932 De Valera's government refused to pay the land annuities to the British government and an embargo on Irish cattle was declared. Six years of great

Mechanical harrowing, County Down

hardship hit the southern Irish farmers who remained in great economic difficulties until 1938 when the matter was settled by a treaty between the governments.

In contrast, the Second World War proved a time of great prosperity as cattle, sheep, pigs, butter and tinned milk were exported to England. After the war, the mechanisation of Irish farming continued with the use of tractors on the farms. Soon the first combine harvesters were used – and then the reaper-and-binders. The need for farm labour was reduced and many young people sought employment in towns or emigrated to England.

The old fairs were replaced by cattle marts. The only fairs to survive were the annual fairs for the sale of horses at the Cahirmee in Co. Cork and in Ballinasloe. The Lammas fair in Co. Antrim is also still held each year.

Finally, Ireland joined the EEC. Farmers were supported with grants, the small creameries were amalgamated and farms were consolidated. Smallholdings vanished as more houses were built around cities, towns and villages. A new and more prosperous way of life was being established.

Hay making in sight of the Mourne mountains County Down

The wit and wisdom of the Irish

A hungry ass keeps his kicking end down

Keep your house and your house will keep you

Folk Wisdom

Life and death

In youth we have our troubles before us; in age we leave pleasure behind.

Twenty years a growing
twenty years at rest
twenty years declining
and twenty years when it doesn't
matter whether you're there or not.

Young people don't know what age is, and old people forget what youth was.

When the twig hardens, it is difficult to twist it.

Whiskey when you're sick makes you well; whiskey when you're well makes you sick.

The herb that can't be got is the one that brings relief.

To die and to lose one's life are much the same thing.

Death does not take a bribe.

There's always one more son of a bitch than you counted on.

Money matters

A shamefaced man seldom acquires wealth.

The doorstep of a great house is slippery.

A heavy purse makes a light heart.

Poverty parts good company.

It's hard to take britches off bare hips.

Poverty is no shame, but shame is ever a part of poverty.

The moneymaker is never tired.

It's no use carrying an umbrella if your shoes are leaking.

Forgetting a debt does not pay it.

Friendship

Tell me who your friends are and I'll tell you who you are.

Pick your company before you sit down.

A friend that can be bought is not worth buying.

A little help is better than a lot of pity.

Don't show your skin to the person who won't cover it.

Two persons never lit a fire without disagreeing.

Promising but not fulfilling is worse than refusing.

A constant guest is never welcome.

Animals

Every cat is gray at night.

It's not easy to put pants on a cat.

A calf's skin often goes to market before his mother's.

In winter the milk goes to the cow's horns.

One cow breaks the fence, and a dozen leap it.

Better an ass that carries you than a horse that throws you.

A hungry ass keeps his kicking end down.

A dead dog won't bark.

A well-trained dog goes out when he knows he's about to be thrown out.

If you lie down with dogs, you'll rise with fleas.

In spite of the fox's cunning, his skin is often sold.

A nod is as good as a wink to a blind horse.

Many a shabby colt makes a fine horse.

A mouse is bold under a haystack.

The cocks crow but the hens lay the eggs.

A turkey never voted for an early Christmas.

Dry shoes won't get fish.

A fly is of little account until it gets into the eye.

Every little frog is great in its own bog.

You can't pluck a frog.

Wisdom and luck

A wise head keeps a shut mouth.

Better knowledge of evil than evil without knowledge.

No fools are so intolerable as those who effect to be wits.

He's a fool who'll not take advice – but he's a thousand times worse who takes every advice.

A scholar's ink last longer than a martyr's blood.

The man who has luck in the morning has luck in the afternoon.

Fortune is a good thing, but it's worth searching for it.

White collars sometimes hide dirty necks.

It is afterwards events are understood.

The river is no wider from one side than the other.

Men, Women and Children

A bad woman knows a foolish man's faults.

Woman was God's second mistake.

Irish women have a dispensation from the Pope to wear the thick ends of their legs downwards.

There are three kinds of men who fail to understand women – young men, old men, and middle-aged men.

An excuse is nearer to a woman than her apron.

A man without a woman is like a neck without a pain.

If you marry at all, marry last year.

The shoemaker's wife and the smith's mare often go barefoot.

Marriages are all happy; it's having breakfast together that causes all the problems.

Irish sexual compatibility is when a husband and his wife both have headaches on the same night.

It isn't a man's clothes that tell how much he earns, but his wife's.

The day you marry your wife, you marry your children.

A light-heeled mother makes a leaden-heeled daughter.

Sex is the only game that becomes less exciting when played for money.

Home and food

Dirty hands make a clean hearth.

A new broom sweeps clean but an old one knows the dirty corners best.

It is easier to demolish a house than to build one.

The old pipe gives the sweetest smoke.

Keep your house and your house will keep you.

Hunger is a good sauce.

He's first at the pot and last at the work.

You can't eat soup with a fork.

A trout in the pot is better than a salmon in the sea.

Wine drowns more men than water.

Drink is the curse of the land. It makes you fight with your neighbour, it makes you shoot at your landlord – and it makes you miss.

Thirst begets thirst.

It's only good to be hungry when you have something to eat.

A narrow neck keeps the bottle from being emptied in one swig.

Work

You'll never plough a field by turning it over in your mind.

Handfuls make a load.

Two never prospered on the same hill.

Making the beginning is one third of the work.

Industry pays debts.

It destroys the craft not to learn it.

Samuel Beckett 1906-1989

Waiting for Godot
We'll always find something, eh, Dido, to give us the impression that we exist?

Malone dies
If I had the use of my body, I would throw it out of the window.

Oliver Goldsmith 1730-1734

Essays: The use of language
The true use of speech is not so much to express our wants as to conceal them.

She Stoops to Conquer
Women and music should never be dated.

George Bernard Shaw 1856-1950

Education
He who can, does. He who cannot teaches.

Marriage
Marriage is popular because it combines the maximum of temptation with the maximum of opportunity.

The Philanderer
The fickleness of the women I love is only equalled by the infernal constancy of the women who love me.

The Rejected Statement
Assassination is the exreme form of censorship.

Annjanska
All great truths begin as blasphemies.

Everybody's Political What's What
Paretage is a very important profession; but no test of fitness for it is ever imposed in the interest of children.

Man and Superman
There are two tragedies in life. One is not to get your hearts's desire. The other is to get it.

Maxims for Revolutionists

Do not do unto others as you would they should do unto you. Their tastes may not be the same.

The Golden Rule is that there are no golden rules.

Richard Brinsley Sheridan 1751-1816

The Rivals
Tis safest in matrimony to begin with a little aversion.

The Perfect Hostess
Won't you come into the garden? I should like my roses to see you.

School for Scandal
Tale bearers are a bad as the tale-makers.

The Critic
If it is abuse – why one is always sure to hear of it by one damned good-natured friend or other!

Jonathan Swift 1667-1745

The Battle of the Books
Satire is a sort of glass, wherein beholders do generally discover everybody's face but their own.

Thoughts on various subjects
Every man desires to live long; but no man would be old.

A Critical Essay upon the Faculties of the Mind.

There is nothing in this world constant but inconstancy.

Laws are like cobwebs, which may catch small flies, but let wasps and hornets break through.

On Poetry

So, naturalists observe, a flea
Hath smaller fleas that on him prey;
And these have smaller fleas to bite 'em,
And so proceed, ad infinitum.
Thus every poet, in his kind,
Is bit by him that comes behind.

Journal to Stella
Tis very warm weather when one's in bed.

Oscar Wilde 1854-1900

Work is the curse of the drinking classes.

Youth is wasted on the young.

The Importance of Being Earnest

Really, if the lower orders don't set us a good example, what on earth is the use of them?

It is very vulgar to talk like a dentist, when one isn't a dentist. It produces a false impression.

On an occasion of this kind, it becomes more than a moral duty to speak one's mind. It becomes a pleasure.

The truth is rarely pure, and never simple.

To lose one parent, Mr Worthing, may be regarded as a misfortune; to lose both looks like carelessness.

All women become like their mothers. That is their tragedy. No man does. That's his.

Never speak disrespectfully of Society . . . Only people who can't get into it do that.

Lady Windermere's Fan

Many a woman has a past, but I am told that she has at least a dozen, and that they all fit.

I can resist everything except temptation.

We are all in the gutter, but some of us are looking at the stars.

The Picture of Dorian Gray

A man cannot be too careful in the choice of his enemies.

It is better to be beautiful than to be good. But . . . it is better to be good than to be ugly.

Anyone can be good in the country.

There is only one thing worse than being talked about, and that is not being talked about.

Sebastian Melmoth and Oscariana
A thing is not necessarily true because a man dies for it.

The Ballad of Reading Gaol
Yet each man kills the thing he loves,
By each let this be heard,
Some do it with a bitter look,
Some with a flattering word,
The coward does it with a kiss,
The brave man with a sword!

Sixteen Self Sketches
He hasn't an enemy in the world, and none of his friends like him.
[on Bernard Shaw]

The Critic as Artist, Part 2

Ah! Don't say that you agree with me. When people agree with me I always feel that I must be wrong.

As long as war is regarded as wicked, it will always have its fascination. When it is looked upon as vulgar, it will cease to be popular.

A little sincerity is a dangerous thing, and a great deal of it is absolutely fatal.

The Soul of Man under Socialism
Democracy means simply the bludgeoning of the people by the people for the people.

A Woman of No Importance
They say . . . that when good Americans die they go to Paris.

Indeed? And when bad Americans die, where do they go to?

Oh, they go to America.

The English country gentleman galloping after a fox – the unspeakable in full pursuit of the uneatable.

Children begin by loving their parents; after a time they judge them; rarely, if ever, do they forgive them.

One should never trust a woman who tells one her real age. A woman who would tell one that, would tell one anything.

Spoken at the New York Custom House
I have nothing to declare except my genius.

Definition of a cynic
A man who knows the price of everything and the value of nothing.

The Decay of Lying
Art never expresses anything but itself.

You'll never plough a field by turning it over in your mind

Youth is wasted on the young

Irish Literature

15th-17th century

In the 15th century there were two strands of literature cultivated in Ireland. One was Gaelic and this was almost exclusively poetry. The other was in English and only a few poems survive from these writings.

The Gaelic poets were heirs of a tradition that had its roots in antiquity and were members of a class that was trained to write poetry in sophisticated metres for patrons. Their poems generally lack lyric quality or passion. It was formal and written to please and flatter patrons. When the Gaelic social and political system collapsed after 1603, this kind of poetry ceased forever.

It was succeeded by a new kind of poetry – one which rang true. Passion and political and social comment arise from its verses, which the new landed gentry no longer rewarded. A whimsical stanza in a poem in translation, expresses:

> *We've received the very worst*
> *But we refuse to be sad;*
> *Since we lack no misfortune,*
> *Let's make ourselves glad!*

Egan O'Rahilly

The last Gaelic poet of real merit was Egan O'Rahilly of Kerry who died circa 1728. He was a cultivated man, who saw the total collapse of his culture confirmed. There was none like him ever again. What was probably his last poem, in translation, has this final stanza:

> *Soon I will be no more*
> *and death is near to me.*
> *Since Munster's warriors*
> *have all been slain;*
> *I'll go to my grave*
> *without these heroes' love,*
> *These princes who ruled my kin*
> *before Christ died*

Brian Merriman

After O'Rahilly's death Gaelic poetry consisted of ballads with the exception of a long and extraordinary erotic poem, *The Midnight Court*, by Brian Merriman (*circa*. 1747-1805). There was no development of the novel or drama in Gaelic. Those who spoke the language were swamped by war and loss of every kind until 1700 and oppressed and impoverished afterwards until the 19th century.

Irish literature in English

Irish literature in English of real worth began with the work of Dean Jonathan Swift, who was born in Ireland 1667 and died in 1745. His best work is satirical, as in *Gulliver's Travels* and much contains savage satire. Although he was a Protestant clergyman in Ireland, he satirised the government's neglect of the poor and the oppression of Catholics.

His work ensured that he was not appointed a bishop nor to any political

William Carleton 1794-1869

office. His attitude towards many people can be summarised in the words:

> *For Gulliver divinely shews*
> *That humankind are all Yahoos.*

Maria Edgeworth

Maria Edgeworth, daughter of a County Longford landlord, was born in 1767 and died in 1849. Her novel, *Castle Rackrent*, appeared in 1800. In the words of a retainer, the story of a landlord family is told. It uncovers the oppressive Irish land system of the time. This novel is the first regional novel in English, a genre which was used later by Walter Scott. Maria Edgeworth is known as a writer on education but on this book her fame rests.

William Carleton

William Carleton was the first writer from among the people to write of them in a realistic manner in English. In his five-volume work, *Traits and Stories of the Irish Peasantry*, he portrays the joys, sorrows and wild ebullience of the common Catholic people. These were published from 1830 to 1833. He had become a Protestant, which was considered an act of betrayal by his former co-religionists. However, in his novel, *Valentine M'Chutchy*, he painted a most unflattering picture of a Protestant minister.

The Nation

In 1842 when the English language was the dominant speech east of a line from Derry to Cork city, *The Nation* newspaper was founded. This promoted nationalism, political and artistic, and also the Gaelic language although all the articles were in English. *The Nation* published patriotic ballads and translations from Gaelic poetry. transferring as much of Gaelic literature and tradition into English as it could. The founders, Thomas Blake Dillon, Thomas Davis and Charles Gavan Duffy became known as the Young Irelanders.

Davis in his short life (1814-1845)

wished to create a literature which disregarded England and was centred on Ireland alone. He wished to unite Ireland in this endeavour and encouraged Irish Protestants to join the movement.

James Clarence Mangan's poems appeared in *The Nation*. These were original poems, translations from Gaelic and from the German poets Ruckert, Heine and Goethe. His poem *Dark Rosaleen* was a Romantic expression of Ireland, which symbolised in some sense the Ireland of the Young Irelanders' dreams. Most of *The Nation* writers had died or had been transported out of Ireland after 1850.

Irish novels

Between 1850 and 1885 four types of Irish novel expressed their artistic Irelands in contrasting ways. There was the melodramatic novel, which presented a full-blooded and grotesque characte, often described as the stage Irishman. The first appearance of this character in a novel was in the works of Charles Lever and Charles Lover before the Great Famine (1845-7). Lover's *Handy Andy* introduced an amusing caricature of the rural Irish Catholic who served his landlord master. This was the predecessor of Dion Lardner Boucicault's work, *The Shaughraun* in 1875. They all spoke a form of English, based on the English spoken in Ireland then.

The other type of novel was based on the daily life of people in rural Ireland but narrated soberly and quietly. *Knocknagow or the Homes of Tipperary* by Charles J. Kickham and published in 1879 is the best example of this. Like Dickens' work, this novel appeared as a newspaper serial and it seems that Kickham wished to do for rural Ireland what Dickens had done for urban England.

The third type of novel is seen in Standish James O'Grady's *History of Ireland – Heroic Period*, published in 1879. O'Grady used the old Gaelic tales which the Gaelic scholar, John O'Donovan, published to describe an heroic Ireland. It was not 'real' history, of course, but it stirred the imagination of many Irish writers.

The fourth type of novel stands alone in Irish literature because it did not have a successor. This was the work of Bram Stoker (1842-1912), whose novel about the Transylvanian vampire, *Dracula*, appeared in 1897.

The Irish Literary revival and The Abbey Theatre

Poems and ballads of Young Ireland was published in Dublin in 1885. Containing a selection of works by the rising generation of poets, it heralded the Irish Literary revival, which was the first coming to maturity of Irish literature in the English language with W. B. Yeats one of the poets. The poetic movement merged into drama in the first years of the 20th century. Lady Gregory of County Galway and W. B. Yeats with Edward Martyn and others founded a national theatre in Dublin, the Abbey Theatre. The new Irish Literary revival was less a revival than the birth of a new sense of nationalism expressed in English.

While Yeats looked into the heroic world evoked by Standish James O'Grady, Lady Gregory based her drama on the lives of the humblest people in Irish rural society. Then John Millington Synge wrote plays for the Abbey, which were anchored on Irish rural society, such as *Riders to the Sea* and *Playboy of the Western World*. Synge gave his characters a form of English, whose syntax and imagery imitated Gaelic. In Synge's work there was something quite new and distinctive but Yeats and others detested the English of the characters in the books of Lover, Lever and Boucicault.

The new Irish literature owed much to Dr. Douglas Hyde's translations of Gaelic poems from Connacht. They were *Love-Songs of Connacht* (1893), *Religious Songs of Connacht* (1903), and *Songs Ascribed to Raftery* (1906). The translations presented the simple and direct language of the writers. Yeats used them for turns of phrase in his poems. The first and last of these books influenced the new poets, while the second one was more or less neglected. They were invaluable for poets, above all others, who sought a distinctive form of English to suit the new poetry.

Joseph Campbell was a Belfastman wrote poetry on religious topics and collected and set to music Ulster folk songs. He also celebrated the beauty of County Wicklow in delicate lyrics.

Canon Sheehan

The works of Canon Sheehan (1852-1913) began in 1899 with *My New Curate* in 1899. He wrote five novels in all and was the only Irish novelist then. He presented a benevolent picture of the Irish priest in the countryside. The power and authority, which were wielded by the priests in Ireland then, is scarcely hinted at. His books were very popular and filled a niche in Irish writing.

Oscar Wilde

Oscar Fingal O'Flahertie Wills Wilde was born in Dublin on 16 October 1854. His first real success was *The Happy Prince and Other Tales* (1888), a collection of fairy stories. It was followed by *Lord Arthur Savile's Crime and Other Stories* (1891) and *A House of Pomegranates* (1892). Wilde's only novel, *The Picture of Dorian Gray* was published in 189). In the following year

Lady Windermere's Fan (1892) showed his prowess as a playwright and soon Wilde wrote three more comedies, *A Woman of No Importance* (1893), *An Ideal Husband* (1895) and *The Importance of Being Earnest* (1895), making him the most popular playwright in London. In May 1895 Wilde was sentenced to two years' hard labour because of his homosexual offences. His prison experiences inspired *The Ballad of Reading Gaol* (1905).

Irish drama movement

The modern Irish drama movement began with the Irish Literary Theatre. This was founded by W. B. Yeats, Lady Augusta Gregory, George Moore and Edward Martyn. In 1889 they had their first production of the *Heather Field* by Edward Martyn. The Irish Literary Theatre was followed by the National Theatre Society, which became known as the Abbey Theatre. This produced W. B. Yeats' *Cathleen ní Houlihan* and G. W. Russell's *Deirdre* in 1902. 'AE' (this was Russell's pen-name) was a great influence on the young poets of his time and was a painter and mystic, as well as an author.

Augusta, Lady Gregory made her house at Coole Park near Gort in Co. Galway, a place where playwrights and poets came together. The 20th century Irish Literary movement was to a large extent directed and inspired from that house. She wished to give the Irish people a literature based on the old heroic tales and the Gaelic peasant culture. The Irish theatre movement was nurtured in a special way from her house. She wrote some short plays of worth. After her death in 1932 the house and grounds were acquired by the Irish State Forestry Department which demolished this historic house.

The Playboy of the Western World by the playwright, John Millington Synge, was produced at the Abbey Theatre in 1907. Its distinctive Anglo-Irish dialect is characteristic of Synge's plays. The audience, taking offence at certian perceived slurs at Catholicism, rioted. It took five hundred policemen to control the angry crowd.

George Moore

George Moore of a County Mayo landlord family came to Ireland in the early years of the Irish Literary revival. His already-published novels were hardly in any Irish literary tradition but now he issued a collection of short stories, which were translated into Gaelic to guide the new writers of the Gaelic revival. When he left Ireland, he wrote *Hail and Farewell* in three volumes from 1911 to 1914. The material is based on fact and the characters include W. B. Yeats, Lady Gregory, Douglas Hyde and the writers of the Irish Literary Revival. Later on in England his *Storytellers' Holiday* was published, which is based on the history of the Gaelic ascetic movement, the Culdees. When it came to Irish affairs, Moore was a biting satirist.

Poetry

The greatest poetry of W. B. Yeats was pub-

lished between 1916 and the 1930s. From 1921 onwards Austin Clarke published poetry which drew on the old Irish sagas. In his poetry he harked back to Early Christian Ireland and he moved on to satirising modern Irish Catholicism. He offered criticism, which was not expected nor much appreciated. Already in 1918 Brinsley McNamara's work, *The Valley of the Squinting Windows*, had portrayed a country village where local gossip drove one person to commit suicide and the other to flight from the unChristain society where the Catholic church ruled.

World War I

World War I took its toll of Irish writers. In 1916 three literary men were executed as leaders of the Easter rebellion that was put down by the British Army. They were P. H. Pearse, Joseph M. Plunkett and Thomas McDonagh, all of them poets. McDonagh's book, *Literature in Ireland*, on the Gaelic influence on Anglo-Irish literature, was published posthumously. Fighting with the British Army Tom Kettle was killed at the Somme 1916 and in 1917 Francis Ledwidge, the sweet pastoral poet of Ireland, fell in action at Ypres.

Austin Clarke

In Ireland in 1917 the work of a new poet, Austin Clarke, appeared when his narrative poem, *The Vengeance of Fionn*, was published. He dipped into the Finn story-cycle for his inspiration and he used Gaelic storytelling in later works. In 1925 his work, *The Cattle-Drive of Connaught and Other Poems* was published when he went this time to the Ulster Sagas for inspiration. In 1929 he had a further volume of poems published, *The Pilgrimage*.

W. B. Yeats

In 1919 *The Wild Swans at Coole*, poems by W. B. Yeats, were published – followed by *Michael Robartes and the Dancer* in 1921. His book of poems, *The Tower* was also published in 1925. His later works were: *The Winding Stair and Other Poems* (1933), *A Full Moon in March* (1935) and in 1936-9 *Last Poems*. The last two volumes show Yeats as the greatest Irish poet that had so far written in English.

W. B. Yeats died at Roquebrune in France in 1939. In 1947 his remains were brought back to Ireland in a corvette and buried in Drumcliff cemetery in Co. Sligo.

James Joyce

One of the greatest world novelists was James Joyce (1882-1941), a Dublin man who fled with his friend, Nora Barnacle, to Trieste before World War I. He had published some works in Ireland but wanted to escape the narrow society in which he grew up. In 1916 his *Portrait of the Artist as a Young Man* was published. This work, built around the character of Stephen Dedalus, was viewed variously in Ireland but H. G. Wells considered Joyce from the beginning as a major writer. Already his short stories, *Dubliners*, had appeared in 1914 in which he depicted Dublin as 'the centre of paralysis'.

The great literary event of the 1920s was the publication of James Joyce's *Ulysses* in Paris. This was based on the voyage of Ulysses and each of the eighteen episodes of the voyage provides a basis for a literary episode with every one exploring another facet of the human experience. Many claim it to be the leading novel in English of the 19th century in which the furthest limits in the use of the English language are explored

It followed a journey through Dublin in one day and is the compendium of styles and views that makes it a summation of the English literary experience. Joyce expressed a male human being in the duality of the young Dedalus and the mature Leopold Bloom. This literary evocation of a man, young as Stephen Dedalus, middle-aged as Leopold Bloom, is set against a Dublin background on a June day. The language is treated in an ordinary manner at times; at other moments it is a mosaic of shattered human expression in words.

Joyce's final work was *Finnegan's Wake*, which was published in full in 1939. In this extraordinary work the English language is sometimes pushed beyond its limits as a mode of expression. James Joyce died two years later in Zurich – where he had fled from Paris at the German occupation and where he is buried. He is still regarded as one of the greatest novelists in the English language.

Right
James Joyce
1882-1941

Centre
George Bernard Shaw
1856-1950

Seán O'Casey

Between 1923 and 1926 the plays of Seán O'Casey, T*he Shadow of a Gunman, Juno and the Paycock* and *The Plough and the Stars*, appeared on the Abbey stage. The plot in each case was based on the warfare from 1916 to 1923. The plays are sited in the slums of Dublin. O'Casey evoked the poor of Dublin, the heroic strength of women and the sham strength of men. *The Shadow of a Gunman* portrayed the rawness of life in the Dublin slums during the years of the national revolution. It was in stark contrast to the heroic dreamland of the Abbey stage which someone called 'Swinging claymores in the Celtic twilight'. This was followed in 1924 by *Juno and the Paycock*. This was so successful that it helped to restore the severe financial situation of the theatre. This situation was further eased by the first annual grant by the

Irish Free State to the Abbey. An annual subsidy has been paid to it by the government ever since. The last play of Seán O'Casey's trilogy, *The Plough and the Stars* was produced in the Abbey Theatre in 1926. This production caused great disturbance in the theatre. People saw an unflattering aspect of themselves. They protested in a riot against what was seen as dishonour being shown to the flag. It was an occasion reminiscent of the riots against Synge's *Playboy of the Western World* in 1907. This was the last play of O'Casey's that was produced at the Abbey. He lived henceforth in England.

George Bernard Shaw

In 1925 George Bernard Shaw received the Nobel Prize for literature. Born in Dublin, Shaw was an Irishman who went to live in London in 1896 at 20 years old. Dramatist, debater, critic and novelist, his plays combine comedy and wit with political and philosophical issues. They include *Arms and the Man* (1894), *Devil's Disciple* (1897), *Man and Superman* (1905), *Pygmalian* (1913) and S*aint Joan* (1924).

Daniel Corkery.

An exploration of the part played by Gaelic culture in the 18th century was the theme of *The Hidden Ireland* by Daniel Corkery. He showed how this hidden element had progressed Ireland's artistic development, bringing the exploration of the subject of McDonagh's *Literature in Ireland* (1916) one step further.

The Gate Theatre

The foundation of a new theatre in Dublin, the Gate Theatre, by Mícheál MacLimmeir, Hilton Edwards, Coralie Carmichael, Geareid O Lochlainn and Madame Bannard Cogley took place in 1925. Here the plays of Paul Vincent Carroll and T. C. Murray were introduced for the first time.

The plays were staged in the Peacock. The object of the Gate Theatre was to create an image of Ireland other than that of 'the cottage and the tenement'. The first play was a production of Ibsen's *Peer Gynt*. An Taibhdherac, a Gaelic theatre, was founded in Galway where it was directed by Mícheál MacLimmeir for three years.

In 1929 *The Old Lady Says No!*, a work

by a major new playwright, Denis Johnston, was produced at the Gate Theatre: His next play, *The Moon of the Yellow River* was performed at the Gate in 1931. The Gate Theatre had moved to new premises in 1930 in the Rotunda, Parnell Street, where Goethe's *Faust* was produced. The theatre company went on tour to England, Malta, Greece, Egypt, Bulgaria and Yugoslavia between 1935 and 1939.

A new theatre company, Longford Productions, was established in 1936 by Lord Longford. It staged its plays sharing the theatre premises with the Gate Theatre.

Paul Vincent Carroll

The Abbey Theatre had to wait until 1930 for its first production of a play by Paul Vincent Carroll: *The Watched Pot* was produced in that year. In 1932 *Things that are Caesar's* was very successful and was in due course staged in USA and London, too. In 1937 Paul Vincent Carroll's best play *Shadow and Substance* was perfomed at the Abbey Theatre. The theme of the play was how a cultured canon abused the power he had over the local teacher.

Frank O'Connor and Seán O Faoláin

Guests of the Nation, a first collection of short stories was published in 1931, the first volume by a talented writer from Cork, Frank O'Connor (the pen-name of Michael O'Donovan). Leading Irish short story writer of his time, O'Connor cultivated 'an outward looking provincialism'. In 1936 and 1944 other volumes appeared and in 1937 he wrote *The Big Fellow*, a biography of Michael Collins.

Seán O Faoláin's collection of short stories *Midsummer's Madness* was published in 1932 and many more followed. He and Frank O'Connor were the greatest Irish short story writers of their time. As well as short stories O Faoláin also wrote *The Great O'Neill, the Earl of Tyrone* in 1942 and *The King of the Beggars, Daniel O'Connell* in 1938.

Francis McManus

Francis McManus wrote three novels, *Stand and Give Challenge, Candle for the Proud* and *Men Withering* in the 1933-39 era. They are the artistic expression of the 'hidden Ireland' that Daniel Corkery wrote about in his 1925 book. He describes the life of an 18th-century poet-schoolmaster who was a 'poor scholar' that lived and loved in these miserable times.

Brian McMahon

The short-story writer and playwright, Brian McMahon of Listowel, County Kerry, was born in 1909 but lived until the end of the century. He drew on the tradition of the people in his native area for his themes. His first play, *The Bugle in the Blood,* produced in the Abbey in 1949, was followed by *The Song of the Anvil* in 1960 and *The Honey Spike* in 1961. His novel, *Children of the Rainbow* was published in 1952 and republished in the USA and Canada. McMahon continued an old tradition of publishing and printing ballad sheets, the old way of propagating newly written and old ballads in the Irish countryside.

Flann O'Brien

At Swim-Two-Birds by Flann O'Brien (the pen-name of Brian O'Nolan) was published in 1939. This is a fantasia of Gaelic literature and folklore interwoven with Dublin life, a great work of literature. It was 1961 before *The Hard Life* was published and in 1965 *The Dalkey Archives*. After his death in 1966 *The Third Policeman* was published the following year. His novels are a blend of mordant humour and satire on the human condition. He also wrote a satirical work on the Ireland of his time, *An Beal Bocht*, that has been translated as *The Poor Mouth*.

The book-censor

In 1942 *The Tailor and Anstey*, a racy account of Irish rural life by Eric Cross, was banned without just cause as obscene by the book-censor. Since 1929 the censor of publications had banned all literary work that contained even the suggestion of bawdiness – no matter how worthwhile it was. This book was a very good example of the wanton prudishness of the Irish censorship system. As Austin Clarke taunted: 'Burn Ovid with the rest!'

Patrick Kavanagh

Patrick Kavanagh's long poem, *The Great Hunger*, was published in 1942. This expressed the hunger for human emotional fulfilment of a bachelor farmer who lived for his mother, his farm and local recognition. His rural background is that of his volumes of poems, which began with *The Ploughman and other poems* in 1936. His collected poems were published in 1964. Kavanagh had two novels published *The Green Fool* and *Tarry O'Flynn*.

Walter Macken

Walter Macken an Abbey actor, returned to his native Galway to manage the Taidhbhearc theatre. He had these novels published: *Quench the Moon* (1948), *I am alone* (1949), *Rain on the Wind* in 1950, *Sunset on the Window Panes* in 1954, *Seek the Fair Land* (1959), *The Silent People* (1962) and *The Scorching Wind* in 1964. He also was a talented playwright, whose fine play *Home is the Hero* was performed in 1953.

Samuel Beckett

Samuel Beckett, a native of Dublin, went to live in France in 1932, as Joyce did, and became friendly with him. Here he wrote mostly in French. His dramatic works in English have had a great influence on European drama. His work, *Waiting for Godot* in 1952 has earned him much praise and fame.

Thomas Kinsella

Thomas Kinsella is one of the better Irish poets of the second half of the 20th century. His poetic works include *The Starlit Eye* (1952), *Another September* (1958) and *Downstream* in 1962. He also composed an English poetic narration of the *Cattle-*. In 1972 he published a long poem on the Bloody Sunday massacre in Derry entitled *Butcher's Dozen: A Lesson for the Octave of*

Widgery written in rhyming couplets.

The Irish Theatre festival

The Irish Theatre festival had its first successful year in 1956. However, in 1958 there were objections and protests in certain quarters when Seán O'Casey's *The Drums of Father Ned* and the Pike Theatre's *Rose Tattoo* were performed at the Theatre Festival. The festival collapsed when Bord Féilte withdrew support. Seán O'Casey and Samuel Beckett refused to have their plays performed in Ireland henceforth. After some time the festival was revived and is nowadays a successful annual event.

John B. Keane

In 1959 the play *Sive*, written by John B. Keane of Listowel, Co. Kerry was first produced. It was an immediate success and led to much controversy. Here was the raw life of rural society revealed on the stage. Keane's next play, *Sharon's Grave* was produced in 1960 and in the years afterwards there were some memorable plays, such as *The Highest House on the Mountain, Many a Young Man of Twenty* in 1961, *The Year of the Hiker* in 1963, and above all *The Field* in 1965: this powerful play was an expression of the land hunger, which could lead to murder.

His novel, *Durango*, was published in 1992. Keane's themes are from the Kerry countryside where he was born and lived.

Edna O'Brien

In 1960 Edna O'Brien's first novel, *The Country Girls*, was published in London. Her evocation of life in rural Catholic Ireland caused many of her novels to be banned by the censor. She also wrote *The Lonely Girl* in 1962, later known as *The Girl with the Green Eyes*. *Girls in their Married Bliss* came in 1964, and *August is a Wicked Month* in 1965. Many of her compatriots had to wait for the banning of her works to be lifted before they could read them. There was, of course, surreptitious smuggling of such books all the time.

WAITING FOR GODOT
SAMUEL BECKETT

John McGahern

John McGahern's first novel *The Barracks*,

published in 1963, won both the AE Memorial Award and a MacCauley Fellowship. *The Dark* in 1865 aroused the anger and condemnation of the Catholic clergy because of how he dealt adolescent sexual experiences and clerical celibacy. This provoked the censor to ban his book. His marriage in a registry office in that year also led to his dismissal from his National School teaching post. Other works are *Nightlines* 1970, *The Leave-Taking* in 1974 and *Among Women* in 1991.

Brian Friel

Brian Friel, the playwright, was born in Omagh, Co. Tyrone, in 1929. The first of his three great plays are *Philadelphia Here I come* in 1964 with the theme of emigration to the USA at its centre. In 1980 *Translations* appeared. The rural Ireland of the early 19th century when the Ordnance Survey mapped and authoritatively named the towns and townlands of Ireland is at the centre of this play. His third and greatest play is *Dancing at Lughnasa* in 1991. This was filmed a few years later.

A new dawn in writing

Three literary men expressed in their work the change from the old to the new Ireland in their mordant criticism of the country where they lived. The high ideals of the revolution were seen to have failed. Patrick Kavanagh (1904-1967) the poet and novelist, Brendan Behan the dramatist (1923-1964) and Brian O'Nolan (1911-1966, novelist and Gaelic scholar, all wrote with bitter humour about Ireland, which had turned in upon itself culturally. None of their books were banned.

The new dawn in writing was underlined by the work of Edna O'Brien of County Clare and her frank portrayal of the Irish countryside girls.

In 1963 John McGahern's first novel, *The Barracks*, was published and the myth of pastoral innocence was torn from the image of Irish country life. Sexual matters were introduced where appropriate and, like Edna O'Brien's works, his books were banned. They had a similar fresh and frank air about them but were also introspective.

The banning of these books helped those who sought the easing of book banning. It was seen as unjust and a brake upon cultural development.

Gaelic revival

The attempt to revive the Gaelic language was to prove a daunting task in the 20th century. There was no developed literary form in the language.

The short story was developed first. The translation of the *Untilled Field* by George Moore provided a model for new writers. Various novels were written but none reached any real standard of excellence. Then in 1949 *Cré na Cille* (The Cemetery Clay) by Máirtín Ó Cadhaín was published. At last a major novel had emerged. ÓCadhaín's volumes of short stories had already appeared but the Irish Press serialised *Cré na Cille* and then it appeared in book form. It presents the

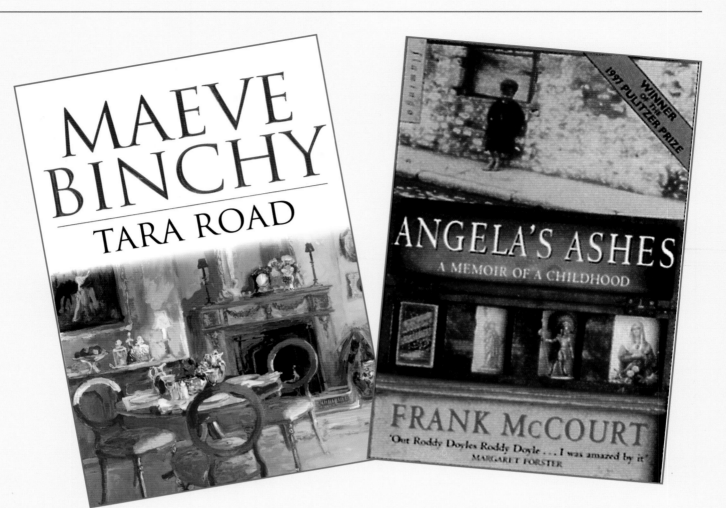

WINNER OF THE 1997 PULITZER PRIZE

Books by two of today's best known Irish authors

dead people of the parish as a community awaiting the next death for news of their village. Thus a whole community is presented through the eyes of the death. Ó Cadháin used the dialect of his native village in Connamara for this unusual work.

*Centre
Séamus Heaney
1939-*

David Hanly

An interesting novel, *In Guilt and Glory*, by David Hanly, was published in 1979. The plot is based on a journey through part of Ireland made by some Irish people who were guiding an American film crew. The Ireland which had grown up and developed in the Republic since 1916 is discussed. For example, one character says, 'Inhibitions are the root and glory of civilisations and I love inhibitions'.

Brendan Behan

Brendan Behan achieved fame in 1956 when his play, *The Quare Fellow*, was produced in London. *The Hostage* confirmed his position as a major Irish dramatist. His autobiography, *The Borstal Boy*, was published in 1958. Posthumous works were *New York* and *The Confessions of an Irish Rebel*. Behan was a native of Dublin city.

Séamus Heaney

Séamus Heaney is a great twentieth-century Irish poet. Born in 1939 in County Derry, his first volume was *Death of a Naturalist* in 1966, and among the others were *North* in 1979, *Station Island* in 1984 and *The Spirit Level* in 1996. In 1995 he was awarded the Nobel Prize for Literature, the third

Irish writer to win it. The first to win this award was W. B. Yeats (1923) and the second Samuel Beckett (1969).

New novelists

The last quarter of the 20th century have seen the rise of many novelists whose works have appealed to the public. Among the more successful of these have been Maeve Binchy who achieved her first success with *Light a Penny Candle*, Patricia Scanlan and Frank McCourt, whose *Angela's Ashes* and *'Tis* have both been extraordinarily successful.

In 1987 *The Commitments* by a Dublin teacher, Roddy Doyle, was published. *The Snapper* (1990) and *The Van* (1991) followed this. His fourth novel,

Paddy Clarke Clarke Ha Ha (1993), won the Booker Prize.

All his novels, but especially the first three, are an evocation of Barrytown, the Dublin suburb that he created. The characters are working class and the modes of expression in each are honestly crude. *The Van* follows the struggle of a man to make an independent living in spite of local difficulties and officialdom while *The Snapper* is a celebration of life, when a teenage girl becomes pregnant and is supported by all her family in spite of local prejudices.

Just a few of the famous Irish authors

Allingham, William	1824-1889
Banim, John	1798-1842
Banim, Michael	1796-1874
Barrington, Sir Jonah	1760-1834
Beckett, Samuel	1906-1989
Behan, Brendan	1923-1964
Berkeley, George	1685-1753
Binchy, Maeve	1940-
Birmingham, George A.	1865-1950
Boucicault, Dion	1820-1890
Bowen, Elizabeth	1899-1973
Burke, Edmund	1729-1797
Campbell, Joseph	1879-1944
Carleton, William	1794-1869
Carroll, Paul Vincent	1900-1968
Cary, Joyce	1888-1957
Colum, Padraic	1881-1972
Corkery, Daniel	1878-1964
Davis, Thomas	1814-1845
Doyle, Lynn	1873-1961
Doyle, Roddy	1958-
Dunsany, Lord	1878-1957
Edgeworth, Maria	1767-1849
Ervine, St John	1883-1971
Farquhar, George	1677-1707
Ferguson, Sir Samuel	1810-1886
French, Percy	1854-1920

Friel, Brian	1929-
Gogarty, Oliver St John	1878-1957
Goldsmith, Oliver	1728-1774
Gregory, Lady	1852-1932
Griffin, Gerald	1803-1840
Heaney, Séamus	1939-
Johnston, Denis	1910-1984
Joyce, James	1882-1941
Kavanagh, Patrck	1904-1967
Kickham, Charles J.	1828-1882
Le Fanu, Sheridan	1814-1873
Lecky,	
William Edward Hartpole	1838-1903
Ledwidge, Francis	1887-1917
Lever, Charles	1806-1872
Lewis, C. S.	1898-1963
Longley, Michael	1939-
Lover, Samuel	1797-1868
Lynd, Robert	1879-1949
Macken, Walter	1915-1967
MacNeice, Louis	1907-1963
Mahony, Francis	1804-1866
Mangan, James Clarence	1803-1849
Maturin, Charles Robert	1780-1824
McCabe, Frank	1955-
McCourt, Frank	1931-
Moore, George	1852-1933
Moore, Thomas	1779-1852
Morgan, Lady	1776?-1859

O'Brien, Flann	1911-1966
O'Brien, Kate	1897-1974
O'Brien, Edna	1936-
O'Casey, Seán	1880-1964
O'Connor, Frank	1903-1966
O'Donnell, Peadar	1893-1986
O'Faolain, Sean	1900-1991
O'Flaherty, Liam	1896-1984
O'Grady, Standish	1846-1928
Reid, Forrest	1875-1947
Robinson, Lennox	1886-1958
Ros, Amanda McKittrick	1860-1939
Ross, Martin	1862-1915
Russell, George	1867-1935
Shaw, George Bernard	1856-1950
Sheridan, Richard Brinsley	1751-1816
Shiels, George	1881-1949
Somerville, E. Œ.	1858-1949
Steele, Sir Richard	1672-1729
Stephens, James	1880?-1950
Stoker, Bram	1847-1912
Swift, Jonathan	1667-1745
Synge, J. M.	1871-1909
Trevor, William	1928-
Waddell, Helen	1889-1965
Walsh, Maurice	1879-1964
Wilde, Oscar	1854-1900
Yeats, W. B.	1865-1939

The poet, W.B. Yeats is buried in Drumcrieff cemetery

Libraries and Museums

Libraries

Belfast Central Library
Royal Avenue
Chester Beatty Library, Dublin Castle
This houses a collection of cuneiform clay tablets, Coptic papyri, Hebrew, Sanskrit, Syriac and Samaritan vellum manuscripts, owned formerly by Sir Alfred Chester Beatty. There are 3,000 Arabic manuscripts also as well as Indian, Siamese and Tibetan documents

Franciscan Library
Killiney
Gaelic manuscripts 11th to 20th century, *Annals of the Four Masters* to AD 1169

Free State Army Records
Cathal Brugha Barracks
Military archives including an army census, 1922

Genealogical Office
2 Kildare Street, Dublin 2

Linen Hall Library
17 Donegal Square North, Belfast
Founded in 1788 and contains a large collection of books dealing with the linen trade. It houses archival material from 1791. It also houses the meteorological records for Belfast during the 1796-1906 era. The first librarian was Thomas Russell, who was hanged in 1803 for rebellion

National Archives
Bishop Street, Dublin 8
This has primary sources, such as State Papers, copies of wills and police papers of the Royal Irish Constabulary. Admission is free

National Library of Ireland
Kildare Street, Dublin 2
One of the copyright libraries, it holds a large manuscript collection, 65,000 catalogues containing 750,000 individual items. It has almost 750,000 volumes in its printed books section

Trinity College Library
College Green, Dublin 2
This is one of the copyright libraries of Ireland, which receives a copy of every book published in Ireland or Great Britain within a year of publication. It has 3,000 ancient manuscripts including the *Book of Kells* and many Egyptian papyri. It has up to one million printed books

County and city libraries
There are also county and city libraries which, in addition to standard works, house collections of local history, files of local newspapers and other local history sources

Armagh County Library

Carlow County Library
Dublin Street, Carlow

Cavan County Library
Cavan town

Clare County Library
Ennis Mill Road, Ennis

Cork Central Library
27 Grand Parade, Cork

Cork County Library
Farranlea Road, Cork

Donegal Central Library
Oliver Plunkett Road, Letterkenny, County Donegal

Dublin City Central Library
Ilac Centre, Henry Street, Dublin 1

County Galway Library HQ
Galway Island House,
Cathedral Square, Galway

Kerry County Library HQ
Tralee, County Kerry

Kildare County Library HQ
Newbridge, County Kildare

Kilkenny County Library HQ
John's Quay, Kilkenny

Laois County Library HQ
County Hall, Port Laoise

Leitrim County Library HQ
Ballinamore, County Leitrim

Limerick City Library HQ
The Granary, Michael Street, Limerick

Longford County Library Annaly
Longford town

Mayo County Library HQ
The Mall, Westport, County Mayo

Meath County Library HQ
Navan, County Meath

Monaghan County Library HQ
The Diamond, Clones, County Monaghan

Offaly County Library HQ
O'Connor Square, Tullamore, County Offaly

Roscommon County Library
Abbey Street, Roscommon

Sligo County Library HQ
Stephen Street, Sligo

Tipperary North &
South County Library HQ
Thurles, County Tipperary

Waterford City Library HQ
Lady Lane, Waterford

Waterford County Library HQ
Lismore, County Waterford

Westmeath County Library HQ
Mullingar, County Westmeath

Wexford County Library HQ
Abbey Street, Wexford

Wicklow County Library HQ
Bray, County Wicklow

Museums

Bank of Ireland
2 College Green, Dublin 2
The Bank of Ireland Arts Centre, in the old bank armoury, Foster Place, is host to the **Story of Banking Museum**. This exhibition reflects the role played by Bank of Ireland in the economic and social development of Ireland over the past 200 years

Cavan County Museum
Virginia Road, Ballyjamesduff, County Cavan
Exhibits include items from archaeology and folklore

Cork Butter Museum Ltd
O'Connell Square, Shandon, Cork

Cork City Museum
Fitzgerald Park
Cork Exhibits mainly confined to Cork city and county

Custom House Visitor Centre
Custom House Quay, Dublin 1
Gandon museum with information and displays on his life and work in Ireland; the history of the Custom House itself, including the 1921 fire and subsequent restoration, and on the many Government offices and important characters who have had offices in the building in the two centuries since it was complete.

Down County Museum
The Mall, Downpatrick, County Down

Drogheda Town Museum
Millmount, Drogheda, County Louth

Dublin Civic Museum
58 South William Street, Dublin 2
Subjects covered in the permanent collection: Streets and Buildings of Dublin, Traders, Industry, Transport, Political History, Maps and Views of Dublin.

Dublin Writers Museum
18/19 Parnell Square North, Dublin 1
The Irish literary tradition is one of the most illustrious in the world, famous for four Nobel prize winners and for many other writers of international renown. In 1991 the Dublin Writers Museum was opened to house a history and celebration of literary Dublin

Dublin's Viking Adventure
Essex Street West, Temple Bar, Dublin 8
Interactive experience of life in Viking Dublin.

Fermanagh County Museum
Enniskillen, County Fermanagh.
Material mostly from the county

Fethard Folk, Farm & Transport Museum
Cashel Road, Fethard

Findlater's Museum
The Harcourt Street Vaults,
10 Upper Hatch Street, Dublin 2
Traces the history of a Dublin Merchant family over the past 170 years

Folk Museum & Heritage Centre
Glencolumcille, County Donegal

Folk Village
Cashel, County Tipperary

Galway City Museum
Spanish Arch, Galway

Guinness Hopstore
James's Gate, Dublin 8.
This is the home of Guinness Stout, the famous black beer with the distinctive creamy head

Heraldic Museum
Office of the Chief Herald, 2 Kildare Street.
This museum illustrates the uses of Heraldry (coats of arms) and is the only one of its kind in the world. Shields, banners, coins, paintings, porcelain and stamps depicting coats of arms are on view

Hunt Museum
Custom House, Rutland Street, Limerick
This collection of items made by John Hunt includes articles from the Stone Age onwards

Irish Jewish Museum
Walworth Road, Off Victoria Street, South Circular Road, Dublin 8.
The museum consists of the restored synagogue and the history of the Irish Jews dating back over 150 years

Irish Museum of Modern Art
The Royal Hospital Kilmainham,
Royal Hospital, Military Road,
Kilmainham, Dublin 8.
Permanent collection and temporary exhibitions, covering international and Irish art of the 20th century

Irish National Heritage Park
Ferrycarrig, Wexford

James Joyce Cultural centre
Parnell Street, Dublin

James Joyce Museum
The Joyce Tower, Sandycove, Co. Dublin
The life and work of James Joyce, who made the tower the setting for the first chapter of his masterpiece, *Ulysses*

Knock Folk Museum
Knock, County Mayo.

Louth County Museum
Jocelyn Street, Dundalk, County Louth
Items of the industrial heritage of the area.

Maritime Museum
Mariner's Church, Haigh terrace, Dun Laoghaire
Historical models, including one of The Great Eastern, and a French longboat captured at Bantry in 1796.

Museum of Irish Transport
College Street, Carlow

National Gallery of Ireland
Merrion Square West, Dublin 2
Collection of some 3,000 paintings, and approximately 10,000 other works in different media including watercolours, drawings, prints and sculptures

National Museum of Ireland
Kildare Street and Merrion Row, Dublin 2
Artefacts and masterpieces dating from 2000 BC to the 20th century. Of particular interest are the Tara Brooch of the 8th century, the Ardagh chalice, the Lismore corzier and the Cross of Cong. There are valuable collections of Irish glass, textiles, ivories, ceramics and lace. An extension to the museum has been opened in the former Griffiths Barracks

National Museum of Ireland
Collins Barracks, Benburb Street, Dublin 7
Ireland's new museum of the decorative arts and of the economic, social, political and military history of the state

National Print Museum
former Garrison Chapel, Beggars Bush
Story of Ireland's printing heritage

National Transport Museum
Howth Castle Demense, Howth,
Co. Dublin
The exhibits range from buses, trams, commercial, utility, military, fire appliances, horse drawn and other memorabilia associated with transport which are on display.

National Wax Museum
Granby Row, Parnell Square, Dublin 1
Heroes of the past and the present 'preserved' in wax

Natural History Museum
Merrion Street, Dublin 2
Collections illustrative of the wild life, both vertebrate and invertebrate, of Ireland.

Pearse Museum
St. Edna's Park, Grange Road,
Rathfranham, Dublin 16
Irish flora and fauna and an audio-visual show

Rothe House
16 Parliament Street, Kilkenny

Shaw Museum
33 Synge Street, Dublin

The Fry Model Railway Museum
Malahide Castle, Co. Dublin
Handmade models of Irish trains

The GAA Museum
Croke Park, Dublin 3
Origins of the GAA and its role in the evolution of the country since 1884: artefacts, trophies and 'tools of the trade'

Tipperary County Museum
Clonmel

Ulster Folk and Transport Museum Library
Cultra Manor, Hollywood, County Down
Contains the horse-drawn tram, *Fintona* and the express locomotive, *Maeve* built in 1939

Wexford County Museum Ltd
The Castle, Enniscorthy, County Wexford

Bibliography and further reading

ADAM, DAVID
The Wisdom of The Celts
Lion Publishing plc, 1996

JOYCE, P. W.
Atlas and Cyclopedia of Ireland

SULLIVAN A. M.
The General History
Murphy & McCarthy, Publishers, 1903

BAIN, GEORGE
Celtic Art The Methods of Construction
Constable and Company Ltd, 1977

BARDON, JONATHAN
A History of Ulster
Blackstaff, 1992

BISHOP, PATRICK
The Irish Empire
Boxtree, 1999

BOYCE, D.
Nationalism in Ireland
Gill and Macmillan, 1982

BRENNAN-WHITMORE, W. J.
*Dublin Burning: The Easter Rising
from Behind the Barricades*
Gill and Macmillan, 1996

BRINDLEY, ANNA
Irish Prehistory: An Introduction
National Museum of Ireland, 1994

BROWN, TERENCE
*Ireland: A Social and Cultural
History 1922-79*
Fontana, 1981

BUCKLAND, PATRICK
A History of Northen Ireland
Gill and Macmillan, 1981

BULL, PHILIP
Land, Politics and Nationalism
Gill and Macmillan, 1996

BYRNE, F. J.
Irish Kings and High-Kings
Batsford, 1973

CROSSMAN, VIRGINIA
*Politics, Law & Order
in 19th Century Ireland*
Gill and Macmillan, 1996

CURTIS, EDMUND
A History of Medieval Ireland
Barnes & Noble, 1983

CUSACK, MARY FRANCES
*An Illustrated History of Ireland
From AD 400 to 1800*
Senate, 1995

D'ALTON, THE REV E. A.
History of Ireland
Gresham Publishing Company

DOYLE, BILL;
NEWLAND, SONYA
The Magic & Mystery of Ireland
DP Dempsey Parr, 2000

DUFFY, SEÁN
Atlas of Irish History
Gill & Macmillan Ltd, 1997

DUFFY, SEÁN
Ireland in the Middle Ages
Gill and Macmillan, 1997

Encyclopaedia Britannica

FOSTER, R. F.
*The Oxford Illustrated
History of Ireland*
Oxford University Press, 1989

GAHAN, DANIEL
The People's Rising, Wexford 1798
Gill and Macmillan, 1995

GRAGLIA, ROSALBA
Past and Present Ireland
Tiger Books, 1997

GREENWOOD, MARGARET;
CONNOLLY, MARK;
HAWKINS, HILDA;
WALLIS, GEOFF
Ireland The Rough Guide
Rough Guides Limited, 1999

HARRIS, NATHANIEL
Heritage of Ireland
Ted Smart, 1998

KEE, ROBERT
*The Green Flag: A History of Irish
Nationalism*
Weidenfeld & Nicholson, 1972

KELLY, EAMONN P.
Early Celtic Art in Ireland
National Museum of Ireland, 1993

KELLY, JAMES
*Prelude to Union: Anglo-Irish Politics
in the 1780s*
Cork University Press, 1992

KENNY, MICHAEL
The 1798 Rebellion
National Museum of Ireland, 1996

KENNY, MICHAEL
The Road to Freedom
National Museum of Ireland, 1993

KILLEEN, RICHARD
A Short History of Ireland
Gill & Macmillan Ltd, 1994

KINEALY, CHRISTINE
*This Great Calamity, The Irish
Famine, 1845-52*
Gill and Macmillan, 1994

LEE, JOSEPH
Ireland, 1912-85
Cork University Press, 1989

LENNON, COLM
Sixteenth-Century Ireland
Gill and Macmillan, 1994

LITTON, HELEN
Irish Rebellions 1798-1916
Wolfhound Press Ltd, 1998

LOVETT, RICHARD
Ireland 100 Years Ago
Bracken Books, 1995

MacCARTHY MORROGH, MICHAEL
The Irish Century
Weidenfeld & Nicolson, 1998

MacENTEE, SEÁN
Episode at Easter
Gill and Macmillan, 1966

MacKILLOP, JAMES
Dictionary of Celtic Mythology
Oxford University Press, 1998

McNAMARA, AIDAN
*The Simple Guide to Customs
& Etiquette in Ireland*
Global Books Ltd, 1996

MEEHAM, BERNAR
The Book of Kells
Thams & Hudson, 1994

MITCHELL, FRANK
*The Shell Guide to Reading the
Irish Landscape*
Country House, 1986

O'GRIOFA, MAIRTIN
Irish Folk Wisdom
Sterling Publishing
Company, Inc, 1993

O'KELLY, M. J.
Early Ireland
Cambridge University Press, 1989

OTWAY-RUTHVEN, A. J.
A History of Medieval Ireland
Ernest Benn, 1968, 1980

POWER, PATRICK C.
A Literary History of Ireland

POWER, PATRICK C.
The Book of Irish Curses

POWER, PATRICK C.
History of South Tipperary

POWER, PATRICK C.
The Courts Martial of 1798-9

POWER, PATRICK C.
Anglo-Irish Poetry 1800-1922

RETZLAFF, KAY
Ireland: Its Myths and Legends
John Hinde Ltd, 1998

ROLLESTON, T. W.
*The Illustrated Guide to
Celtic Mythology*
Studio Editions Ltd, 1993

ROUSE, SARAH
Into the Light
National Library of Ireland, 1998

SULLIVAN, SIR EDWARD
The Book of Kells
Studio Editions, 1986

TODD, LORETO
Celtic Names for Children
The O'Brien Press Ltd, 2000

VAUGHAN, W. E.
*A New History of Ireland VI: Ireland
Under the Union II, 1870-1921*
Oxford University Press, 1996

WALLACE, MARTIN
Famous Irish Writers
Appletree Press Ltd, 1995

WOOD, JULIETTE
The Celts Life, Myth and Art
DBP, Duncan Baird Publishers, 1998

WOODHAM-SMITH, CECIL
The Great Hunger
Hamish Hamilton, 1987